"*The Fabric of Faithfulness* is a profoundly important work. Profound because it is rich in biblical wisdom and nearly palpable truths. Important because there has perhaps never been a time when the academic community has so resigned itself to the inevitability of fragmentation and intellectual incoherence. It is a tragedy which most avoid and some lament. But who is offering wise counsel? Dr. Garber does so without apology or hubris; just tons of common sense. And I am deeply grateful."

STANLEY GAEDE, SCHOLAR-IN-RESIDENCE, CENTER FOR CHRISTIAN STUDIES, GORDON COLLEGE, AND AUTHOR OF *WHEN TOLERANCE IS NO VIRTUE*

"Here is the best book on moral education I have ever encountered. No dry treatise this! Garber's guide to character development is both well illustrated and profoundly reflective. It is filled with stories of real people whose lives are seen in the light of the insights of good movies, literature and academic pundits. The themes of history of ideas, sociology of knowledge and ethic of character thread their way through all the stories. Though reflection on moral education today might well lead to despair, this is a vibrantly upbeat challenge to all who yearn to see students develop spiritual and moral depth."

JAMES W. SIRE, AUTHOR OF *THE UNIVERSE NEXT DOOR*

"Attentive to the peril of the gap between belief and behavior over time, Garber offers a thoughtful, challenging, passionate and well-written look at how the worldviews we teach can, do and must become ways of life for our students."

SHARON DALOZ PARKS, AUTHOR OF *BIG QUESTIONS, WORTHY DREAMS: MENTORING YOUNG ADULTS IN THEIR SEARCH FOR MEANING, PURPOSE AND FAITH*

"If there is any book I would want to give to a son or daughter going off to college, it would be this one. In an extraordinary way Garber weaves together theological commentary on contemporary literature and events to help form the imagination of Christians. Hopefully this book will be read not only by the young but by us all who need such wisdom."

STANLEY HAUERWAS, GILBERT T. ROWE PROFESSOR OF THEOLOGICAL ETHICS, DUKE UNIVERSITY, AND AUTHOR OF *A COMMUNITY OF CHARACTER*

"Steve has written a marvelous book. I gladly recommend it and will make it required reading for our students here at Covenant Seminary. He is very creative in setting forth the need for conviction, character and community. . . . I especially like his combination of careful analysis, true stories, masterfully chosen quotes and Calvin and Hobbes cartoons as he presents and answers this challenge."

JERRAM BARRS, DIRECTOR, FRANCIS SCHAEFFER INSTITUTE

"*The Fabric of Faithfulness* only becomes more relevant each year, as we recognize that our own faithfulness—and that of our students—is enacted and sustained in community. Garber's exploration of the central importance of a robust worldview, authentic models and mentors, and living communities for cultivating character has been and continues to be inspiring to students, college leaders, churches and anyone who wants to think more deeply about the embodied and embedded nature of meaningful human life."

CLAUDIA DEVRIES BEVERSLUIS, PROVOST, CALVIN COLLEGE

"*The Fabric of Faithfulness* has become something like a standard primer for the spiritual formation of university students. Everywhere I go in the world of campus ministry practitioners, this book provides the background source for our work. Steve Garber poses the most important questions, sees the spiritual formation of students from a large enough vista, and engages learning in ways that are creative and provocative. In these pages a learning is honored that is reflective, serious, conversational, hopeful and wise."

KEITH ANDERSON, ACADEMIC DEAN, MARS HILL GRADUATE SCHOOL, AND AUTHOR OF *SPIRITUAL MENTORING*

"No living author has done a better job than Steve Garber in presenting a workable, sustainable plan for closing the gap between profession and behavior. His answer lies not in more American grit and guts determination, but rather Spirit-born, communal patterns of intentionality lived out as coherent, sustainable stories. Trust me, this book connects with the human soul like very few books do. For those with ears to hear and eyes to see, Garber's prophetic and artful thoughts will be life-changing."

CHARLIE PEACOCK, MUSIC PRODUCER, AND AUTHOR OF *NEW WAY TO BE HUMAN*

"For ten years now I have seen this indispensable book transform the loves and lives of many students. But first it changed me. It rescues us all from a flaccid religious pragmatism with its revolutionary vision of Christian moral education that is at once theologically informed, culturally relevant and pedagogically constructive. This book is Steve Garber's soul writ large, his calling encapsulated."

DAVID NAUGLE, PROFESSOR OF PHILOSOPHY, DALLAS BAPTIST UNIVERSITY, AND AUTHOR OF *WORLDVIEW: THE HISTORY OF A CONCEPT*

"This book was my field manual through college. Steve Garber's deep understanding of students authentically guides them through the difficult years of questions and confusions about purpose and life direction. Inside the written wisdom is a mentor who cares for students and will equip them to do what is true and right. My work today grows out of the inspiration of this wise man and his guiding work."

JENA LEE, EXECUTIVE DIRECTOR, BLOOD:WATER MISSION, AND AUTHOR OF *HOPE IN THE DARK*

WEAVING TOGETHER
BELIEF AND BEHAVIOR

The Fabric
of Faithfulness

EXPANDED EDITION

Steven Garber

IVP Books

An imprint of InterVarsity Press
Downers Grove, Illinois

InterVarsity Press
P.O. Box 1400, Downers Grove, IL 60515-1426
World Wide Web: www.ivpress.com
E-mail: email@ivpress.com

InterVarsity Press® is the book-publishing division of InterVarsity Christian Fellowship/USA®, a student movement active on campus at hundreds of universities, colleges and schools of nursing in the United States of America, and a member movement of the International Fellowship of Evangelical Students. For information about local and regional activities, write Public Relations Dept., InterVarsity Christian Fellowship/USA, 6400 Schroeder Rd., P.O. Box 7895, Madison, WI 53707-7895, or visit the IVCF website at <www.intervarsity.org>.

Design: Cindy Kiple
Images: Jim Wehtje/Getty Images

ISBN-13: 978-0-8308-3319-1

Printed in the United States of America ∞

Library of Congress Cataloging-in-Publication Data

Garber, Steven.
  The fabric of faithfulness: weaving together belief and behavior
during the university years / Steven Garber.—2nd ed.
      p. cm.
  Includes bibliographical references (p.   ) and index.
  ISBN-13: 978-0-8308-3319-1 (pbk.: alk. paper)
  ISBN-10: 0-8308-3319-6 (pbk.: alk. paper)
  1. Christian college students—Religious life. 2. Church work with
students. 3. Education (Christian theology) 4. Church and the
world. 5. Evangelicalism. 6. Garber, Steven. I. Title.
  BV4531.3.G37 2007
  248.8'34—dc22

                                                                 2006030491

| P | 19 | 18 | 17 | 16 | 15 | 14 | 13 | 12 | 11 | 10 | 9 | 8 | 7 | 6 | 5 |
| Y | 22 | 21 | 20 | 19 | 18 | 17 | 16 | 15 | 14 | 13 | 12 | 11 | 10 | | | |

For my children

Eden, Elliott, David, Jessica and Jonathan

with the deepest hope that you will learn

to love what is real and true and right

Contents

Remember your Creator
in the days of your youth,
before the days of trouble come
    and the years approach when you will say,
    "I find no pleasure in them"——
before the sun and the light
    and the moon and stars grow dark,
    and the clouds return after the rain;
when the keepers of the house tremble,
    and the strong men stoop,
when the grinders cease because they are few,
    and those looking through the windows grow dim;
when the doors to the street are closed
    and the sound of grinding fades;
when men rise up at the sound of birds,
    but all their songs grow faint;
when men are afraid of heights
    and of dangers in the streets;
when the almond tree blossoms
    and the grasshopper drags himself along
    and desire no longer is stirred.
Then man goes to his eternal home
    and mourners go about the streets.
Remember him——before the silver cord is severed,
    or the golden bowl is broken;
before the pitcher is shattered at the spring,
    or the wheel broken at the well,
and the dust returns to the ground it came from,
    and the spirit returns to God who gave it.

ECCLESIASTES 12:1-7

When I grow up I won't have to think
I won't have to see unpleasant things
It'll all be perfect just like on TV
When I grow up I won't feel a thing
I won't trifle in other people's pain
I'll put all these childish things away
    When I grow up, when I grow up,
    When I grow up I won't have to
    think so much
When I grow up I'll look out for me
It's a small lifeboat and baby, it's a great big sea
And your tears are nothing, don't put that guilt on me
    When I grow up, when I grow up
    When I grow up I won't have to
    think so much
The one who dies with the most toys wins
The one who dies in unspeakable sin
While the hungry multitude is condemned to live
Loaves and fishes and fairy tales
Let them eat cake, let the strong prevail
Let me alone, let them help themselves
I wanna kill this little voice inside of me
The crazy little bastard saying things I will not believe
I wanna slide just like a snake into the driver's seat
I'm so glad I'm living in the USA
With my BMW and my MBA
Driving over these slums high on the new beltway
    When I grow up, when I grow up
    When I grow up I won't have to feel so much

"WHEN I GROW UP"
PIERCE PETTIS
WINDHAM HILL RECORDS, 1988

Preface

D o you need to go? Can you talk to me?" Bai Meng looked very much the *artiste,* with his very cool coat and cravat. But the words were weighty, and came from his heart; that was plain to see. In the blink of an eye, I thought about how late I'd been out the previous night speaking at St. John's College in Annapolis, talking late into the night with students there, and wondered —but I knew I needed to stay.

So I told him that I was glad to talk with him. His next words surprised me: "I feel so guilty to be alive." For the next three hours we talked about his guilt, and at the same time, with unusual candor, about the possibility of grace.

That evening, in the company of twenty-five young Chinese ex-patriots, I had reflected on a question that has become the core of my own calling, namely, why is it, in the face of situations that seem too complex, too broken, that human beings sometimes still choose to enter in—knowing that they will suffer, knowing that it will cost them—that for love's sake they still choose responsibility?

I did so telling the tale of Tolstoy's *Two Old Men.* In a short story the great Russian novelist recounts the pilgrimage of two friends who decide that before they die they must make a pilgrimage to Jerusalem. Gathering supplies, they begin their journey—and they walk and walk and walk. At the end of a long day they enter a small village but see no one. Wondering where the villagers are, they knock on a nearby hut. No one answers, and one of the pilgrims, Elisha, steps in. In the dark he hears a groan, and smells death. He returns to his friend, gets water and food, and goes back into the hut, offering his gifts to the family that he has found.

What he discovers is that the family is starving, but even more starkly that the village is too. With great insight into what it means to have "eyes that see," Tolstoy allows us to ponder what it is that connects what Elisha knows with what Elisha does, that allows him to understand that he is implicated in what he sees and hears and smells. I finished by commending these young Chinese for the courage of their convictions, for understanding that they too had been implicated in history—as had Tolstoy's Elisha.

When we broke for the evening, my conversation with Bai Meng began. Rarely have I entered so deeply into someone's hopes and dreams, griefs and sorrows, as I did with him. But it is also rare to spend hours like I did that night, and other nights like it, listening to the leaders of the Tiananmen Square protest, gathered together to wonder about the past and the future in light of the deepest questions that human beings ask and answer.

Bai Meng had been the leader of the student journalist association of China during the spring of 1989, and had been one of three carrying a banner leading thousands of students into Tiananmen Square for the initial demonstration in April. As he told me his tale, I winced in my heart, hearing about the unusual cruelty of the Chinese government as they suppressed the students in what we now call the Tiananmen Square massacre. His best friend had died, bloodied, in his arms. It took him two years to "crawl out of China" as he put it; several years later, when I met him, he was studying film at Columbia University.

This was my second time meeting with a group like this; a year earlier I had been asked by a noted China specialist to spend an evening with "the Havels of China," as she described them. They were the intellectual leaders of the Tiananmen generation, a diaspora, scattered across North America— from Vancouver to Boston. Not allowed to return because of the public character of their protest, some were working in journalism and business while others were studying in relevant disciplines that would enable them to return someday to China. One of them gave me his card, which included all of the needed information, with these words in italics on the bottom: *China for the 21st-century.* Since Tiananmen, he had already finished a first Ph.D. at UC Berkeley, and was working on a second at Harvard.

As I sat there listening to their stories, I was overwhelmed. On the one hand, they had suffered so much. The depth of their sadness ate away at my heart. But at the same time, the seriousness of their desire to return home, and its motivation, was amazing. They simply said: "We love China—and we want to go home and be part of the rebuilding of our culture." I heard that again and again.

But they had a question that brought them to Washington: "We have been reading the philosophers of the world, and are not satisfied. We want to return to China, and know that we might be imprisoned or die if we do. But we love China, and so we will go home. The more we read it seems to us that the Christian vision of human nature and history might give us a basis to return, a raison d'être that makes sense to us philosophically—what do you think?"

Nothing cheap could be said.

As I pondered their question, I thought back one week to the previous Thursday night, when I had taken my two older sons, Elliott and David, and some of their friends to a Smashing Pumpkins concert, during the "Mellon Collie and the Infinite Sadness" tour. It was stunning, in many ways. The pulsing of the red/black/purple/green light show behind the stage, the energy of thousands of Virginia adolescents pressed together waiting to hear what was the biggest music in the world that year, and the skillful lyricism of the band feeling the feelings of their audience with incredible ability—all in all it was quite a show.

When we got home I asked my sons about the concert, particularly wondering what they thought was the "climax"—the high point of the playlist of songs. In different rooms, so neither knew what the other had said, they quickly offered, "Zero." I had thought the same thing. With lines like, "I'm in love with my sadness," Billy Corgan and his band had tapped into the melancholy of the human heart at the end of the century—but with almost Pentecostal fervor. No song that night had as much energy as that one.

Much of Walker Percy's work reflects that same reality, namely, that we are a surprisingly sad people, "lost in the cosmos" as we are, with Prozac being the cultural drug-of-choice. Through pop culture eyes, the Pumpkins were seeing "the homeless mind" of the sociologist Peter Berger; not being scholars but singers, and rock stars at that, they were shouting their critique across the arenas and auditoriums of America. I understood that part of their gift, and honored it.

What bothered me was that they were making so much money doing so. I told my sons, "The nihilism may be honest; I don't know them well enough to know. But it doesn't seem right that they should make a fortune off of sadness. If they really believe that 'God is empty just like me' (another line in the song 'Zero'), then they should stop celebrating the sadness in huge concert venues—and live with its starkness."

That evening was still rumbling through my heart a week later when I sat in the room with the young Chinese. Sadness? Yes, again. But it seemed so very different from the "mellon collie and infinite sadness" of the Smashing Pumpkins, full of adolescent angst as it was.

Those Thursday nights still ripple across my soul, almost ten years later.

A few weeks ago a friend invited me to a dinner with a group of Chinese visitors. A former politician, he still has global interests, with China leading the way. He described them as leaders, and because of my history with the Tiananmen students, I was intrigued. Over a feast, I listened to their stories. It soon became clear that these were "Havels" too; in fact, one was the translator of Havel's work into Chinese.

Each one had literally put his life on the line for the sake of the future of China. One was an attorney, another a professor, still another a human rights activist. In the literal handful, two had been named "Person of the Year in Asia" by *Newsweek*. Over dinner I sat next to Yu Jie, the translator of Havel and one of China's bestselling novelists whose work, ironically, is banned in his own country, and a pastor of an underground church in Beijing. Described in the *International Herald Tribune* as "the most courageous writer in China," he seemed so young to have such a reputation.

But the longer I listened, the more sure I was that I wanted to contact a journalist friend, one of the most respected voices in foreign affairs in Washington, D.C., and have him meet this group of leaders. A couple years earlier I had written him, wondering about his "Havel-like" vision. Unlike almost every other writer who is predictably conservative or liberal, this man seems to have a different compass, a "north star" informed by notions like good and evil, truth and falsehood, justice and injustice, and therefore refuses to be put in a partisan box.

He invited us to meet him at his home in Georgetown later that week. For almost two hours he listened to them, asking clarifying questions that drew them out even more fully. Their central thesis was this: after the devastating disillusionment of Tiananmen, their generation had two choices, either to return to Communism or to embrace Confucianism. Neither seemed sufficient, given the yearning they had to engage history, to take up both the suffering and responsibility that was their common vocation. And overwhelmingly, these young intellectual and cultural leaders had come to believe in the gospel of the kingdom, embracing the Christian faith. It had given them a place to stand.

Given the question that I had been asked years earlier (did I think the Christian vision of human nature and history could provide a sufficient basis to return to China?), hearing the testimony of these men was astounding. They were the incarnation of the answer to the question; it was being embodied in their lives. And I felt as if I was in the presence of saints.

Having known personal and political heartache, and knowing that any honest account of the present and future implicated them more, they had found in their faith a way forward. For the sake of love—in imitation of Christ—they could suffer, even as they acted responsibly in and for history, hoping for the way the world ought to be.

◆ ◆ ◆

It has been almost ten years since *The Fabric of Faithfulness* was published. By God's grace it has had a wide reading, in this country and beyond. I have traveled from corner to corner of the United States—San Diego to Boston, Seattle to Miami—speaking about the book and its themes. I have traveled to Latin America, to Great Britain, to Central and Eastern Europe, talking about the challenge of deepening one's vocation over a lifetime. I have watched professors gather on the historic lawn of Mr. Jefferson's University of Virginia, in the hallowed halls of MIT and the University of California at Berkeley (where as a boy I spent many happy days), and in the medical school of the University of Florida, as well as in the auditoriums and classrooms of scores of liberal arts colleges across the country, each time pondering the book's vision for life and learning.

But as I have followed the response over the years, listening to people who have indwelt its thesis, this has struck me: men and women who sustain visions of faith over a lifetime learn to take into their hearts the disappointments and sorrows that come to them, finding a deeper, truer faith as they do so. Rather than being shipwrecked by the brokenness of the world, they learn to navigate their way through, holding onto the integrity of their vocations through life. Indeed, they have *woven together belief and behavior into a fabric of faithfulness* that has kept their hearts alive in the face of evil and injustice, grief and pain. And in this now-but-not-yet world, no one is exempt. As Bob Dylan once lamented, everything is broken—and everyone is broken. These are younger people and older people, men and women, students and professors, young professionals and senior executives, craftsmen and farmers, doctors and lawyers. I have had almost countless conversations and correspondence with people who have wanted more after reading the book.

When I wrote it I was a professor myself, teaching undergraduates semester by semester at the American Studies Program on Capitol Hill. As interest grew for interaction over the book, I was asked by the Council for Christian Colleges and Universities to become its scholar-in-residence, a position I held for several years. In that time I spent weeks of my life on university and college campuses—many deeply Christian and some profoundly secular—and had hours of conversation with administrators, faculty and students. In many ways, their cares became my cares.

As I listened, I found that my own vocation was becoming clearer—perhaps deeper and more embodied in the practices of my own labor of love as I journeyed among students and among those who taught them. This question began to emerge, becoming the thread I followed in all that I read, in every presentation I made: is there a spirituality of learning that grows out of the gospel of the kingdom? Or to press the point: if the Christian vision of life and the world is true, what ought learning to be like?

To see it in those terms made the ideas and issues that the book explored seem broader. Yes, the pilgrimage into adulthood begins in late adolescence, but its meaning is only understood as our loves are lived out over time. People whose vocations were beyond the university found their way to me, wondering about the book's argument for their own lives—as butchers, bakers and candlestick-makers . . . and as musicians and politicians, as businessmen and women, as mothers and fathers, as pastors and journalists. *What do you think it means for me in the situation I am in? What ought our institution be like, if we take the thesis to heart?*

Eventually these questions grew into relationships that over time have given birth to The Washington Institute for Faith, Vocation & Culture, the setting of my life and work today. Embedded in a community of good friends with diverse vocations, we have committed ourselves to a common calling. As we care for the culture and the world through our vocations, we care for each other. Our worship and work take us to different places—some of us are neighbors, some are scattered across the city—but we are bound up with each other in common loves.

And in a proximate way, we are able to be what I have long longed for: a community that invites people in. I have traveled a lot, and spoken in many places. I do not disdain that life, primarily because I have met so many good people wherever the planes, trains and automobiles have taken me. But it is deficient as a way of learning. "Come and see" was the pedagogy of Jesus. The truest learning is incarnational; we learn the deepest lessons looking "over the shoulder" and "through the heart," seeing that a worldview can become a way of life.

We are not perfect, and what we are doing is not perfect; but we are serious, and we welcome conversations about things that matter. And best of all we have wonderfully imagined rocking chairs, and beautiful places to walk. *Come and see.*

◆ ◆ ◆

Even as I write, my engagement with the Chinese dissidents continues. This morning the Washington journalist called, wanting clarification on two points, as he plans to write his weekend column on the conversation. Of course he's exploring its political implications for the United States and China, even as he attends to the plight of the men whose commitments and cares have given them eyes to see their responsibility for the way China is and ought to be.

Their convictions have cost them, and continue to put them and their families at risk. Seeing that strain, the question I was asked that Thursday night—do you think there is something different about the Christian vision that might give us a sufficient basis to return to China, giving ourselves to its rebuilding?—seems all the more sobering, all the more important. It was not a cheap question, and there are no cheap answers.

What did I say to those gathered around the living room, wondering whether the Christian faith might answer their deepest hopes? I told them of a conversation I once had with the theologian and bishop Lesslie Newbigin, who spent forty years of his life in India. He had a friendship over many years with a Hindu scholar who, after reading the Bible, wondered aloud to Newbigin, "Why is it that Christian missionaries have given us this book, saying, 'Read it and add it to your supply'? I have finished it and it is a completely unique book. Its vision of universal history, of a story that makes sense of life from beginning to end, is unique. But also unique is its understanding of the human person as a responsible actor in history. And the two go together, don't they?" I told those Chinese leaders that their intuitions were right, that the Christian vision does give people the contours for genuine human flourishing, from the most personal areas to the most public of arenas of life. That at the heart of the Christian understanding of human nature and history is the possibility of a life of responsibility marked by love, "of gladness and singleness of heart," as the Book of Common Prayer puts it.

And China for the twenty-first century? And the young man, eschewing education as a passport to privilege, with longings so profound that his post-Tiananmen years were spent in Ph.D. programs wanting to prepare for the renewing of his culture? The last I heard he did return, and was imprisoned—a finite sadness, but a very real sadness.

But like the rest of life and the world, history is full of tensions: past, present and future. For people who care about the globalizing political economy of the twenty-first century it is virtually impossible to ignore China—even with its record of oppression. It is a messy world, and Tolstoy's tale continues to teach us. Remote villages with darkened huts on the steppes of Russia become a metaphor for China in the twenty-first century—a place with hurts and wounds and suffering, and yet with the potential for becoming a nation of unparalleled opportunity. Experienced world-watchers wonder aloud, "Will this century belong to China?"

A very good friend of mine is the CEO of a corporation that does substantial business with China, and for twenty years he has chosen to enter into its life with the social, political and economic complexities that are there. Determined to "tear a little corner off of the darkness"—to quote Bono of U2, as he reflects on his own vocation as a musician—through his company's involvements across China, my friend is passionate about the renewal of its culture, and prays and works toward that end. Over the last several years I have done work for his company, joining him in that hope. Another friend is a senior executive in a firm with extensive responsibility for the Beijing Olympics, which will give the world a window into a China that could not have been imagined in the spring of 1989. She serves on our board, and now her life and labor is bound up with mine. The challenges of acting responsibly in our globalizing world are very real for my friends, but they take up that task with unusual integrity, living day by day with the implications of that for both personal and public life—and remembering Tolstoy as they do. And finally, implicating myself even more in the contemporary complexity that China is, *The Fabric of Faithfulness* has been translated into Chinese, at the request of Chinese students who have wanted a different paradigm for understanding life and learning.

Worldviews are not abstractions; they become ideas with legs that have metaphysical and moral muscle, enabling real people to make the hardest choices possible. Mentors are not an interesting idea; rather they become the primary means by which beliefs are interpreted and understood, especially when what one believes is a matter of life and death, when what one believes has consequences for the way the world is and ought to be. Community then becomes the laboratory in which our hopes and dreams become real; we do not keep on keeping on without people of kindred heart and mind pledging their own lives toward the same end, holding us up when the world, the flesh and the devil call into question our core commitments and cares.

To say it plainly: in the concreteness of their choices over time, each one of these young Chinese men and women is an incarnation of the thesis set forth in the book. A worldview, a mentor, a community—these are the habits of heart that grow and sustain a faithful life, that so nourish a soul that a career can become a calling that gives coherence to the whole of life. Not by happenstance, but because, as gifted scholar and friend Stanley Gaede observed in his early review of the book, the truths are palpable. The embodied beliefs of these men and women instruct all of us. They become our teachers as we learn from them where the lines in the sand are.

For integrity's sake—philosophically, politically, psychologically—we hunger for beliefs that can make sense of life. Every son of Adam, every daughter of Eve, longs for that kind of coherence. In despair or frustration, most give up on the possibility.

A year ago I had a conversation with Billy Corgan, no longer with his band, as not long after their "Mellon Collie" album they broke up. In fact, on their last tour they made a surprising decision: to give away all their profits to charities. Now traveling on his own as a poet and songwriter, he came through Washington, and we had a conversation at a beautiful, historic home in Georgetown called Evermay, a place offering itself as "a living room in the nation's capital."

I found him to be a remarkably thoughtful man, able and willing to engage the most serious questions about politics and faith, art and culture. My intuitions about why the Pumpkins had disbanded proved right: mainly, they could not sustain the nihilism and make so much money at the same time. (And of course personalities and egos were all bound up in that decision, making it quite complex.) As he left I gave him a copy of *The Fabric of Faithfulness,* and he said that he hoped we could talk again. I hope so too.

Whether one's calling is to music or to the marketplace, to the academy or to the pulpit, to the gallery or to the construction site, to the city or to the plains and the mountains, these questions—which I first asked on the pages of the book ten years ago—are there for each of us, waiting for a response: do I have a *telos* that is sufficient to meaningfully orient my *praxis* over the course of life? Or in the language of the street, and therefore a little more playful: why do I get up in the morning?

They are questions for the Bai Mengs and the Billy Corgans, and for every one of us.

May 2006
Washington, D.C.

Acknowledgments

Like all good work in a fallen world, this book has had its pleasures and pains. When it became specially hard, I found these words from a Puritan sermon to be a great grace: "Weakness with watchfulness will stand out, when strength with too much confidence faileth. Weakness, with acknowledging of it, is the fittest seat and subject for God to perfect his strength in; for consciousness of our infirmities driveth us out of ourselves to him in whom our strength lieth." So said Richard Sibbes in "The Bruised Reed and Smoking Flax" in 1630. Thanks be to God.

Among his servants whose commitment and care have been sustaining, my wife, Meg Elliott, stands first. She is the woman whom I love to love.

Good work and good friends go hand in hand, and for many years, I have been blessed with both. In my "extracurricular" study as a college dropout in the early 1970s, George McEwen opened his home—and library—in the beautiful coastal community of Portrush, Northern Ireland. During the days I spent there reading in Calvin's *Commentary on Genesis,* I first began to understand the meaning of faithfulness. Years later Denis Haack's teaching to InterVarsity Christian Fellowship staff and students on faithfulness—insights which later became the book *The Rest of Success*—was a good gift to me. Longtime friends whose own vocations are a journey among students, Jim Sire and Bonnie Liefer, encouraged me at many important times and places. In their own unique ways they represent many beloved colaborers in InterVarsity and the Coalition for Christian Outreach.

My colleagues at the Council for Christian Colleges and Universities supported me in the writing of this from the very beginning, chief among them Jerry Herbert, Cheryl Kienel Jackson and Rich Gathro. I am grateful. Several friends have been, like Jonathan to David, very dear to me: Tod Moquist,

Mark Rodgers, Margie Haack, Tom McWhertor, Charlie and Andi Ashworth-Peacock, Beau Boulter, Dave Kiersznowski, and Gideon Strauss. With very different personalities and in many different places, they are reminders to me that the vision of the book can be embodied. Over the last several years Ray Blunt has come alongside me in my hopes and dreams, my sorrows and disappointments, with remarkable faithfulness. His servant leadership within The Washington Institute has been a great gift, perhaps most in helping me understand even more fully the meaning of the thesis at the heart of this book. And Ben Guthrie, who first began praying for my writing as a six-year-old when he was on his way night after night into the land of Nod, has continued on for many years, and I am still profoundly grateful. Thanks to him and to his parents, Don and Mary, for teaching him to pray.

In addition to these friends, there are communities of Christ's people that have nourished me along the way in Greeley, Colorado; Shafter, California; Lawrence, Kansas; Pittsburgh, Pennsylvania; and Washington, D.C. They include Presbyterians, Mennonites and Anglicans, and in different ways they incarnate the vision of the kingdom that is now-but-not-yet. The Falls Church, an almost-three-hundred-year-old Anglican congregation in Virginia, has for many years been the context of our common life, a people and a place where worship and work are twined together. Our rector, John Yates, is a true pastor, loving us as he shepherds us, and I am so very grateful for his friendship.

One gift of this study has been a deepened understanding of the role that my own teachers have played in my life. Ever since adolescence people have opened themselves, allowing me to see that the Christian vision of life and the world is more than rhetoric. That I believe that it is rooted in the reality of human life under the sun is substantially due to the ways they have incarnated its truths—even through a glass darkly—and so to Milt Cole, John Penrose, Bruce Hemphill, Bob Tweed, David Carson, Dean Smith, Paul Martin, Surrendra Gangadean, Jack Crabtree, Jerram Barrs, Donald Drew, Knox Hyndman, Ted Tripp, Bill White, Os Guinness, Paul Woodard, Bob Mann, Alden Hathaway, Ken Smith, Grady Spires, Calvin Seerveld, Joseph Kocklemans, Henry Johnson, Jim Martin and James Houston, thanks. And a special thanks to John Stott, whose pastoral care, even from afar, has allowed me to understand the priority of living in the world under the Word. His vision benevolently broods over every page.

At significant points along the way I received grants from the Mustard Seed Foundation of Washington, D.C., the John G. Bennett Memorial Foundation of Vancouver, B.C., and the Lilly Endowment of Indianapolis, Indiana. A special thanks to Thelma Herbert Weaver of Whittier, California, whose generosity to her children touched my life too. And to Gaylen Byker, who, as the president of Calvin College in Grand Rapids, Michigan, invited me into his college's life: "Come listen to us." The relationship with him and his school was a great grace. In addition, I was given the gifts of quiet places to read and write in Charles and Kay Bascom's log home in the Flint Hills of Kansas, George and Victoria Hobson's garden flat in Oxford, England, and Ward and Suzanne Scull's "Anathoth" on the Chesapeake Bay. One other very good gift came from Marianne Geers, who transcribed hours and hours of tape. "Thank you" seems small, and yet it is from my heart.

To my parents, Richard and Elizabeth Garber and Howard and Winifred Elliott, thanks be to God for their faithful love for me and mine.

The manuscript was given the thoughtful attention of InterVarsity Press editors Rodney Clapp and Linda Doll, and their gifts are gratefully received.

And finally, the questions and concerns that grew into this book have come from knowing and loving hundreds of students on a wide variety of campuses over many years. As I have listened to you, I have learned from you. May this be for you, and for many more, who have set out to explore the vocations that now call you into the world.

Introduction

Perhaps in providence all students are gifts, and yet some stand out as gifts of grace: their eagerness for God and eagerness to learn make them a joy to teach.

Just a few weeks ago I got a letter from one whose name on the envelope brought to mind a young woman whose student days were marked by her articulate, passionate commitments about the meaning of life, and of her own life. Unusual in her maturity, Lori already knew that education had to be, for students who take the gospel of the kingdom seriously, more than a passport to privilege. She was so good at understanding the nuances and writing about the complexities that I read her papers to my faculty colleagues. Like me, they needed to know that some students take it all seriously, really wrestling with the reading and its implications for life and the world.

Lori's letter came in response to an essay I had written for *The Washington Notes,* a publication sent to alumni and faculty friends of the American Studies Program. "Embracing the Brokenness" was a reflection on the centrality of that call for all vocations—even as we, in imitation of Christ, face the fallenness of the world in its tragedy, injustice and sadness. In particular, I had written about how incredibly hard it was for several students I had taught over the previous year, from institutions as diverse as Stanford, Harvard and Calvin, as they moved from the academic arena into the world of work, trying to meaningfully connect their faith with their vocational visions.

Lori wrote:

> Where to begin? I cannot believe that a year-and-a-half has passed since my convicting semester in Washington. . . . So many memories of my learning, laughing, and discovering parts of myself, new per-

spectives, and the face of God. Oh, how I miss the stimulation, challenges, mental exercises, guidance and controversy of that joyous and unforgettable fall. So many times I have started letters to you that were never mailed for one reason or another. I was so excited to find the American Studies Program newsletter on my kitchen table when I returned from a long day at work, and I sat down after dinner to read it. I was but halfway through your article when I started to cry, and Scott asked me what I was reading. I could not explain to him how your words grabbed on to my heart, and I cried for my own exhaustion and frustration with the brokenness I see daily. . . . How do you keep at it? How do you keep going? What words do you use to pray?

She went on for many pages, telling of her new marriage and her job as a social worker. Of the job she wrote, "I'm sure you can imagine that I have certainly seen some brokenness." The weight of her letter, though, came in the next paragraph:

I do not hate my job. Our caseloads are low here, I enjoy the staff, and the pay and benefits are generous. I just don't find the work rewarding. I have seen and heard so much in the families I work with and "help," and the problems seem so mammoth. I do appreciate the relationships I've built with some of my clients, but I am so overwhelmed. I realize that one reason I'm so unhappy is that I miss the mental stimulation and intellectual discussion of college and my hospice internship. Steve, if I remained mentally alert and absorbed in all that I deal with, I couldn't get up in the morning!

A few pages later her last words were these: "I hope you and your family are doing well. Your secrets for dealing with the brokenness are coveted by one who has been blindsided by the reality of the world."

Why do you get up in the morning? For nearly twenty years I have been teaching university students in many different kinds of settings—both those laboring away at secular-spirited institutions and those within Christ-centered colleges and universities, both undergraduates and graduate students, both within the classroom as a professor and outside as a campus minister—and in a variety of ways I have asked this question. It gets at the relationship between what one believes about the world and how one lives in the world, particularly as that dynamic interaction is being formed as young people begin to move out of their parents' worlds and worldviews and take up their own convictions as frameworks within which to live and move and have their being. But it also focuses a student's attention, asking for a good reason to get up beyond the call of the cafeteria or the classroom.

At heart that more playful question is rooted in more substantive ones: Which commitments will give shape to my life? Is my life about something that matters? What do I really care about? In this vocation of talking to students about the issues of life, I have had countless conversations like the one in this letter. Often they are face-to-face, but more often they come in correspondence; typically the world of higher education is not a place where ideas and consequences are clearly connected, and so "the reality of the world" has not yet been faced in all its fallen fury.

But it does come, every time and for everyone. The good news is that my student friend wrote, conscious of her need to work through the difficulty of coherently connecting what she had learned with how she would live. That has always been the challenge for those whose callings take them through the university on their way into the rest of life.

Hundreds of years ago, on the northern coast of the Mediterranean Sea, a young African named Augustine took up this journey into the academy and beyond. A brilliant student, he was torn between the pressures from his father to succeed, achieving along the way all of the human honors attainable to someone so young and able; his mother, whose vision of her son's success was rooted in her own love for God, yearning that academic achievement might be the means by which he would come to embrace her own deepest loves; and his friends, whose selfishness and vanity only served to stimulate him to his own natural vices, Augustine found himself retrospectively self-conscious of the transformation he was undergoing: he was entering into a crucible in which *moral meaning* was being formed.[1]

In *Confessions,* after acknowledging an especially grievous time of telling "lies to my tutors, my masters and my parents," he recalls,

These were the ways of the world upon whose threshold I stood as a boy, and such was the arena for which I was training—more concerned to avoid committing a grammatical error than to be void of envy in case I did commit one and another did not. . . . This I say and confess to Thee, O My God: and in this I was praised by those whom my one idea of success was to please. I did not see the whirl of vileness into which I had been cast away from Thy eyes: for what was more unclean than I. . . . Is this boyhood innocence? It is not, Lord. I cry Thy mercy, O My God. Yet as we leave behind tutors and masters and nuts and balls and birds and come to deal with prefects and kings and the getting of gold and estates and slaves, these are the qualities which pass on with us, one stage of life taking the place of another as the greater punishments of the law take the place of the schoolmaster's cane.[2]

In every generation the years between adolescence and adulthood have been ones in which people have asked the cosmic questions and wrestled— for better or for worse—with answers. This period of intense self-scrutiny led Augustine to reexamine his deepest assumptions about God, human nature and history. From his academic mastery of Cicero to his delving into the philosophy of the Manicheans, through those years between boyhood and manhood he was aware of what, in our time, Erik Erikson has called "the existence of developmental crises."[3] As Augustine looked back on that experience, from the perspective of years later, his heart was full of the lament:

O God, my hope from my youth, where were You all this time, where had You gone? For was it not You who created me and distinguished me from the beasts of the field and made me wiser than the birds of the air? Yet I walked through dark and slippery places, and I went out of myself in the search for You and did not find the God of my heart. I had come into the depths of the sea and I had lost faith and all hope of discovering the truth.[4]

And yet through the faithful love of his mother, Monica, the "dark and slippery places" were not endpoints, but only points along the way. With "the courage of piety . . . she multiplied her prayers and tears that You should hasten Your help and enlighten my darkness. . . . She took it for granted that I had to pass on my way from sickness to health, with some graver peril yet to come, analogous to what doctors call the crises."[5]

Erik Erikson, professor emeritus of human development at Harvard until his recent death, influenced a generation of scholars with his seminal thinking on the meaning of the life cycle. About "crises" in the stages of human development he wrote:

> I must briefly define this ancient little word. In clinical work (as in economics and politics) crisis has increasingly taken on half of its meaning, the catastrophic half, while in medicine a crisis once meant a turning point for better or for worse, a crucial period in which a decisive turn *one way or another* is unavoidable. Such crises occur in man's total development sometimes more noisily, as it were, when new instinctual needs meet abrupt prohibitions, sometimes more quietly when new capacities yearn to match new opportunities, and when new aspirations make it more obvious how limited one (as yet) is. We would have to talk of all these and more if we wanted to gain an impression of the difficult function—of functional unity.[6]

It is this notion of "functional unity" in the face of crisis that connects Augustine and Erikson, bridging the centuries and the cultures which separate them.

And it is this vision of "functional unity," particularly as it is formed during the university years, that this book explores. In Erikson's understanding, an individual could develop an identity that stood against the "disorder, dysfunction, disintegration, anomie" of the modern world, thereby coming to be "the strong person" whose life was marked by a deepening integrity which, in his words, "can balance despair."[7]

Wherever one listens in on the world of today's students, there are echoes of anomie. But if we listen closely enough, we notice that these deep-seated worries about existential choices and their eternal consequences are not new, much as they do in fact characterize the student experience in the contemporary world. Rather, in some sense they are endemic to that unique period of time between adolescence and adulthood when choices about meaning and morality—what one believes to be real and true and right—are being made (choices which, more often than not, last for the rest of life). Whether it is Augustine wrestling with the "crises" of his own life and faith fifteen hundred years ago, or countless others whose stories chronicle the developmental dynamics of these critical years, time and again we are allowed in to view, as Erikson saw it, "a crucial period in which a decisive turn *one way or another* is unavoidable."

One of the most widely respected observers of the modern world, as it was coming into being a century and a half ago, was the Frenchman Alexis de Tocqueville. His memory of "an incident in my youth that marked me deeply for the rest of my life" is one more story of a student straining for an identity and integrity of his own, and painfully aware of his stumbling along the way.

> I heaped pell-mell into my mind all sorts of notions and ideas which belong more properly to a more mature age. Until that time, my life had passed enveloped in a faith that hadn't allowed doubt to penetrate into my soul. Then doubt entered, or rather hurtled in with an incredible violence, not only doubt about one thing or another in particular, but an all-embracing doubt. . . . I was seized by the blackest melancholy, then by an extreme disgust with life—though I knew nothing of life—and was almost prostrated by agitation and terror at the sight of the road that remained for me to travel in this world. . . . I see the world of ideas revolving and I am lost and bewildered in this universal motion that upsets and shakes all the truths on which I base my beliefs and my actions.[8]

His biographer writes, "Suddenly let loose in the world of ideas, he felt his own universe totter."[9]

Augustine, Tocqueville—and Billy Corgan? As I wrote the first edition of this book, *Rolling Stone,* the pop culture chronicle of rock music, had a cover story on one of the most hip groups doing music in the 1990s: Smashing Pumpkins. Their newest album at the time was titled *Mellon Collie and the Infinite Sadness;* they consciously appeal to kids moving through the awkwardness of adolescence. Though they are embarrassed by their reputation as "the poster band for dysfunctional America,"[10] their lyrics are in fact a sad reflection of the "disorder, dysfunction, disintegration, anomie" which Erikson argued shape our experience in the modern world. In their concerts Corgan would proudly wear a T-shirt bearing the name of his song "Zero." Its vision of human life under the sun—"god is empty just like me . . . I'm in love with my sadness"—is an eerie echo of Augustine's "O God . . . where had you gone?" and Tocqueville's "I was seized by the blackest melancholy."[11]

The "dark and slippery places" of Augustine's youth are there for every generation, as the years between adolescence and adulthood are a tumultuous time, anywhere and everywhere. Many students, perhaps most, emerge from their university experience ready to take on the world; the idealism of youth, we call it. But then somewhere along the way the reality of life in the fast lane of adult responsibility hits—sometimes like a ton of bricks, sometimes like acid rain. In a thousand ways they see how hard it is to be faithful to family, at work, in politics. Day in and day out they experience disappointments in every part of life—*every* part of life—and see how hard it is to be hopeful (and therefore responsible) actors in human history as they try to be neighbors to those next door and to those around the world.

The cartoon "Non Sequitur" captures this brilliantly, allowing us to smile even as we see its sober realities. Titled "Post Graduation," it shows the hallway of an academic building with an open classroom door identified by the words REAL LIFE 101. Six feet below, an undergraduate is lying face down on the sidewalk, smashed flat against the concrete, his papers strewn all about. Nearby is a sign that reads: WARNING. NO LIFEGUARD ON DUTY EVER.

And yet there are students who come through that crucible with habits of heart and mind so in place that they move on into the responsibilities and privileges of adulthood without compromising their basic integrity or giving in to the cynicism of "realpolitik," "realeconomik" or "realaesthetik."

Who are they? What happens during their university years that so forms their vision and virtues that they make it through the proverbial "valley of the diapers" of their twenties and thirties with their convictions and character intact? How does a person decide which cares and commitments will give shape and substance to life, for life? How do students learn to conscientiously connect what they believe about the world with how they live in the world?

It is the exploration of these questions that forms the substance of this book. My study takes its place within a literature that ranges from sociology to psychology to educational theory to philosophy and theology.

The thesis amounts to this: The years between adolescence and adulthood are a crucible in which moral meaning is being formed, and central to that formation is a vision of integrity which coherently connects belief to behavior, personally as well as publicly (chapter one); the conditions of modern consciousness, especially as they are manifest in the modern university, make it increasingly difficult for young people to come through those years with the habits of heart required to develop and sustain that kind of integrity (chapters two and three); the perspectives of the history of ideas, the ethic of character and the sociology of knowledge provide windows for understanding the challenge people face in forming a coherent life (chapter four); and it is those who develop a worldview that can address the challenge of coherence and truth in a pluralist society (chapter five), who find a relationship with a mentor who incarnates that worldview (chapter six), and who choose to live their lives among others whose common life is an embodiment of that worldview (chapter seven) who continue on with integrity into adulthood. Finally, the White Rose tells of students whose vision and virtues enabled them to see into their own moment in history and to act with unusual courage in the face of one of the greatest horrors of the twentieth century (chapter eight).

Weaving together belief and behavior during the university years is no small thing. And yet in every generation lovers of Christ have given heart, soul, mind and strength to that task. After the dark and slippery places of his adolescence and early adulthood, by amazing grace Augustine finally found the God of his heart. In the years that followed, his study and service eventually led him to an appointment as the bishop of Hippo. In that setting his deepening understanding of God, human nature and history, and his analytical ability—so finely tuned over the years of his academic training in rhetoric—made him much sought after as an arbiter of orthodoxy in his own time. Among those whose questions wound their way to Hippo was a well-educated Roman layman who asked, "What do we believe?" As an answer to Laurentius, and as a gift to the centuries that have followed, Augustine wrote a long letter in which he wove together the Apostles' Creed, the Lord's Prayer and the theological virtues of faith, hope and love. The *Enchiridion*, a handbook on Christian belief, has served the church in every generation since. The Benedictines saw it as "verily a book of gold, to be kept in hand night and day." Recently one Augustinian scholar remarked: "Of all the works of St. Augustine, no other one, surely, has occupied the attention more continuously than the *Enchiridion*."[12]

Toward the end of his letter, Augustine sums up his lifelong reflection on the meaning of Christian doctrine and discipleship: "For when there is a question as to whether a man is good, one does not ask what he believes, or what he hopes, but what he loves." Simply and profoundly, Augustine brought together what my own more limited experience and ability has concluded, as I have wondered how we can teach students a worldview that will become a way of life.

If we could hear him asking Laurentius a question in return, it would be this: "What do you love?" It is in that question and the spiritual dynamics implicit in its answer that belief and behavior are woven together.

Learning to Care

*Remember your Creator during your youth: when all possibilities lie
open before you and you can offer all your strength intact for his service.
The time to remember is not after you become senile and paralyzed!
Then it is not too late for your salvation, but too late for you to serve
as the presence of God in the midst of the world and the creation.
You must take sides earlier—when you can actually make choices, when
you have many paths opening at your feet, before the weight of necessity
overwhelms you.*

JACQUES ELLUL, *Reason for Being: A Meditation on Ecclesiastes*[1]

W̶hat do you care about?" asks Sabina of Tomas, in Milan Kundera's
novel-made-film, *The Unbearable Lightness of Being.* The two are sitting in a
club and have had a long conversation about Oedipus and political responsibility. Tomas argues that Oedipus blinded himself after he saw what his
wrong choices had done to his country, while the Communist Party officials
eating and drinking at a nearby table had no sense of responsibility or shame
for the havoc they had wrought upon Czechoslovakia. He concludes by saying, "I don't care about politics!"[2]

What do you care about? The question is in its own way the thread that
connects the story from beginning to end. On one level the plot is about a
man who wonders if sex must be connected to love; in the end, after literally
countless "light" liaisons, he decides that it must be, choosing for fidelity.
That itself is a point worth pondering. But on another level it is a meditation

in metaphysics, in the weightiest issues of life in the world. (The novel allows for this in a way that the film never can as it gets lost in the imagery of sex with or without love.) This deeper dimension revolves around a play on words that takes place in the fourth movement of Beethoven's last quartet, Opus 135. The famous "Muss es sein? Es muss sein!" motif—which Beethoven introduced with the phrase "the difficult resolution"—is all about the deepest questions of the cosmos, which Kundera raises on page one and continues asking throughout his novel.

Kundera assumes that Nietzsche was right when, a century ago, he argued that it was senseless to contend for moral meaning in a world without God. With that as a backdrop Kundera walks his way through a discussion of Beethoven's "Must it be? It must be!" motif, which is a reflection on the nature of human responsibility, namely, What does it mean to choose? Do my choices matter?

As the first chapter concludes, we are left with a "profound moral perversity . . . for in this world everything is pardoned in advance and therefore everything cynically permitted."[3] As the author develops his thesis in the life of Tomas—who in the face of political persecution chose to give up his vocation as a brain surgeon to become a window-washer—it becomes fixed upon the question of the importance of "an overriding necessity" in life, and in his life.

Leaving Zurich for Prague a few years earlier, Tomas had quietly said to himself, "Es muss sein!" He was thinking of his love for Tereza. No sooner had he crossed the border, however, than he began to doubt whether it actually did have to be. Later, lying next to Tereza, he recalled that he had been led to her by a chain of laughable coincidences that took place seven years earlier (when the chief surgeon's sciatica was in its early stages) and were about to return him to a cage from which he would be unable to escape. Does that mean his life lacked any "Es muss sein!"—any overriding necessity? In my opinion, it did have one. But it was not love, it was his profession. He had come to medicine not by coincidence or calculation but by a deep inner desire. Insofar as it is possible to divide people into categories, the surest criterion is the deep-seated desires that orient them to one or another lifelong activity.[4]

For Tomas—as for all of Kundera's characters—the question "What do you care about?" is a question answered by those "deep-seated desires that orient them to one or another lifelong activity." For every human being under the sun, it is a question asked within the context of one's answers to the most profound questions of meaning and morality.

WHAT DO YOU CARE ABOUT—AND WHY?

How does someone decide which cares and commitments will give shape and substance to life, for life?

In the years of my teaching mission among graduate students in engineering disciplines at Carnegie-Mellon University, one of the students I got to know best was, at one and the same time, both European and Latin—tall and blond, but also Alberto. His grandfather had been a politician in pre-Nazi Germany. Before most of his countrymen knew what was going on, this man had seen through the nationalistic rhetoric of Hitler to the horrors of its totalitarian logic. Risking his career and life, he protested in public. Through the 1930s he was forced to live underground in his homeland, and he was twice captured by the Gestapo before finally fleeing to Brazil. Two generations and two continents later, his grandson speaks five languages and is as proficient in literature, history and theology as he is in computer engineering.

Alberto and I loved going to films together, and one night we saw Uri Barbash's *Beyond the Walls,* a microscopic view of the centuries-old tension between Palestinian and Jew.[5] Called "the most honored film ever made in Israel," it tells its story from the perspective of a group of prisoners in a maximum-security prison. Some are imprisoned for criminal causes, others for political. It is not a happy film. The hardships of prisons and prisoners the world over—the injustices in the name of justice, the abuse of prisoners by each other and their keepers—are poignantly portrayed.

At one point in the story, a Palestinian prisoner says to another, pouring out his frustration, "You only care about ideologies and national pride—not human beings!" On any night, and in any company, it was worth pondering.

But it was a remarkable statement given my companion for the evening and his own family's history of caring about human beings, not about ideologies and national pride. Alberto has deeply wrought convictions which have led him to live a certain kind of way—his heart is as big as a bear's when it comes to people in need, but he has very little patience for duplicity, in persons or polities. In the tapestry of his life his family, his countries, his education, his time in history, all are woven together with a million choices he has made to make Alberto, now in his forties, who he is.

But how does someone decide which cares and commitments will give shape and substance to life . . . for life?

Alberto's story is its own, of course. But he represents a kind of person who has developed habits of heart that give his life coherence, from the most personal areas to the most public arenas. Though his life and education are reflections themselves of the dynamic effects of modernity on humanity— the Holocaust as a powerful admixture of technology and bureaucracy, affecting the sources of his self in profound ways; Ph.D. studies in artificial intelligence at Carnegie-Mellon University's Robotics Institute—he has come into his maturity as a man with his integrity intact, caring about his faith and his family while at the same time professionally competent and politically conscious. And yet, at every significant point along the way, he has struggled deeply in his effort to connect what he *believes* about life and the world with how he *lives in* the world.

What do I believe and why do I believe it? During Alberto's university years in Brazil, the social and political awareness nurtured by his family reached a crisis point as he searched for a meaningful raison d'etre. He found answers through the help of InterVarsity Christian Fellowship on his campus. And there he was introduced to the writings of Francis Schaeffer. In *The God Who Is There* he found an intelligent apologetic that could make sense of the world of ideas and experiences he was discovering at the university.

What kind of life am I going to have? Nine years later, the decision to leave a university teaching position in Brazil for further schooling in the United States meant leaving his widowed mother for several years. *Do these cares and commitments still make sense, given how hard it really is?* As he settled into the rigor of his study and work at the Robotics Institute, the pressures of graduate school on his marriage and family were intense; at points there were great strains upon his wife and his children. *What does this all mean, after all?* He saw his vocation as a calling to service and stewardship—not just as a career and a passport to privilege. So as the time came to begin thinking of life after school, he tried to understand his responsibility as a First-World-educated member of the Two-Thirds World as he responded to the job offers that came to him. The most interesting places to work in the world, for someone with his background and interests, were opened to him. For a time he stayed on in the U.S., working at IBM's think tank, but he has now returned with his family to work in Brazil, commissioned to "connect" his country to the information superhighway.

Through the two decades which have passed since he left home to begin to make his own home—now emerging out of "the valley of the diapers" in his forties—he is still keeping faith with the choices and decisions about moral meaning that he made as an undergraduate.

How is it that someone decides which cares and commitments will give shape and substance to life, for life? This question and its answer are the heart of this book; it is also a question that has grown out of my own life.

UNDERSTANDING THE WORLD AND MY PLACE IN IT

I dropped out of college after my sophomore year. At heart, I simply did not have a good reason to be in school. For the first time in fifteen years, I did not start school in September but instead began working as the managing editor of a small magazine called *Renaissance*. The staff all lived together "in community"—as we called it—in Palo Alto, not far from the Stanford University campus. We were married, married with children, and unmarried like me. We described our magazine as "a radically Christian critique of culture," and in our feature articles and reviews of films, books and plays, we tried to make sense of the Bay Area and America in the early 1970s.

That year I learned a lot about myself and my world. The San Francisco Bay region—with Berkeley at its epicenter—was a heady place in those days. Every major culture shock of the previous decade had begun there. I reveled in it all, going to lectures, films and discussions that challenged my own developing consciousness about what was real and true and right.

As we were all living very simply, I hitchhiked most everywhere that I could not bicycle. During the year I traveled up and down the Pacific Coast Highway several times and in and around the Bay Area week by week. Taking the adventures of the road as an opportunity to sharpen my own beliefs and commitments, characteristically I would engage my ride in a conversation about the meaning of the cosmos. More often than not, I came out of those a bit bloodied intellectually and increasingly aware of how much I did not know.

In those months of listening and learning while living through the best and the worst of a communal experience in the last days of the counterculture, my view of the world and my place in it was expanding. From the Stanford Chapel, where I sat on the floor to hear Daniel Ellsberg and Joan Baez speak about Vietnam, to "hippie houses" in Berkeley where I met gurus representing a world of worldviews, to long conversations in "on-the-cheap" restaurants in San Francisco's Chinatown, I began to sort through what I wanted to learn about life and the world.

And so I began to read with a new reason for reading. For the first time I saw that "ideas have legs"; that there was always a connection between worldviews and ways of life; that in fact there was an integral connection between education and life.

In the mountains above Santa Cruz, that wonderful place along the California coast where in ten minutes one can be in redwood forests or on the beach, a little house along the highway called itself L'Abri (in French "the shelter"). For a few years it served as an American version of its Swiss counterpart, which was a community of writers, lecturers and artists who prayed day by day that God would send those of his choosing to their doorstep— and then took in those who came.

I was intrigued, and I began finding rides there so that I could take part in weekly discussions and lectures. They offered a simple setting and rich conversation; that was our constant fare. And yet, as I watched and listened, it seemed that the living room was full of people who were *not* there: conversations always went back to Francis and Edith Schaeffer, Hans Rookmaaker, "Birdie" Bird, Donald Drew and Os Guinness. Being intellectually curious, I knew some of the names (I had even met the Schaeffers); these people and the ideas associated with them drew me in. They were as interested in the evolution of rock and roll as they were in the reliability of the Scriptures; they wrote as knowledgeably of Camus as they did of Calvin; they understood the protests of contemporary students as well as they understood the theological protests of the sixteenth century. A match was lit in my heart which still burns now, more than thirty years later.

CAMUS, A GREEK CAFÉ AND CRITICAL CONSCIOUSNESS

The next fall I went to Europe to study in the L'Abri community. Located in a small village in the Swiss Alps, it had been founded by Francis and Edith Schaeffer in the 1950s as a place for young people to "ask honest questions and get honest answers." By the early 1970s, there were L'Abri communities in England, Holland and Italy, and they were typically full of university-and-beyond folk who wanted to make sense of their lives and of life. In part that desire was fed by the revolutionary spirit of the socially tumultuous 1960s. But in any decade, the span of years between adolescence and adulthood are "the critical years" in human development—as Sharon Parks has called them—where basic beliefs about life and the world are settled as one begins to live in the adult world.[6]

My study that fall opened up a new universe to me. For the first time I studied ideas that I cared about, issues that really mattered to me. The previous year I had come to see that people lived their lives on the basis of what they believed about human nature and destiny. The meaning of work, of family, of the arts, of economics, of politics—all of life was rooted in assumptions about the meaning of persons. As the literary critic George Steiner has written in *Real Presences*, "To ask 'What is music?' may well be one way of asking 'What is man?'"[7]

I knew my tradition well enough to know that its answer to those questions was that human beings were made in the image of God. But I did not know what one would say after that was said. The question I came to L'Abri with was "What does it mean to be made in the image of God?" and so under the tutelage of Jerram Barrs I read in philosophical and theological anthropology.[8] In many ways the intellectual world I began to explore in those months is the one I am still exploring years later; it gave me questions and categories sufficiently complex that I have not yet come to their end.

In and through my experiences in Europe that fall sleeping in old church-yards in Scotland, seeing a film of Camus's *The Stranger* in London and dis-cussing it for hours in a Greek café, being lost in the Paris subway, hearing bombs blow up in Belfast, talking with a Jungian psychologist on the train to Geneva—I was all the time listening and reading, deepening my under-standing of what I believed and why I believed it.

When I returned to college the next year I knew what I wanted to pursue. I developed an interdisciplinary course of study which drew upon theology, philosophy, history and psychology. As I worked away at my studies, I began to read Schaeffer, Rookmaaker, Drew and Guinness with new eyes.[9]

The mist had cleared. I understood what they were saying and what dif-ference it made in my life and in the world around me. By the time I finished that third year of undergraduate study, I was on my second reading of Guin-ness's *The Dust of Death* (a comprehensive critique of Western secularism, the response of the sixties counterculture, and a proposal for "a third way") and had proposed to the academic dean that he allow credit for a reading group for the next fall which would focus on that book and the ideas and ideolo-gies critiqued within it. And so we read Albert Camus, Franz Fanon, Aldous Huxley, Jacques Ellul, B. F. Skinner and Herbert Marcuse.

In their respective writings and in their practice of an open-hearted community, the L'Abri folk set me on a course of seeing the connections between presuppositions and practice. I have been pursuing that course ever since. Inspired by the vision of "thinking christianly"[10] about my life and world, and prompted by courses in the history of science and the phi-losophy of history, I did a senior thesis titled "From Instauration to Alien-ation." A study of "the two Francis Bacons"—the English philosopher of the seventeenth century and the English painter of the twentieth cen-tury—took most of my energy that year, but it served to integrate my stud-ies in a way that gave meaning to my academic labor, which by that time was a labor of love.

It was clearly a time for developing what Paulo Freire has called "critical consciousness."[11] What is it I believe about the world? Why do I believe it? What difference does it make, to me and the world around? That critical consciousness influenced what I read, whom I talked to and where I traveled. I wanted to understand the world and my place in it. I began graduate school still pursuing questions in philosophical and theological anthropology, questions such as *What do I believe about human nature, and what difference does it make?*

THE FORMING OF A QUESTION

With those questions as context, I began to teach. For thirty years now I have lived my life among students, serving them in a variety of capacities: pastor, teacher, friend. As I gave myself to that vocation, I came to love both my students and my subject. It was not too many years, though, before a question began to form within me as I lectured and listened. *How do we help students learn to connect what they believe about the world with how they live in the world?* I was just beginning to see that it was not enough to give students good books and take them to great lectures.

Those were years of "circuit riding" around the state of Kansas, visiting staff and students in my position as area director for InterVarsity Christian Fellowship. I came to know the interesting bookstores and cafés in the university towns of Lawrence, Topeka, Manhattan, Hays, Wichita and Emporia, with occasional stops in between at small community and church-related colleges scattered across the plains of the Sunflower State.

The question of how to help students learn to connect belief to behavior became more focused as I spent summers at InterVarsity's Bear Trap Ranch in the mountains above Colorado Springs, teaching in the School for Discipleship Training, a residential study program for university students from the Mississippi River to the Rocky Mountains. There I would meet the sophisticated seekers from Washington University and Rice University, the responsible ranch kids from the University of Wyoming and Kansas State University, the serious students from Baylor and Bethel—the whole spectrum of institutions was represented, from large and urban to land-grant and rural to small and liberal arts.

For several years the question germinated as I worked as staff specialist for the Coalition for Christian Outreach in Pittsburgh, in a teaching mission among graduate students. There I spent my days walking between medical and law students at the University of Pittsburgh and engineering students at Carnegie-Mellon University, with occasional forays into the undergraduate world of places like Chatham College and Penn State University. During that time I sponsored a lecture series called "Knowing and Doing: Crucial Questions for the Modern University" which was set in the Heinz Chapel, right in the middle of Pittsburgh's academic and artistic center.

Over the years we listened to J. I. Packer, Bishop Alden Hathaway, Jim Sire, Nigel Goodwin, John Perkins, Os Guinness and John Stott speak on the relationship of knowledge to responsibility. For me it was a time of starting to see my question as a public question, with institutional implications for the world of higher education.

Later a friend asked me to help him develop a summer residential study program which would focus on this same question. We called our month-long effort "Knowing and Doing." Sponsored by the C. S. Lewis Institute in Washington, D.C., we invited key students to come spend time with us studying the relation of belief to behavior. As we had access to a beautiful farm on the Eastern Shore of the Chesapeake Bay, where the sun could be seen stretching out over the bay from sunrise to sunset, it was not hard to find folks who wanted to come. The program changed some over the years of its existence, later drawing eager adults who wanted a week or two of a learning vacation, but its theme was the same: in the context of the cultural challenges of the modern world, how do we connect what we know with what we do?

And then for the next fifteen years I taught at the American Studies Program, an interdisciplinary semester on Capitol Hill which has the aim of nurturing in undergraduates a vision for responsible public involvement. Begun by a young foreign service officer in the State Department in the mid-1970s, it developed into an intense living/learning experience, drawing forty students who spend four months studying why and how to "make connections" between personal faith and public life. One alumnus described our efforts as "an urban, intellectual Outward Bound." There I was given the freedom to spend several summers studying the historical and philosophical issues which are implicit in the question that started so small, so long ago now.

From there I began a pilgrimage among students and faculty across the country and beyond, visiting many schools, but always with the same question at hand—namely, can you help us understand this relationship of worldview to way of life in the formation of visions of education and vocation? Much of my work in that time was as the scholar-in-residence for the Council for Christian Colleges and Universities, though I continued to journey among the more secular-spirited institutions as well, feeling a profound loyalty to both worlds. At least as I saw it, while the sociological context for learning was remarkably different for students at the University of Chicago and Wheaton College, the cultural challenge was the same: will they have learned the skills of heart and mind to avoid the compartmentalization of faith from life that seems written into the social contract of the modern-becoming-postmodern world? The question grew out of face-to-face conversations with students, on the one hand, and on the other, from relationships with people beyond their university years who had eyes to see more clearly what learning, and life, are all about.

Over those years of teaching students and others in a variety of settings, I saw that some learned to link belief to behavior and that some did not. But even more troubling to me as a teacher was that some appeared to understand the relationship between worldview and way of life—they read all the right books, went to all the right conferences and gave all the right answers, with seeming sincerity—and then slowly, inch by inch, they began to disconnect what they said they believed from how they lived. It is those stories which are the most painful to me. I am chilled in my soul as I remember these people whom I have loved, prayed with and played with, who have read "the right books" but no longer believe them to be true to the way the world really is.

How are we to understand this phenomenon, that some make the connection between belief and behavior in a way that is sustained and some do not? What is it that happens when a person, moving from student years into adulthood, continues to construct a coherent life? How does a worldview become a way of life? How do students learn to connect presuppositions with practice—belief *about* the world with life *in* the world—in the most personal areas and the most public arenas? In a variety of ways, these questions all revolve around one's definition of integrity.

LESSONS ON LEARNING

As I worked to understand why and how those connections are made and
not made, I began to read. A mentor of mine suggested the Marxists, offering
their view of *praxis* as an avenue of exploring the relation between knowing
and doing. I began exploring the history of ideas—that *what I believe is the
result of the philosophers and theologians I have read.* Inevitably, over the course
of years, that reading led me to the centuries-old conversation called the
ethic of character—that *what I believe is most clearly seen in how I live.* For several years I worked within those two perspectives, working to understand
how they contributed to the formation of a life of integrity. But it was not
until I began to read in the sociology of knowledge that a critical third lens
was brought to bear upon the question—that *what I believe is deeply affected
by my social experience:* my family, community, city, society and century. And
so I began to examine the issue of connecting belief to behavior through the
perspectives of

- the history of ideas
- the ethic of character
- the sociology of knowledge

Each offers a unique vantage point from which to understand what we believe and how we behave.

I also began interviewing people who had developed into the kind of
people I always wanted my students to become: folk who were intentional
about connecting what they believed with how they lived, across the spectrum of their responsibilities as human beings, personally as well as publicly.
The criteria that I set were these: (1) they needed to be twenty or more years
beyond their university experience, as less time would not allow for habits
of heart to be substantially established, and (2) they needed to be people
who consciously cared about making the connections between belief and
behavior. And they must not have given up on the effort to do so, even
amidst the tremendous pressures—from the world, the flesh and the devil—
to stop trying.

Each person responded to a series of questions that asked them to reflect
on their "cares and commitments" at this point in their lives, and what had

happened during their university experience that gave "shape and sub-stance" to them. In a variety of ways, this question was asked again and again: What is the relation between how you are living today—particularly your sense of what is most important, what you most care about—and the tapestry of influences on you during your university years?

PATTERNS OF INTENTIONALITY

So around the orbit of the question "What do you care about?" was an attempt to understand what Craig Dykstra has called "patterns of intentionality": the habits of heart that characterize the individual's effort to live a coherent life over the course of life.

If intentionality is an essential feature of faith, then what one looks at to discern growth in faith is the whole constellation of the self, not just structural features. . . . What I mean by intentionality is not discrete, isolated "intentions," but the total orientation of the self that gives it whatever coherence and integrity it has. Intentionality also suggests the idea that who we become is to a major extent our own responsibility. . . . What one would look for, then, if one wished to analyze change or growth in a person's faith, would be the patterns of intentionality that constitute a person's fundamental orientation in life. . . . By the use of such questions, one would be trying to discern the narrative of a person's life and see how the different themes, events and experiences in it hold together. And one would analyze that narrative in order to discern what patterned orientation or fundamental intentionality is imbedded in it, rather than structural capacities abstracted from it.[12]

Dykstra's definition here is not so different from Kundera's observation that "the deep-seated desires that orient them to one or another lifelong activity" are "the surest criterion" for understanding the cares and commitments that distinguish one person from another. For everyone under the sun—those who go to the university and those who do not—the deep-seated desires are shaped by the dynamic interaction between belief and behavior. But for those who do go into the academy following adolescence, their experiences there are critical in establishing "the patterns of intentionality that constitute a person's fundamental orientation in life."

Dykstra's discussion of this orientation takes its place within a discipline called "faith development theory."[13] A daughter of Lawrence Kohlberg's moral development theory, it is an effort to understand human development by means of centering on the formation of faith. Though conceptions of the life of faith have been offered in each generation—*The Quest for the Holy Grail* and *Pilgrim's Progress* are two examples—our century's preoccupation with "scientific" bases for anything and everything has produced a paradigm for understanding the contours of religious belief which takes its place alongside other "theories" within the modern university. As a theory its primary proponent has been the theologian James Fowler, whose study of the works of Jean Piaget, Erik Erikson and Lawrence Kohlberg gave him models of interpretation to understand what he called "faith development."[14] Fowler's work is imaginatively rich, drawing on both ancient and contemporary sources to examine the question "What are the stages of faith?"[15]

The kind of people I interviewed represent a stage that Fowler calls "a normative image of maturity"[16] within the Christian vision of life and the world. In their own ways, time and again, their stories reveal articulate, passionate people who live their lives for the sake of the kingdom of God—their fundamental orientation in life—and see that as an image which determines particular behavior, both personally and publicly.

I interviewed an academic-activist who lives his life for the sake of educating Christian leaders in the Two-Thirds World (as he insists that it be called), drawing them to his Oxford setting for creative, cutting-edge theological training; a "calling" consultant who spends his days helping individuals and institutions understand the vocational threads that make work more satisfying; an artist who lives and breathes aesthetically, even while she spends her occupational hours in a Washington think tank; an American living in rural England who has "rediscovered" his vocation as the pastor of a lively church; a professor at a large research university in Pennsylvania whose thoughtful, committed care for his colleagues and his community is exemplary; a White House attorney whose excellence allowed him to survive the change of administrations; a school teacher in Cyprus whose vision of cultural responsibility begins with his vision of nurturing his family in responsible living; a Malaysian with a deep sense of calling to public service within his nation's Ministry of Trade and Commerce; and others whose stories will be told on these pages.

Their lives continue to be marked by a "radical commitment to justice and love and . . . selfless passion for a transformed world."[17] In contrast to most, they are not people who lost their way before they even finished their university years,[18] nor did they get lost in "the valley of the diapers," the years of settling into the responsibilities of adulthood.[19] For a number of good reasons, they did not lose the vision with which they set out from college, that of a coherent life centered in their deepest convictions about what is real and true and right. Their "patterns of intentionality" caused them to deepen, not discard, their understanding of the meaning of life and its consequent moral vision.

But what are those "good reasons"? If understanding how belief becomes behavior is the result of a textured reading of the history of ideas, the ethic of character and the sociology of knowledge, then understanding those who have kept faith over the years—who with substantial integrity have connected belief to behavior, personally as well as publicly—requires the weaving together of these three strands: *convictions, character* and *community.* In the tapestrylike stories of the experiences of those interviewed, these three factors were the major influences, as seen retrospectively, on the construction of their respective visions of what is real and true and right, especially as they live out of and with that vision twenty years later.

- Convictions: They were taught a worldview which was sufficient for the questions and crises of the next twenty years, particularly the challenge of modern and postmodern consciousness with its implicit secularization and pluralization.

- Character: They met a teacher who incarnated the worldview which they were coming to consciously identify as their own, and in and through that relationship they saw that it was possible to reside within that worldview themselves.

- Community: They made choices over the years to live out their worldview in the company of mutually committed folk who provided a network of stimulation and support which showed that the ideas could be coherent across the whole of life.

Woven together, convictions, character and community nourish a vision of moral meaning which can stand against the most destructive forces of the contemporary world.[20]

As I have listened to these folk who are working to coherently connect their lives—people from the northern and southern hemispheres, Europeans and Asians, people whose vocations have them day by day in rural health clinics, universities, churches, businesses, think tanks and government—again and again I have heard them talk about their college years as ones where they were asking basic questions about meaning and morality, about belief and behavior. But most importantly, over the twenty years since then they are people who have lived out the convictions formed in those years.

ANCIENT WISDOM FOR MODERN STUDENTS

This book is about how people learn to translate what they believe about the world into how they live in the world. My conclusions are shaped by both deductive (the perspectival lenses) and inductive (the interviews) approaches to the question. I have listened to the philosophers reflect on the shaping of belief and behavior, and to the practitioners remember the shaping of their own belief and behavior.

Though my question has a particularly modern context of twentieth-becoming-twenty-first-century influences, the dynamics that bring it to life are very ancient. The questions that human beings ask and answer are perennial, whether we see ourselves as premodern, modern or postmodern.[21] "Remember your Creator in the days of your youth." So wrote Qoheleth the Teacher centuries ago, in his examination of the meaning of meaning. In Jacques Ellul's *Reason for Being: A Meditation on Ecclesiastes,* he offers an exposition of Qoheleth's three intertwining themes: vanity, wisdom and God. Those who know the world of contemporary higher education know that though they are not always explicit in the conversation, frontally addressed in seminars and scholarly journals, these themes are always there, implicit at every important point—because they are themes so deeply rooted in the human heart. It is not a question of *whether* one will address these themes; instead it is *how* one understands them—both for those who keep faith and for those who fall along the way.

Ellul's own years of service among students, both through his long tenure on the faculty of the University of Bordeaux and as a scholar in the fields of law and sociology, give him an honored place from which to write about the meaning of the university experience and of youthful choices in the modern world—even as he has himself wrestled with vanity, wisdom and God. His study of the final chapter of Qoheleth's meditation includes these words, which serve as *alpha* and *omega* for this book:

> Remember your Creator during your youth: when all possibilities lie open before you and you can offer all your strength intact for his service. The time to remember is not after you become senile and paralyzed! Then it is not too late for your salvation, but too late for you to serve as the presence of God in the midst of the world and the creation. You must take sides earlier—when you can actually make choices, when you have many paths opening at your feet, before the weight of necessity overwhelms you.[22]

This labor of love has as its goal that people—students and those who care for them, as well as the many who have moved beyond their student years—might understand how to more faithfully and effectively nurture a vision of being "the presence of God in the midst of the world and the creation." That is a reason for being, and for being lifelong learners, remembering that the point of learning—rooted as it is in the word for "disciple"—is that we become people who sustain our commitments, with gladness and singleness of heart.

The Problem and Its Parameters

Tis all in peeces, all coherence gone;
All just supply, and all relation:
Prince, Subject, Father, Sonne, are things forgot
For every man alone thinkes he hath got
To be a Phoenix, and that then can bee
None of that kinde, of which he is, but hee.

JOHN DONNE, *An Anatomie of the World*[1]

It was a wonderful title, and I did not resist. "Beavis, Butthead & Budding Nihilists: Will Western Civilization Survive?" In this op-ed piece in *The Washington Post* the Harvard junior lamented that the world is already passing him by, and he is barely into the "twentysomethings"! He writes:

> Meet the Beavis Generation. I have, and it scares me. Sad to say, the ascent of Beavis and Butthead marks the dethroning of Bart Simpson as the king of adolescent rebellion. This is profoundly significant. Bart, for all of his run-ins with Principal Skinner, is as smart as he is tough. Beavis and Butthead boast IQs safely in the two-digit range—a fact that this new generation revels in.

And who are Beavis and Butthead? "Two teenaged losers—the eponymous B & B—mindlessly watch videos, and they snicker. Like this: 'ehehehehehehehe.' Or sometimes like this: 'hehehehehehehe.'" In a perceptive analysis of what the show represented, the undergraduate understood that

B & B help us "understand what the next century will be like. The founding principle will be nihilism. Rampant disregard for other living things (e.g., hitting frogs with a baseball bat) will be in. Taking responsibility for one's actions will be out." But his most telling line comes at the end: "It's proof that there is a whole new generation out there that completely understands all of this society's foibles. And can only snicker."[2]

WHY BEAVIS AND BUTTHEAD IS NOT A GOOD ANSWER

And can only snicker. One only has to hear the cries of people who feel overwhelmed with the brokenness of the world, as I do year after year, to feel the force of the challenge from Beavis and Butthead. While their humor is like dew in the morning, and other poets and prophets, comic as they are, have taken their place, the cynicism that characterizes their critique is perennial, growing as it does out of a fear that to hope will only bring sorrow.

I remember a conversation with a young Asian American woman, born in Hong Kong and now living in the U.S., who came in to talk about her studies. She is typical of so many with her background: strong parental involvement in her life, raised with high expectations of excellence in life and learning, responsive and responsible in many wonderful ways. We were trying to understand the role of the U.S. in helping emerging democracies in Eastern Europe—now, after the fall of communism, we see that it is tremendously difficult for the former Soviet bloc countries to break free from decades and generations of systemic injustice, and the question is "How is the U.S. to help in a way that does justice and loves mercy?" It was not long before her academic queries got all mixed up with her deepest beliefs about life and the world. With anguish in her voice and tears running down her cheeks she blurted out, "The whole society is wrong . . . whether it's this reform or that reform . . . it's not going to change anything!"

The next year another student came in to talk, this time in the context of our study of the welfare reform debate. How are we to mend the cracks in capitalism which allow for some of the most powerful people on earth to live and work and have their being literally within blocks of some of the most powerless people in our society? The neighborhood I describe is Capitol Hill, and for just these sociological dynamics it is often "reality therapy" for our students to live and study and work with the contradictions and tensions of the world "in their faces," so to speak.

This student was a bright young Californian from an African American family that had nurtured him in thoughtful, responsible commitments. As we talked I could see that the dilemma had dropped down on his shoulders. The complexities of continuing racial discrimination, of economic empowerment, of partisan political debate, all had worn him down. As he faced the prospect of trying to sort it all out on paper for me, he began to cry, murmuring, "What's the use? What difference does it make anyway?"

Not all my conversations with students end in tears, of course. But for those who begin to understand the implications of belief for behavior, and who see how tremendously complex the challenge is, the intellectual tension sometimes becomes spiritual pain. And the questions and the tears flow.

How is it possible to see into the meaning of one's moment in history and to act responsibly, rather than be overwhelmed by either cynicism or sorrow because the brokenness seems so deep, the pain so profound? In a certain sense, everything we do as human beings is rooted in that question. Decisions we make within families either nourish or destroy our connectedness. Choices we make about our vocations lead to deeper commitments or greater dissatisfaction. Attitudes we nurture about "common good" responsibilities cause us either to be more fully engaged or to retreat into the sphere of those who do not care. Day by day we are forming characters and forming cultures in the way we respond to the world. If we are to avoid the paralysis of destructive cynicism and debilitating sorrow, somehow, somewhere, we have to make sense of the world—not only of our own lives, but of life.

THE QUESTION OF *TELOS* AND *PRAXIS*

Do you have a *telos* sufficient, personally and publicly, to orient your *praxis* over the course of life? Spending several months reading Alasdair MacIntyre's *After Virtue* and Richard Bernstein's *Beyond Objectivism and Relativism*—both serious efforts to make moral sense of our times—persuaded me that the relationship of *telos* to *praxis* was a critical one for people of our century, and every century.[3] As I began to understand the importance of their arguments, and as I continue to listen to the groaning of young men and women year after year, I have asked this question as they come and again as they go.

True education is always about learning to connect knowing with doing, belief with behavior; and yet that connection is incredibly difficult to make for students in the modern university. The historical context of university life in the early twenty-first century, with all that we now know of the post-Enlightenment challenge facing those who labor as students and professors, offers a huge challenge: If we are in fact a culture "after virtue" and "beyond objectivism and relativism," then how is it possible to form moral meaning at all, particularly within the university years—with all its social pressures that bear down on young people learning to make their way in the world?

This issue and how we resolve it matters. For those whose vocations give them responsibility for students, it is not enough to know that they are able to answer all the questions posed during their university years—either those that come formally within the classroom or those that come late at night in a café. Walker Percy's warning about the modern person's "getting all A's but flunking life"[4] is a possibility lurking around the corner of everyone's life. The vocation of teacher requires one to nurture cares and commitments which can be and should be sustained, ones that will last for life because they are worthy of a life. If our culture is to recover the meaning of education, it will be as those who teach begin anew to understand that vocational vision. To labor along with students through the ups and downs of their emergence from adolescence, one has to have a longer view of the meaning of the college experience. The challenge is to translate that vision in ways that students can understand, ways that connect with their sense of what they are doing and why they are doing it.

In this chapter we will begin to look at the cultural conversation brought on by modern consciousness that makes this such a difficult task for today's students. In particular we will examine the *telos* and *praxis* dynamic, both historically and in the context of the works by MacIntyre and Bernstein. In the end we will argue that the questions raised by George Steiner, Robert Bellah and Lesslie Newbigin—rooted as they are in a commitment to transcendence—offer more light to our path.

One spring day, "Frank and Ernest," the comic strip bums, find themselves on a bench, musing over the meaning of life in the world, as a little
boy walks by with schoolbooks under his arm. Out of the mouth of one of
these disheveled characters comes the wisdom of the ages: "School is mostly
true/false, kid, but real life is all essay questions." He is profoundly right. The
question of one's *telos* and its relation to one's *praxis* must be wrestled
through during the critical years in which students are making sense of life
for life, answering questions about what is real and true and right—essay
questions, each one.

ON HAPPY ENDINGS

Over the course of one week, I saw two films that in remarkably different
ways address the challenge of coherently connecting *telos* to *praxis* amid the
pressures of the modern world. A young friend, knowing my interest in film,
begged me to see Robert Altman's *The Player.* A satire on the Hollywood culture and full of cameo performances by most of its famous folk, it is a story
about the "real" bottom line in the film industry. Altman maintains that, in
the end, it is not primarily profits or power which drive the making of movies; instead, it is the requirement of a happy ending. And so, while there are
requisite murders and mysteries in the film, it is the "happy ending" which
emerges as its raison d'etre.[5]

Browsing through Blockbuster a few days later, I came across a new Jeremy Irons film, *Waterland.* The Irons character teaches twentieth-century
history through the lens of his own family's history in this century, a story
begun in England and told in Pittsburgh. While this method has its own
strength as a pedagogical tool, Irons abuses his students with it, failing to do
justice to the curricular requirements of his discipline. While he raises important questions about the meaning of history, too many class hours are
spent in the sad and sordid details of his family life. In the end, his contract
is not renewed. He is asked to speak at the graduation ceremony and, as always, speaks from the heart:

> But as for what really bothers some of you, the end of the future, the
> final end . . . How can I help you? I can't. I'm the same as you . . . I

don't expect much from my future . . . I'm history. But at your age, Price [here he apparently directs his comments to one student, Price, the "rebellious" student who became intrigued by his teacher, hoping that his questions would be answered], I sometimes think all this storytelling is something like a disease . . . I caught it from my father, who caught it from his father. . . . It seemed to keep my father going through his life, telling stories . . . though they never ended well. . . . It was always blood and horror, or sadness and despair. I said to him once, "Don't you know any stories that have a happy ending?" He said, "Nope, nope." And he said if I was ever to find one, I should be sure to let him know.[6]

Two films, two views on "endings." The one laments the commercialization of cinema and the need for happy endings, while the other laments the impossibility of any happy endings. In both, there is an implicit understanding of the relationship of one's view of the end, *telos,* with life, *praxis.* For Altman, a whole industry, individually and institutionally, has prostituted itself for a particular "end." The teacher in *Waterland* gets lost in the cosmos, and loses his job in the process, due to his inability to find a sufficient "end"— an end, that is, that can orient his *praxis* in a way which is meaningful and satisfying to him and to those he works with and for.

The question of *telos* is a question of one's "end." The Westminster Catechism asks, "What is the chief end of man?" In our own time, it might sound more like this: What is the purpose of life? What is human existence all about, anyway? Or as I ask my students, Why do you get up in the morning? *Telos* takes that beyond the trivial and asks one to have a reason for getting up, a reason for being, that can be sustained over the course of life and can meaningfully direct one's personal and public responsibilities. Do you have a *telos* sufficient, personally and politically, to orient your *praxis* over the course of life?

It is an old, old question, going back to our most ancient musings about the meaning of life and the world. Out of Hebrew history, the patriarch Job and the Teacher of Ecclesiastes were people who asked the deepest human questions, pressed as they were by the problems of their own times and places. For those with ears to hear, their stories are full of the question of a sufficient *telos,* a meaningful reason for being, for oneself and for humanity. With his heart full of the greatest of human pains, Job cried out to God, "My days have no meaning" (Job 7:16) and "Why then did you bring me out of the womb?" (10:18). Faced with his horrible losses, he asks, "Why do I exist? What is the point of my life?" As the story unfolds he engages his friends in conversation over his question; eventually God himself engages Job with the question "Do you think you really understand the meaning of your life, and of life?"

The Teacher begins his meditation on life in the universe by crying out, "Meaningless! Meaningless! . . . Utterly meaningless! Everything is meaningless" (Eccles 1:2). He later continues, "Enjoy life with your wife, whom you love, all the days of this meaningless life that God has given you under the sun—all your meaningless days. For this is your lot in life and in your toilsome labor under the sun" (9:9). Apart from their intentional appeal to adolescents, the Smashing Pumpkins, in their artful articulation of angst, offered nothing new under the sun. And yet the sober epilogue of the Teacher's study of human life is that there is a meaningful end: "Now all has been heard; here is the conclusion of the matter: Fear God and keep his commandments, for this is the whole duty of man. For God will bring every deed into judgment, including every hidden thing, whether it is good or evil" (12:13-14).

The first words in Aristotle's *Ethics* are his own ponderings about the question of a *telos* that can meaningfully orient human life.

> Every art or applied science and every systematic investigation, and similarly every action and choice, seem to aim at some good; the good, therefore, has been well defined as that at which all things aim. But it is clear that there is a difference in the ends at which they aim. . . . Of medicine the end is health, of shipbuilding, a vessel, of strategy, victory, and of household management, wealth. . . . Now, if there exists an end in the realm of action which we desire for its own sake, an end which determines all other desires; if, in other words, we do not make all our choices for the sake of something else—for in this way the pro-

cess will go on infinitely so that our desire would be futile and point-less—then obviously this end will be the good, that is, the highest good. Will not the knowledge of this good, consequently, be very important to our lives? Would it not better equip us, like archers, who have a target to aim at, to hit the proper mark?[7]

W. F. R. Hardie's commentary interprets the discussion of *telos* in this way:

> Aristotle, in describing the nature of his inquiry, tries to persuade his hearers to accept at the outset the doctrine that there is one supreme end of action, a final good for man. He seems to suggest that, when this central doctrine has been grasped, there will be a clear programme for what remains to be done, like the filling in of the details in a map when the main lines have been drawn.[8]

It is that teleological vision which threads its way throughout Aristotle's work, as he argues that there is in fact a *telos* which can orient *praxis* over the course of life, what he calls a "complete life." "For one swallow does not make a spring, nor does one sunny day; similarly, one day or a short time does not make a man blessed and happy."[9]

We could walk through the centuries, listening to articulate and passionate people who in every era have wondered aloud, "What is the point of my life?" And though they could come to us representing different voices and visions, again and again they would ask about the relationship between *telos* and *praxis*. Written in stone above Harvard University's Emerson Hall, home of the philosophy department, are the words of the Hebrew poet and king David, "What is man that thou art mindful of him?" (Ps 8:4). The query reverberates over the years, asking each generation to wonder about the relationship between one's answer to the most cosmic questions and one's daily duties and desires, between one's *telos* and one's *praxis*.

And in the modern world, the possibility of that relationship is deeply challenged on a number of fronts—and there are clear consequences for students.

WEEPING FOR STUDENTS
Several years ago I spoke at a retreat for students from Rice University in Houston; we spent the weekend studying the New Testament letter Colos-

sians, trying to understand the worldview and way-of-life dynamic. Over the first meal together we all introduced ourselves. One young man said, "I'm Marc, and I'm an artist." He paused, then added, "But it is all so meaningless."

We talked over the weekend, and I arranged to visit his studio on the Rice campus before going to the airport. With excitement he walked me through the department, showing me various works in progress in the student studio. And then finally we came to his own space, and he announced, "Well, here's my work." The canvases were large, wall-size paintings. One was purple, another blue, still another green. I asked him to tell me about what he was trying to do in his work. For an hour we talked about how his professors had taught him that the meaning of painting was in the technique of applying paint to the canvas. And it was all "so meaningless."

Few in our century have understood the *reductio ad absurdum* of technique as an end in itself with the prescience of Jacques Ellul. In *The Technological Society,* his grand critique of the meaning of technology for the modern world, he writes:

> Technique has become a reality in itself, self-sufficient, with its special laws and its own determinations. Let us not deceive ourselves on this point. . . . Technique tolerates no judgment from without and accepts no limitation. . . . The power and autonomy of technique are so well secured that it, in its turn, has become the judge of what is moral, the creator of a new morality. Thus, it plays the role of creator of a new civilization as well.[10]

From a different vantage point than that of Ellul in the social sciences, Aleksandr Solzhenitsyn, as a great contemporary artist, has brought his considerable prophetic insight to bear on what my friend Marc was experiencing during his university years in Texas. The *New York Times Book Review* gave his remarks upon receiving the National Arts Club medal of honor for literature the title "The Relentless Cult of Novelty and How It Wrecked the Century."

> Every age and every form of creative endeavor owes much to those outstanding artists whose untiring labors brought forth new meanings

and new rhythms. But in the twentieth century the necessary equilibrium between tradition and the search for the new has been repeatedly upset by a falsely understood "avant-gardism"—a raucous, impatient "avant-gardism" at any cost. Dating from before World War I, this movement undertook to destroy all commonly accepted art—its forms, language, features and properties—in its drive to build a kind of "superart" which would then supposedly spawn the New Life itself. It was suggested that literature should start anew "on a blank sheet of paper." (Indeed, some never went much beyond this stage.) Destruction thus became the apotheosis of this belligerent avant-gardism. It aimed to tear down the entire centuries-long cultural tradition, to break and disrupt the natural flow of artistic development by a sudden leap forward. This goal was to be achieved through an empty pursuit of novel forms as an end in itself, all the while lowering the standards of craftsmanship for oneself to the point of slovenliness and artistic crudity, at times combined with a meaning so obscured as to shade into unintelligibility.

Solzhenitsyn continued:

Looking intently, we can see that, behind these ubiquitous and seemingly innocent experiments of rejecting "antiquated" tradition there lies a deep-seated hostility toward any spirituality. This relentless cult of novelty, with its assertion that art need not be good or pure, just so long as it is new, newer, and newer still, conceals an unyielding and long-sustained attempt to undermine, ridicule and uproot all moral precepts. There is no God, there is no truth, the universe is chaotic, all is relative, "the world as text," a text any postmodernist is willing to compose. How clamorous it all is, but also—how helpless.[11]

It was helplessness that I heard in Marc. On the plane home, as I pondered what I had seen in his studio, I found myself becoming very sad—and very mad. The sadness came as I thought of the waste of time and talent in Marc's life. These were to be his "best years," the ones in which he was to learn his art and what its meaning was for life and for his life. The anger came as I thought about his professors and their "emperor's new clothes" approach to the teaching of art. That helplessness-become-meaninglessness should make us weep for students, under the impact of contemporary consciousness, who do not have the critical tools necessary to understand their cultural context with "the relentless cult of novelty" as one of its faces—and what that context means for their efforts to make sense of life for life.

THE CRITIQUES OF MACINTYRE AND BERNSTEIN

It is in the midst of this malaise that MacIntyre and Bernstein have written their books. From different traditions, they have chosen to study a common problem: In the face of the pressures of modern consciousness—what MacIntyre identifies as the effects of the "the Enlightenment Project" and what Bernstein calls the crisis caused by "the Cartesian Anxiety"—how is it possible to think and act in ways which are personally and politically meaningful? Central to both critiques is the thesis that the dynamic relationship of *telos* to *praxis* has been lost over the last few centuries, with devastating cultural consequences. What do they offer to us as we look at the challenge facing students in the modern university?

After Virtue has been one of the most widely read works in moral philosophy in the last generation. Arguing that we are a culture "after virtue" and on the brink of a new dark age, MacIntyre reworks a synthesis between Aristotle and Aquinas as his way out of the morass. Maintaining that even though we still use the same moral language to make sense of our world—a language that arises out of the Greek/Christian worldview—it is no longer meaningful because the language is now disconnected from any moral reality. Instead we have come to live by an ethic of emotivism, one which asserts that "all moral judgments are nothing but expressions of preference."[12] He argues that the failure of the "Enlightenment Project" was its inability to provide an adequate moral basis for modern life. In a profound way, MacIntyre takes up the deepest questions we have as human beings—What is real? What is true? What is right?—and out of his foundational commitments about reality comes a vision of self and society. Like all personal and political visions, it is framed by the question of *telos,* that is, by what standard can human life be meaningfully measured? To what end is human life meaningfully directed?

Bernstein spends himself on the task of developing a moral vision that will escape the facts/values paralysis of the Enlightenment. He identifies the thread of *praxis*—in both its personal and political dimensions—as the important end of his analysis of the hermeneutical movements in modern science. And he does so explicitly in interaction with the Aristotelian tradition, drawing on both the *Ethics* and the *Politics*.

As Bernstein charts his way out of the "Cartesian Anxiety"—the either-or epistemological vision of Descartes ("Either there is some support for our being, a fixed foundation for our knowledge, or we cannot escape the forces of darkness that envelop us with madness, with intellectual and moral chaos")[13] he begins by calling on Aristotle, interpreted through the perspectives of the twentieth-century philosophers Hannah Arendt, Hans Gadamer, Jurgen Habermas and Richard Rorty.

The threads he weaves together bring him to the position that it is only in understanding the interrelations between "science, hermeneutics and praxis" (the subtitle) that one can get free of the objectivist/relativist bind. This thesis is unfolded page by page as he keeps directing the reader to "the new conversation" which, he maintains, moves us beyond objectivism and relativism. In the end, he does not depend on Aristotle for any final answer to his question, though, as with all of us, his answer is framed with the famous philosopher looking over his shoulder.

MacIntyre, on the other hand, conscientiously engages Aristotle and at every point roots both his critique—*after virtue*—and his construction of a way out in the Aristotelian tradition. As with the teleology/moral vision relationship, he does this as he addresses the facts/values dichotomy.

> Aristotle's *Ethics* and *Politics* . . . are as much treatises concerned with how human action is to be explained and understood as with what acts are to be done. Indeed within the Aristotelian framework the one task cannot be discharged without discharging the other. The modern contrast between the sphere of morality on the one hand and the sphere of the human sciences on the other is quite alien to Aristotelianism because, as we have seen, the modern fact/value distinction is also alien to it.[14]

For MacIntyre, the teleology/moral vision discussion and the facts/values discussion are the very same. The resolution of the latter is in a recovery of the meaning of the former: that a meaningful moral vision—one which is not flawed by emotivist doctrine—is one which is necessarily framed by a teleology based on the classical/Christian synthesis.

Bernstein focuses his work in uncovering the hallowed ground of the objectivist and relativist worldviews. Like MacIntyre, he works hard at examining the fundamental philosophical questions and their relevance for personal and public life. As he studies the "either/or" inheritance—which is his major point of critique, as the Enlightenment Project is for MacIntyre—he sees that it has been a constricting one, forcing its one-dimensional view of reality onto the whole of reality, on both sides of the debate. The objectivists' genuine insight into the natural world—that observable patterns of life can be both repeatable and quantifiable—for them became the only way to determine trustworthy information about any and every part of the world. The relativists' understanding that no historical situation is exactly the same as past ones and so each requires a "relative" response became, for them, the means by which every situation is morally judged—thus, no judgment. Bernstein characterizes this no-win situation in this way:

> Once we are caught into thinking that the subjective-objective distinction is a fundamental one that arises as soon as anyone reflects . . . we pursue the variations of this distinction until the subjective becomes virtually synonymous with the private, idiosyncratic and arbitrary. . . . Knowledge must be objective—or else it is only pseudoknowledge. When values enter, they must be treated as noncognitive emotional responses or private subjective preferences.[15]

The "no-win" nature of the facts/values polarization is death to truthful conversation in the public square, be it within the university, the media or the government. Year after year, when my young friends ask, from the deepest places in their being, "How do I coherently connect what I believe about God, truth, history and so on with the *realpolitik* of the public square?" they are coming face to face with the impact of having their most basic beliefs about the nature of life and the world "treated as noncognitive emotional responses or private subjective preferences." More than any other one dilemma, it is this one which causes my students to stumble as they take up the challenge of their studies in this city.

And yet it is not only Washington; it is also Cambridge and Berkeley, New York and Hollywood. In every major center of culture-forming power, the possibility of coherence across the concerns of life is discouraged—not as a plot against or for anyone, but by the very nature of the consciousness-shaping influences of modernity with its disintegrating dichotomies. On the other hand, there are places which intentionally push this facts/values dualism toward its logical end. One example is deconstructionism, an academic apologia for "incoherence," for the meaninglessness of Marc's art.

Whether it is explicit or implicit, in the books they read or the air they breathe, there is a sense of disconnectedness felt by countless students who are stumbling out of the starting blocks in their efforts to be people of integrity in the modern world.

MacIntyre and Bernstein are asking questions that thoughtful modern people must answer. Given the failure of the Enlightenment Project and its emotivist inheritance, is it possible to make sense of our world not only individually but corporately? Are we so far "after virtue" that a new dark age is all we can expect? What does it mean for us to face the failure of both the objectivist and relativist visions? Is there a way forward—both personally and politically—that can meaningfully disentangle the facts/values morass? There are few questions which search our societal soul more deeply than these.

RAISING THE ANTE: AN ALTERNATIVE READING

In "The Year 2000: Is It the End—or Just the Beginning?" Henry Grunwald, former U.S. ambassador to Austria and former editor-in-chief of Time Inc., observed,

> One of the most remarkable things about the twentieth century, more than technological progress and physical violence, has been the deconstruction of man (and woman). We are seeing a reaction against that phenomenon. Our view of man obviously depends on our view of God. The Age of Reason exalted humankind but still admitted God

as a sort of supreme philosopher-king or chairman of the board who ultimately presided over the glories achieved by reason and science. The humanist nineteenth century voted him out. It increasingly saw reason and science irreconcilably opposed to religion, which would fade away. Secular humanism . . . stubbornly insisted that morality need not be based on the supernatural. But it gradually became clear that ethics without the sanction of some higher authority simply were not compelling. The ultimate irony, or perhaps tragedy, is that secularism has not led to humanism. We have gradually dissolved—deconstructed—the human being into a bundle of reflexes, impulses, neuroses, nerve endings. The great religious heresy used to be making man the measure of all things; but we have come close to making man the measure of nothing.[16]

Grunwald makes no grand proposals in the four pages *Time* gave to his lecture at the New York Public Library. He is simply speaking about "the world without windows" of modern consciousness—the world in which my student friends seemingly live and move and have their being. Grunwald understands the moral meaning of this worldview: "It gradually became clear that ethics without the sanction of some higher authority simply were not compelling. The ultimate irony, or perhaps tragedy, is that secularism has not led to humanism." But if not to humanism, then to what? Surveying the same terrain as MacIntyre and Bernstein, he concludes that the logic of this moral vision is profoundly inhuman.

But if Grunwald's analysis has the tone of an end-of-life look at the end of a century, then George Steiner's work takes on the quality of one whose vocation has been to explore the haunting relationship between humanism and barbarism in the modern world. He observes that "art, intellectual pursuits, the development of the natural sciences, many branches of scholarship flourished in close spatial, temporal proximity to massacre and the death camps."[17] And then he asks,

What good did high humanism do the oppressed mass of the community? What use was it when barbarism came? What immortal poem has ever stopped or mitigated political terror—though a number have celebrated it? And, more searchingly: Do those for whom a great poem, a philosophic design, a theorem, are, in the final reckoning, the supreme value, not help the throwers of napalm by looking away, by cultivating in themselves a stance of "objective sadness" or "historical relativism"?[18]

In his *In Bluebeard's Castle: Some Notes Toward the Redefinition of Culture*— lectures "intended in memoration" of T. S. Eliot's *Notes Towards the Definition of Culture*—Steiner surveys the Enlightenment culture. As a literary critic, Steiner uses tools different from those used by MacIntyre and Bernstein. But it is more than his tools that distinguish him, as Steiner presses this point very sharply: Is moral meaning possible apart from a transcendent reality?

If the gamble on transcendence no longer seems worth the odds and we are moving into a utopia of the immediate, the value-structure of our civilization will alter, after at least three millennia, in ways almost unforeseeable.[19]

Steiner's own moral vision is one which sees an integral connection between values and transcendence. Clearly, his questions are the very same questions which brought books out of Bernstein and MacIntyre. But with an eye that sees more clearly the starkness of the choices, he asks, "Can civilization as we know it be underwritten by an immanent view of personal and social reality?"[20]

His own simply stated answer is, "To argue for order and classic values on a purely immanent, secular basis is, finally, implausible."[21] Bernstein and MacIntyre never see it as clearly, for all their understanding and eloquence. Bernstein plainly pleads for "order and classic values on a purely immanent, secular basis." His deepest hopes are pinned on the possibilities arising from "the new conversation." Even very good philosophers in conversation together is, when all is said and done, a conversation on this side of the transcendent. MacIntyre's syncretism ultimately defeats his own argument: order and classic values—read "the virtue culture"—are, simply said, dependent on transcendence. For all his brilliance, does Aristotle ever offer a virtue culture on any other basis than an immanent one? To so fix one's hopes on the marriage of the classical and Christian traditions is finally futile.

To agree with Steiner does not answer all the questions either. But it does draw a line in the sand on issues of cosmic importance. These are "the essay questions" of life, which the comic characters Frank and Ernest remind "the kid" that school does not typically address. These are the ones we "gamble on" with our deepest aspirations as human beings. From the most personal areas of human responsibility on to the most public arenas, our answers to these questions are the most critical, as they foundationally shape our understanding of reality and therefore of human responsibility. "What is real?" informs "What is true?" which informs "What is right?" Metaphysics shapes epistemology which shapes ethics, and in the complexity of human belief and behavior they work back on each other as well. It is precisely because of this that the lines in the sand are drawn: *what* we believe about the world affects *how* we live in the world.

But when Steiner writes of "personal and social reality," he understands that there are "common good" consequences, as well; in their own ways, with equal integrity, MacIntyre and Bernstein each argue the same point. Personal beliefs have public faces. In *Ethics and Policy,* Robert Bellah understands that the *telos* conversation is one that is full of political implications.

> Without the regulative notion of a true nature and final end I believe we are left in a Hobbesian world of conflicting individual desires and peace based on violent coercion. . . . I believe, contra Hobbes, that there really is a good out there, and that though we can never know it wholly we can know it in part.[22]

Like Steiner, Bellah places his bet—and his life—on the side of transcendence, understanding that what one believes about God, human nature and history affects persons as well as the *polis.*

One of the most perceptive inquiries into the nature of the gamble comes from Bishop Lesslie Newbigin in *The Gospel in a Pluralist Society.* His questions take their place alongside those of MacIntyre, Bernstein and Steiner, though his pretheoretical commitments lead him to a different conclusion. Raising the ante on their discussion, he addresses himself to the problem posed by modernity for those whose meaning system is shaped by the centuries-old confession of faith, "Christ has died, Christ is risen, Christ will come again." How is it meaningful to speak of the gospel—which makes claims to being true for everyone and for all time—in a pluralist society that distinguishes between private beliefs and public truths and is polarized over facts and values? Ad hominem, he characterizes the contemporary world in this way:

> Only what can stand up under the critical examination of the modern scientific method can be taught as fact, as public truth; the rest is dogma. One is free to promote it as personal belief, but to affirm it as fact is simply arrogance. How, in this situation, does one preach the gospel as truth, truth which is not to be domesticated within the assumptions of modern thought but which challenges these assumptions and calls for their revision?[23]

Writing in his eighties, and having spent half his life in India, Newbigin came back into the West with sensitivities highly tuned to the interrelation between worldview and way of life. Addressing the same cultural dilemma as MacIntyre and Bernstein, he argues that the dichotomy between private beliefs and public truths, facts and values, which so dominates the modern discourse, is, at its heart, false. It does not take into account the rethinking of the nature of knowing brought about by the work of Thomas Kuhn and Michael Polanyi,[24] and so it fails to see that every moral language is framed by a priori commitments about the nature of the universe, and therefore that facts can never be separated from values—as the public square seems to require. Brilliantly, and also somewhat playfully, Newbigin writes,

> The world so understood is the world of what are called "facts," the facts which we "know" and which everyone needs to learn. It is a closed world of cause and effect, a world from which purpose has been excluded as a category of explanation, and in which—therefore—there can be no judgment of "good" or "bad." It is a world, as we say, of value-free facts. . . . Most ordinary people, and many practitioners of the human sciences such as sociology and economics, still operate with the myths of "value-free facts" and a mechanical universe. And in such a universe, the rules regarding human conduct

which were based on a different and earlier view of what is the case
have lost their ontological grounding. They have no firm basis in reality as science understands it. They can only be "values," matters for
personal choice. They are what some people believe. They are not part
of the world of "facts" which all human beings will have to take account of whether they like it or not.

The facts are "value-free" because the world of which they are a part
is not the product of any purpose, but is the accidental result of the
operation of the twin factors of chance and causality. Yet it does not
take much reflection to see the absurdity of this. It has been seriously
argued that a monkey with a typewriter could—given time—produce
by chance all the plays of Shakespeare. I have not yet heard a scientist
saying that the monkey could have manufactured the typewriter by
chance. But the example is a nice one to end with, for the machine—
a favorite model for this kind of thinking—is precisely that which can
never be explained without invoking the concept of purpose. A complete mechanical, chemical and physical analysis of the parts of a machine and of the interrelation between them is not an explanation of
the machine. It is inexplicable without some concept of the purpose
for which these pieces of metal were put together in this way. A machine which creates itself and exists for no purpose is something
which in most periods of human history would have been thought to
exceed the imagination of even the most credulous. Yet it is widely dif-
fused and is still given credence by respected scientists. It is the concept of a cosmos without purpose which provides the validation for
the division of our world into two—a world of facts without value and
a world of values which have no basis in facts.[25]

THEORIZING FOR THE SAKE OF THEORIZING

This notion of "a cosmos without purpose"—with all of its inherent implications for the formation of moral meaning—is at the heart of the challenge
facing human beings today. Without an intelligible *telos*, the possibility of
forming a meaningful *praxis*, personally and politically, seems a cruel joke
that at best can evoke a cynical laugh: on a trivial level Beavis and Butthead's

snickering, while more seriously, according to Kundera, "The devil laughs because God's world seems senseless to him; the angel laughs with joy because everything in God's world has its meaning."[26]

And yet this cosmic purposelessness permeates and penetrates the daily discourse of university life, from the earliest entry points on through to the farthest reaches of graduate education. Sometimes it is overt, as with those who are apologists for the deconstructionist critique; often it is more subtle, for example, Marc's experience in the art department at Rice University, and my students tearfully asking, "What difference does it make?" And yet we only have to hear from Harvard's former president Derek Bok—"Relativism and individualism have rewritten the rules of the game; they have extinguished the motive for education"—to understand the interwovenness of the facts/values and objectivist/relativist pathologies and the cultural consequences of the loss of purpose and meaning.[27] This is what the *telos* and *praxis* discussion is all about.

One student whom I have loved over the years gives me the gift of long, thoughtful letters every few months. He is now in the last stages of his graduate work; in his first year he wrote a lengthy lament, which included these words:

> The last several months have been a huge adjustment for me. And while they have certainly been a time of growth, they have also been incredibly frustrating and really not very enjoyable at all. . . . Political science at this level is a completely different subject than it is at the undergraduate level. No one seems to be concerned with anything that's really going on in the world, except as evidence for this or that theory. Prescriptive statements of any sort are automatically dismissed because of their normative overtones. Talking about public policy is out of the question—we'll leave that for the technocrats. Thus, there seems to be little purpose behind what we're doing. . . . It often seems like theorizing just for the sake of theorizing. It's appropriate that our department is on the twelfth, thirteenth and fourteenth floors of the social science building. The image of an ivory tower presents itself quite easily.[28]

"There seems to be little purpose behind what we're doing . . . theorizing

for the sake of theorizing." Without a sufficient *telos* it is not possible to form
a coherent vision for life, one that can meaningfully connect the personal
with the political, the individual with the institutional. As Mark Schwehn
has written in his remarkably wise book *Exiles from Eden: Religion and the Academic Vocation in America,* "Ways of knowing are not morally neutral but
morally directive."[29] If pretheoretical commitments are not embedded in a
vision of responsible action in the world, then their purposes may devolve
into "theorizing for the sake of theorizing."

It is here that Newbigin offers good news, a way of standing against theorizing for the sake of theorizing. He tells the story of a Hindu scholar who
complained to him that "you Christians have misrepresented the Bible. . . .
As I read the Bible I find in it a quite unique interpretation of universal history and, therefore, a unique understanding of the human person as a responsible actor in history."[30]

Given what the Hindu knew of his own worldview, Newbigin could see
that the distinguishing feature of the worldview embedded in the Bible was
one which gave a unique basis for responsible action in the world. In the
next pages Newbigin walks through the modern world, assessing its debts
to Augustine and the varieties of Enlightenment influences, including Marxism. He then comments,

> One searches contemporary European literature in vain for evidence
> of hope for the future; rather . . . it is characterized by cold despair,
> loss of vision, resignation and cynicism. My Hindu friend saw in the
> Bible a unique vision of universal history and the place of the human
> person as a responsible actor in history. The two belong together. You
> cannot have hopeful and responsible action without some vision of a
> possible future. To put it another way, if there is no point in the story
> as a whole, there is no point in my own action.[31]

Very few are willing to live with the moral meaning of cosmic purposelessness.

Someone who saw the starkness of the choices more plainly, feeling in his
very bones the disease caused by an unresolvable tension between his *telos*
and his *praxis*, was Bob Kramer (one of those interviewed in this study). A

campus leader for the student protest at Harvard in the late 1960s, he remembers being inspired by the political visions of the Kennedy brothers.

I came to college as a very naive, very idealistic young person who expected that by being raised in a very civic, involvement-oriented, very political family, and getting the best education, I would therefore be able to take my place in a substantive way by causing positive change in society. . . . I really looked forward to getting the credentials so I could get on with it. Then came college, and two things happened. First, the late sixties made me see the inadequacies of bringing about change through all the traditional channels. Second, as a political theory major, the first two years of college undermined the foundations or underpinnings to any beliefs I had, in terms of the basic values I was committed to in Western liberal democracy, values like right and wrong, truth and justice. In writing a paper on Nietzsche's *Beyond Good and Evil*—at the same time that I was encouraging a student strike against the university over rent controls in Cambridge—it all came together for me, meaning it all came tumbling down. There was no real foundation for what I believed—beyond that I believed it.

Behavior and beliefs, praxis and presuppositions. Bob had eyes to see that how he lived—"to take my place in a substantive way by causing positive change in society"—needed to be coherently connected to what he believed. And when he saw the disjunction, he dropped out.

Education for What Purpose?
Competence to What End?

Beyond the consciousness of everyday reality, or perhaps more accurately, beneath it, submerged below the stream of thoughts and perceptions that occupy normal waking attention, lies a system of symbols and images that evokes a larger coherence and meaning than that found in everyday reality. This level of consciousness derives from the impulse for "something more" in which to embed the reality of day-to-day existence.

ROBERT WUTHNOW, *The Consciousness Reformation*[1]

That is the Raskolnikov complex."

While speaking to a group of private school students at the FOCUS Study Center on Martha's Vineyard one summer, I met a young man who was on his way to college in the fall.[2] Day by day we had discussions about life and learning. One morning, lingering over breakfast on the veranda of the study center, he referred to the "Raskolnikov complex" and went on to apply it in the context of our conversation. His reference intrigued me as I had brought the book, planning to use it in my teaching. Later that week I invited him to participate in a lecture on the nature of a Christian worldview, in which I was particularly hoping that the students would see the relevance of truth and the difference it makes for persons and polities.

DOSTOYEVSKY'S RASKOLNIKOV

I asked the student to explain the Raskolnikov complex to the group. And so we talked about the student Raskolnikov from Fyodor Dostoyevsky's murder mystery *Crime and Punishment*. Raskolnikov had written a paper, later published in an academic journal, which argued that certain people "have a perfect right to commit all sorts of enormities and crimes and that they are, as it were, above the law."[3] Central to his thesis was the notion that "in accordance with the dictates of his conscience . . . [a person has] a right to commit a crime."[4] A person even has a right to commit a crime like murder, which is the heart of the story of Raskolnikov's crime *and* punishment.

It was, of course, over the question of conscience that I engaged the young student. What does it mean? Where does it come from? How is it violated? What kind of universe do we need to live in for Raskolnikov's crime to receive the punishment of a wounded, roaring conscience? Do we have to believe in God? Do we have to believe that human beings are made in the image of God? What kind of worldview is required to make sense of this story?

What is most intriguing about Dostoyevsky's story, to me as a teacher, is that its central theme involves a student theorizing about the nature of the world and of his place in it. That is the heart and soul of the academy in every generation. In the long conversation that Raskolnikov has with the detective Porfiry, when both begin to know that the other knows, the student qualifies the crudity of his thesis by saying, "I only believe in my principal idea." That is to say, this thesis cannot be lived with across the spectrum of human responsibilities; it is a theory, not something we could all practice. His argument does not die the death of a thousand qualifications; only one is required—but that is fatal as it deals a death blow to the worldview he has constructed. In the last pages of the book—after hundreds of pages of wrestling with the punishment of his crime on his soul—Dostoyevsky writes that Raskolnikov

> suddenly remembered Sonia's words: "Go to the crossroads, bow down to the people, kiss the earth, for you have sinned against it, and proclaim in a loud voice to the whole world: 'I am a murderer!' He trem-

bled all over as he remembered it. And so utterly crushed was he by his feeling of hopelessness and desolation and by the great anxiety of all those days, but especially of the last few hours, that he simply plunged head over heels into this new and overwhelming sensation. It seemed to come upon him as though it were some nervous fit; it glimmered like a spark in his soul, and then, suddenly, spread like a conflagration through him. Everything within him grew soft all at once, and tears gushed from his eyes. He fell to the ground just where he stood.[5]

The difference between what he believed about the world and how he lived in the world produced a profound tension for Raskolnikov—and it broke him.

TOLSTOY'S NEKHLYUDOV

Tolstoy's tale of the student-prince in *The Resurrection* is a fascinating study in the formation of moral meaning, set in nineteenth-century Russia. Tolstoy paints pictures with words, offering us in the character of Prince Nekhlyudov a view of the human person that is both familiar and haunting. Heir to a large fortune in farms, the prince seems an unusually sensitive young man. His studies nourish a framework of belief which places a strain on his relationships with family and friends, particularly because of their self-absorbed materialism: "Thus, when Nekhlyudov used to think, read and speak about God, about truth, about wealth and poverty, everyone round him had considered it out of place and in a way ridiculous, and his mother and aunt had called him, with kindly irony, *notre cher philosophe.*"[6]

As he makes his way out of adolescence into the responsibilities of adulthood, Nekhlyudov spends several years in the military as a young officer. They are not good years for him; his worldview is insufficient for the challenges he faces as a young professional out in the world. Stopping by to see his aunts, whose country estate had been the setting for many happy memories as a boy,

he was now a very different person from the one who had spent the summer with them three years before. Then he had been an honest, unselfish lad, ready to devote himself to any good cause; now he was a dissolute accomplished egoist, caring only for his own enjoyment. Then he had seen God's world as a mystery which with excitement and delight he strove to penetrate; now everything in life was simple and clear and depended on the circumstances in which he happened to be. Then he had felt the necessity and importance of communion with nature, and with men who had lived, thought and felt before his time (philosophers and poets); now worldly affairs and social intercourse with his comrades were the necessary and important things. Then women had seemed mysterious and enchanting creatures—enchanting because of their very mystery; now his idea of a woman, of any woman except such as were of his own family or the wives of his friends, was precisely defined; women were a familiar means of enjoyment. Then he had not required money and less than a third of what his mother gave him would have sufficed, and it was possible to refuse the property inherited from his father and give it to the peasants; but now his monthly allowance of fifteen hundred roubles was not enough, and there had been some unpleasant interviews with his mother over money matters. Then he had regarded his spiritual being as his real self; now his healthy, virile animal self was the real *I*.[7]

It is not until he comes face to face, ten years later, with a young woman who had been "precisely defined," and therefore whom he had miserably used, that he begins to see the consequences of his convictions. The worldview which has served him through his young adult years, allowing him to justify a "healthy, virile animal self" comes crashing down on his head as he must deal with the implications of his ideas. The young woman is now on trial for theft and murder—after years of prostitution—and Nekhlyudov is on the jury assigned to hear her case. As he listens, he is shocked into awareness of the responsibility he has for the dissolution of her life. "Without removing his pince-nez he stared at Maslova, while a complex process took place in his soul."[8]

The difference between what he believed about the world and how he lived in the world produced a profound tension for Nekhlyudov—and it broke him.

SOLZHENITSYN'S VOLODIN

Inner feelings of satisfaction and dissatisfaction are the highest criteria of good and evil. Innokenty Volodin mused over the meaning of the words which had shaped his young career in the diplomatic corps of Stalin's Russia. In the mid-twentieth century they were already ancient wisdom and had given guidance to generations of students over the centuries.

First taught by Epicurus to his disciples in the third century B.C., it was a moral vision Volodin had embraced as an undergraduate, one which had "made sense" of his life thus far. Still in his twenties, he had risen quickly through several levels of advancement and already enjoyed a life of luxury and pleasure unknown to the average Soviet citizen. His standing allowed him the privilege of travel throughout Europe, where he stayed at only the finest hotels and villas—while representing the proletariat revolution of Marx and Lenin.

The young diplomat read on, especially interested in his own notes on the famous Greek philosopher.

> Before closing his notebook, he read what he had noted down at the very end: "Epicurus influenced his pupils against participating in public life."
>
> Yes, how easy. To philosophize. In gardens . . .
>
> Innokenty threw back his head, just as a bird tilts back its head so that water will flow down its throat.
>
> No! No![9]

For many years I told this story at the beginning of our study together in the American Studies Program as a window into the relationship between belief and behavior. Innokenty Volodin is a character in Aleksandr Solzhenitsyn's *The First Circle,* a morally rich account of a week in the lives of several Russians in the late 1940s. A wonderfully well-told story, it is at heart a study in moral meaning. What do I believe? Is it true? What difference does it make, personally and politically? These are questions students ask and answer in every generation and every culture.

The novel begins in Moscow, in an office of the diplomatic service. In his European travel Volodin has learned that an honored Russian scientist had promised to send the results of his research to a colleague in the West. Even though the information had already been published in a scientific journal, to have contact with "the West" would result in the scientist's imprisonment. The scientist—an old man who had labored in a laboratory for most of his life—was politically unaware and had no idea that passing on his research notes would be seen as a crime against the state. Volodin, on the other hand, knows the reality of *realpolitik,* Stalin-style. And it has put him in great moral turmoil: he knows, but will he be responsible? To link knowledge with responsibility does not "make sense" if he is to maintain integrity with his creed; the potential cost to his own career, not to speak of his life, will not lead to "inner feelings of satisfaction." And since satisfaction, for Epicurus, meant "the enjoyment of pleasure and the absence of pain,"[10] a decision to act in a way that would lead to personal pain would be inconsistent with his deepest commitments about what is real and true and right.

After only a few pages, Volodin resolves his dilemma, acting more as a human than an Epicurean. In the second chapter the story dramatically changes, and Volodin does not return again for four hundred pages, though, as Solzhenitsyn tells the tale, it is only a few days in December in the lives of a handful of prisoners. But the crisis of his creed—can it meaningfully connect my private world with the public world?—moves Volodin to reexamine his university texts and notes, and it is that task which he has taken up when we meet him again.

Not long after the "No! No!" Volodin is captured by the MGB (an earlier version of the KGB) and taken to the Lubyanka, where political prisoners are taken, never to be seen again. In the hours that follow, he poignantly recalls his undergraduate philosophy: "Inner feelings of satisfaction and dissatisfaction are the highest criteria of good and evil."

That meant, according to Epicurus, that what one liked was good and that what one didn't like was evil.

The philosophy of a savage.

Stalin enjoyed killing—did that mean that for him killing was a virtue? And since being imprisoned for trying to save somebody did not, after all, produce satisfaction, did that mean it was evil?

No! Good and evil had now been substantively defined for Innokenty and visibly distinguished from one another—by that bright gray door, by those olive walls, by that first prison night.

From the heights of struggle and suffering to which he had been lifted, the wisdom of the ancient philosopher seemed like the babbling of a child.[11]

Pushed to the wall, Volodin is caught by his own humanness. He sees his undergraduate ideas as "philosophizing in a garden" and profoundly irrelevant to his public responsibilities ten years later. The ethic he has lived with since his student days—personal pleasure as the aim of life—now seems hollow and deeply inhuman. Being young, urban and professional simply was not enough.

The difference between what he believed about the world and how he lived in the world produced a profound tension for Volodin—and it broke him.

How is it possible to see into the meaning of one's moment in history and to act responsibly? In times and places very different from our own, the Russian students Raskolnikov, Nekhlyudov and Volodin each wrestled with what they believed about the world and what difference it made in how they lived. Each felt the tension created by the incoherence between behavior and beliefs, praxis and presuppositions—and it broke them.

In this chapter we take the question up more fully. If thus far we have established that the formation of moral meaning is critical during the university years, and that the modern world makes accomplishing that incredibly hard, then this next part will look at what it is in the contemporary university that militates against students' finding and forming moral meaning.

In particular we will argue that higher education, under the impact of modern consciousness, more often than not excludes the deepest human questions—those of meaning and morality—from the curriculum. And finally, we will reconnect to the larger question of the book, asking, "Is it possible to so educate students that they are prepared for making sense of life over the course of life, developing the necessary integrity and coherence to stand against the pressures of modern and postmodern life?"

EDUCATION: A PASSPORT TO PRIVILEGE?

I had expected a quiet evening with a book. After a long day of work, I found a pub with outdoor tables not far from the Bodleian Library and settled in with Thomas Hardy's *Jude the Obscure*.[12]

For months I had been looking forward to reading this novel while doing some summer study and work in Oxford. Set in nineteenth-century Oxfordshire, it is a portrait of the life and times of Jude the stonecarver. More deeply it is a study in the meaning of education, which on a more theoretical level was the direction of my study.

But my quiet was interrupted with the question "What are you reading?" I looked up and saw a young, earnest face. He introduced himself as a second-generation Keble College student; though Indian, he had grown up in Rome. I told him that I was reading about another young man who had come to the city of steeples and spires with high hopes of being a scholar at Oxford. But, though Jude had diligently prepared himself through a regimen of self-disciplined study—learning Greek and Latin and reading all the required texts—he was not able to get in because he had neither connections nor money. And we talked for some time about the intellectual snobbery which had so defeated the obscure Jude.

"What are you studying at Keble?" I asked. It was obvious within a few sentences that this young man was unusually articulate. He told me of his studies in political theory, and I asked more questions. The longer we talked, the more ironic our conversation seemed. I was talking about a book that explored the question "What's the point of education?" with a student who seemed remarkably insensitive to the responsibility of knowledge. His own studies were extremely self-oriented, with no concern for people: political theory, with no apparent concern for the *polis*. In the most selfish way, he saw his education as a passport to privilege.

I pressed the young student, hoping—as Hamlet taught, that "the play's the thing to catch the conscience of the king"—to tell enough of Jude's story to help him see himself more truthfully. We parried back and forth for a long time, but throughout he seemed as hard-hearted as he was articulate. I shook my head sadly as I watched him walk away, knowing that he had little if any sense of the stewardship of his gifts in service to the world.

What is *the point* of higher education? *What is it all about?* Oliver Stone has made a career of films which are a form of autobiography, charting the evolution of his own convictions and commitments from the sixties on. The "personal-is-the-political" approach to history has its own unique pitfalls, of course, and Stone's prejudices have been plainly, and sometimes painfully, portrayed. *Platoon* told the story of Vietnam, drawing on his own memories of the war. As the helicopter takes the wounded young hero up into the sky, he observes that now he and his battle-worn colleagues must "try with what's left of our lives to find a goodness and meaning to this life."[13] *Wall Street* is in part the story of his father's world, as seen through the so-called greed decade, the 1980s. In it Stone has a Michael Milken/Ivan Boeskylike character overpower a stockholders' meeting with the business version of *realpolitik:* "The point is, ladies and gentlemen, that greed is good." The Wall Street insider later tells his apprentice, "It's all about bucks, kid. The rest is conversation."[14]

What is the point of life and education? Did "the masters of the universe"—as Tom Wolfe called the Wall Street traders—have it right after all? Or was their experience, prototypical of the eighties, in reality a "bonfire of the vanities"?

In the last several years the ethics curricula at both Harvard and the Naval Academy have been called into question in light of the behavior of prominent graduates. The former Securities and Exchange Commission chairman, John Shad, offered $30 million to Harvard Business School after the Wall Street scandal. His assumption was that if something was wrong on Wall Street, then Harvard Business School needed to be "fixed." Shad hoped that his money would help his alma mater address the propensity to felonious behavior on the part of its graduates.

During the social uproar caused by the insider trading scandal, most of those who regularly write about our national life offered their insights into why and how it all happened. A particularly thoughtful piece appeared in *The New Republic,* titled "Ethics for Greedheads: B.S. at Business School."

In fact, it doesn't matter *how* you teach ethics, if what you are teaching is muddled. In business school, ethics is taught as a matter not of morality but of pragmatism. Consider a course that takes off from Shad's belief, in his words, that "crime doesn't pay." This approach tries to convince students that if they factor in the costs of getting caught, they will see the folly of doing the wrong thing and therefore not do it. But crimes are committed precisely because the offender thinks he will not be caught (especially if his wrongdoing is buried in a maze of stock transactions). Pragmatism may be the only language MBAs understand, but it misses the point that crime is wrong even when you are unlikely to be caught.[15]

Arguing that the $30 million is "aimed at cold, hard cash changing hands"—not the moral gray areas in business—Fareed Zakaria wryly notes: "That a course in ethics could prevent that—by itself, integrated, part of the case study method, or as an adjunct to a course in Power—is a hopeless goal. By the time they arrive at business school, students are a bit old for basic character formation."[16] A harsh assessment but, pedagogically speaking, plainly in line with the judgment of Aristotle, who centuries ago had a policy of taking as his students only those whose characters were already virtuously formed.

Following the convictions of Oliver North and John Poindexter in the Iran/Contra scandal during the Reagan administration, a thorough evaluation of the ethics curriculum at the Naval Academy was ordered. The question was this: How could an education committed to "develop midshipmen morally, mentally and physically and to imbue them with the highest ideals of duty, honor and loyalty" have produced people who would lie to the Congress and the nation over a partisan political position?[17]

The supposition in both situations was that education has a social responsibility, that there is a connection between learning and life that has moral consequence. These institutions were not taken to court, of course, as if they were legally responsible for the behavior of their graduates, but there was an assumption that something was wrong with the learning if something was wrong with the life. The critical question is this: Is that a relationship between the two that is rooted in reality, or is it meaningless moralism?

In his landmark study of higher education, *College: The Undergraduate Experience in America*, Ernest Boyer (of the Carnegie Foundation for the Advancement of Teaching) asked two questions which search our societal soul:

Education for what purpose? Competence to what end? At a time in life when values should be shaped and personal priorities sharply probed, what a tragedy it would be if the most deeply felt issues, the most haunting questions, the most creative moments were pushed to the fringes of our institutional life. What a monumental mistake it would be if students, during the undergraduate years, remained trapped within the organizational grooves and narrow routines to which the academic world sometimes seems excessively devoted.[18]

They are haunting questions because they are important questions. And they are important questions because they wonder at the meaning of education; the meaning of education, in turn, is grounded in a conversation about meaning itself.

Only weeks after the conversation about *Jude the Obscure,* I was back in Washington. Far from the quiet of Oxford, I met with another student over pizza at an outdoor restaurant amidst the busyness of Capitol Hill. An undergraduate at the University of California, he too came from a family steeped in Oxbridge education. Part English, part Burmese, his articulate earnestness reminded me of the young man from Rome. He had just finished a summer internship in a think tank given to studying international relations. Early on he asked, "So tell me about the relation of spirituality to politics." His uncle is an Anglican rector and is a good friend to both his nephew and to me. Knowing both of us, he had suggested the subject in a letter to his nephew. It was obviously an honest question, wanting an honest answer.

I discovered that this young man had spent the last two summers in Washington and the academic year between in Eastern Europe. The longer we talked, the more obvious it was that he was searching for a larger reason for responsible involvement in the world. Because he had seen so much with such young eyes (exposure to politics typically leads to disillusionment with politics) he was wondering, *What is the point, after all?* And so I asked him if he had read Milan Kundera.

He brightened, saying, "Oh yes, and I've seen *The Unbearable Lightness of Being* three times."

Kundera is the Czech novelist who has written so perceptively about the meaning of personal and political life in the modern world. My question seemed to deepen the conversation immediately, and he talked at some length about his studies in political science and what purpose they had in a world like ours. He had thought deeply enough about his questions to understand that if meaning and truth were written out of political discourse, then his educational plans and vocational dreams were seriously called into question. He had seen that those haunting questions—the ones of real social and political consequence—were not important questions in either politics or education. And though his unusual intelligence and initiative had already put him on the "fast track," he wondered instead about the relation of spirituality to politics.

In fact, he yearned for something more.

THE QUESTION OF MORAL MEANING

"There's got to be more to life than quietly waiting for death . . . is there, though?" Very popular in the university and arts theaters, the much-acclaimed Canadian film *Jesus of Montreal* portrays a group of young actors who take up the production of a play about Jesus—not the Jesus of Palestine and the first century, but of Montreal and the twentieth century. After the resurrection scene, an actress says to the audience: "They were ready to die for their convictions. They too were crucified, beheaded, stoned. They were steadfast; Jesus awaited them in his kingdom. . . . They personified hope, the most irrational and unyielding of emotions. Mysterious hope . . . that makes life bearable, lost in a bewildering universe."

Their play is well received, but the priest who commissioned the play tells them they cannot perform it, after all, at the shrine above Montreal on Easter. The church hierarchy has forbidden it.

Actor: They wore you down in the end?

Priest: It's understandable. Institutions last longer than individuals. At my stage of the game, I think people should just live happily as long as they can.

Actress: So long as they're happy.

Actor: (walks away in frustration) There's got to be more to life than quietly waiting for death. I may be naive, but there must be more. Is there, though? Or are we in reality "lost in a bewildering universe"?[19]

The film *Reality Bites,* with its double-entendre title, was billed as the defining film of that cultural phenomenon known as "Generation X," though its themes run through most generations, as there really is nothing new under the sun. The questions are perennial, as are the answers. It is at one and the same time a statement about the fears facing the newly graduated and a critique of the possibility of having a coherent understanding of life and the world. In a word, the best one can hope for is "reality bites." Set in Houston, the opening scene is the graduation ceremony at Rice University. Valedictorian Winona Ryder's commencement address is like a thousand before her, full of the challenges facing Texas's best and brightest as they move from the hallowed halls into the world beyond. As she moves to the climax of her speech, the crescendo builds until she finally says with great passion: "And the answer is . . ." and then she loses her place in her notes and stumbles. Again, "And the answer is . . ." but once more she cannot find her next card. Finally, much more subdued, she simply says, "And the answer is, I don't know."[20]

As Kundera has put it, with a sobering starkness: "The devil laughs because God's world seems senseless to him; the angel laughs with joy because everything in God's world has its meaning."[21] Whether or not one is willing to bet "the farm" on Kundera's alternatives, his perspective on the possibilities is not sectarian, in any sense. In *Real Presences*—which asks, "Can there be major dimensions of a poem, a painting, a musical composition created in the absence of God?"—Steiner writes, "This study will contend that the wager on the meaning of meaning . . . is a wager on transcendence."[22]

Contending that "to ask 'what is music?' may well be one way of asking 'what is man?'" he understands that "one must not flinch from such terms" and so see the issues as they truthfully are.[23] My young friend who had immersed himself in politics and who was also familiar with Kundera was uncannily able to see the issues as they truthfully are—and he did not flinch.

But where does this leave us? And why is it the way that it is? And in particular, what is the place of education in all this? Whether the young Canadian drama students, the newly graduated Rice students or my own young friend, each in their own ways felt betrayed by their university experience. How is it that we have strayed so far from educational visions that saw the formation of moral meaning as at the heart of learning? What happened to the integral connection between "veritas et virtus," as the University of Pittsburgh's motto still reads?

Anyone who knows that university, or a thousand more like it, knows that the understanding of education as concerned with the formation of "truth and virtue" still sells sweatshirts with Latin mottoes but is a worldview away from the actual commitment of the university. The shriveled visions of universities under the impact of modernity—particularly the effects of bureaucracy and technology—seem more concerned to produce people who are technically competent but who have little interest in the whys and wherefores of their competencies.

Education must be oriented to preparation for a calling and not just training for a career. The difference is one of substance, not semantics. Walker Percy's memorable metaphor captures the irony inherent in our individual and social expectations of the meaning of education when he writes of "the one who gets all A's but flunks life." That difference and the difference it makes is what moral meaning is all about.

One of the disciplines we maintained as faculty at the American Studies Program was eating meals with our students. It was written into our expectations, in terms of both time and money. Capitol Hill has enough interesting places to eat that we can meet any student's desire. A few years ago I had lunch with a student in a café somewhere between her internship at the Department of Health and Human Services and my office. We talked about her reading and the questions which had arisen in the first weeks of the program. Quite explicitly we ask students to wrestle with "What do I believe? Is it true? What difference does it make, personally and publicly?" They are questions intended to probe a student's working assumptions about life and learning, especially about notions like coherence, purpose, meaning and interconnectedness. As we pursued her responses, at one point she exclaimed: "This isn't like school. My roommates and I have been up until two every night talking about class! This is not just academic! This is about my life . . . my future . . . the future of the world!"

What is it about higher education in the modern world that would cause this bright young woman to say, "This isn't like school—this is not just academic"?

THE FORMATION OF MORAL MEANING IN THE MODERN UNIVERSITY

One of the most interesting voices in America on the meaning of education—what it is, why it is, what it ought to be—is Neil Postman, who for three decades has written with great understanding about the nature of education in a technological society. From *Teaching as a Subversive Activity* on through *Amusing Ourselves to Death* and *The End of Education*, he challenged America to think about the impact of modern consciousness on life and, particularly, on education.[24] Throughout, his concern was to stand against the subtle seductions inherent in our culture's inescapable negotiation with technology, which "in sum, is both friend and enemy."[25] And perhaps nowhere more so than in schools and schooling.

In *Technopoly: The Surrender of Culture to Technology*, he argues that technology redefines what we mean by religion, art, family, politics, history, truth, privacy and intelligence—becoming, in effect, a "technopoly." The final chapter suggests that education take up the task of developing "loving resistance fighters." *Loving* because they need to love the best about American society—to understand why the Chinese students built a "statue of liberty" in Tiananmen Square. *Resistance fighters* because they need to feel a profound tension with the friend/enemy nature of technopoly, which flourishes in America like nowhere else on earth. Acknowledging that "in the United States, as Lawrence Cremin once remarked, whenever we need a revolution, we get a new curriculum. And so I shall propose one," Postman writes,

> In consideration of the disintegrative power of Technopoly, perhaps the most important contribution schools can make to the education of our youth is to give them a sense of coherence in their studies, a sense of purpose, meaning and interconnectedness in what they

learn. Modern secular education is failing not because it doesn't teach who Ginger Rogers, Norman Mailer and a thousand other people are but because it has no moral, social or intellectual center. There is no set of ideas or attitudes that permeates all parts of the curriculum. The curriculum is not, in fact, a "course of study" at all but a meaningless hodgepodge of subjects. It does not even put forward a clear vision of what constitutes an educated person, unless it is a person who possesses "skills." In other words, a technocrat's ideal—a person with no commitment and no point of view but with plenty of marketable skills.[26]

To give them a sense of coherence in their studies, a sense of purpose, meaning and interconnectedness in what they learn.

Postman adds his voice to Kundera's and Steiner's in asserting that the secularist vision of life and education fails "because it has no moral, social or intellectual center."[27] When all is said and done, is it really "all about bucks, kid . . . and the rest is conversation"? Or is the deeper reality that that moral vision is profoundly immoral, impoverishing individuals and institutions because it is always and everywhere a "bonfire of the vanities"?

To the latter question, the authors of *Habits of the Heart* and *The Good Society* answer a loud yes.[28] Their groundbreaking study of the relation of individualism and social commitment, in the first volume, grew into a second study that offered a rich assessment of the importance of individuals' assuming institutional responsibility in order for "democracy in America" to survive into the next century. In their chapter "Education: Technical and Moral" they analyze the "bonfire of the vanities" view of education explicit in Stanford University's prospectus for its new Institute for Higher Education Research. In particular, they examine the statement of William Massy, Stanford's vice president for finance, a professor of education and the chief instigator of the new institute, who writes, "I have become really fascinated with higher education as an industry":

He rejects any notion of the university as a community of moral discourse. One can imagine that in his university the notion that higher education has anything to do with a coherent view of the world or the meaning of life would be absent—and one must hope that indeed student services and psychological counseling would be available. Unfortunately, given the culture of therapy today, the help the students get would be oriented to strengthening their autonomy in a difficult world, rather than to finding a larger meaning or a more socially viable context for their education.[29]

Education for what purpose? Competence to what end? Developmentally ready to sort through the serious questions of life and the world—Who or what is God? What about me? What does life, and my life, mean anyway? Is truth possible and knowable? On what basis will I decide right and wrong?—students hunger to be taken seriously and to be given time and space within the curricular requirements to explore those questions. If instead they are offered, in Postman's critique, "marketable skills"—with no moral, social or intellectual center to give shape and substance to those skills—they have become the "technocrat's ideal." That is not a small thing, for persons or polities.

In *The Abandoned Generation: Rethinking Higher Education*, William Willimon and Thomas Naylor, writing out of their long experience at Duke University, argue that institutions of higher education—like their own—naively nurture an academic atmosphere in which an inarticulate but deeply felt nihilism is rampant. Looking at the study hard/play hard ethos, where students link their disciplined study and high hopes for careers marked by power and privilege with nights and weekends of binge drinking, Willimon and Naylor maintain that universities desperately need to recover their sense of calling as settings in which students can pursue questions that matter. In a chapter eerily titled "Meaninglessness," they quote Edward Long Jr., whose book *Higher Education as a Moral Enterprise* contends:

> Higher education dares not become merely the avenue to success; it must be the gateway for responsibility. It should not be concerned with competence alone, but with commitment to civic responsibility. An academic degree should not be a hunting license only for self-advancement, but an indication of abilities to seek, cultivate and sustain a richer common weal. It is not enough to achieve cultural literacy; we must en-

gender social concern. It is not enough merely to open the mind; it is necessary to cultivate moral intentionality in a total selfhood.[30]

Their book is full of stories that painfully illustrate the reality of their thesis. Telling one from Duke's School of Business, where students were asked, "What do you want to be when you grow up?" the authors confess:

> With few exceptions, they wanted three things—money, power and things (very big things, including vacation homes, expensive foreign automobiles, yachts and even airplanes). Primarily concerned with their careers and the growth of their financial portfolios, their personal plans contained little room for family, intellectual development, spiritual growth or social responsibility. Their mandate to the faculty was, "Teach me how to be a moneymaking machine." "Give me only the facts, tools and techniques required to ensure my instantaneous financial success." All else was irrelevant.[31]

Where does this "it's all about bucks, kid; the rest is conversation . . . so let's get drunk" raison d'etre come from? The answer is complex, of course, and Willimon and Naylor do justice to that complexity, analyzing the fraying fabric in families and society as part of the social context that contributes to the morally hollow aspirations. But they also clearly charge that much responsibility is due to the impoverished educational visions that animate the Duke Universities of the world. Quoting a student, "We've got no philosophy of what the hell it is we want by the time somebody graduates. The so-called curriculum is a set of hoops that somebody says students ought to jump through before graduation. Nobody seems to have asked, 'How do people become good people?' We need more leadership from faculty and administration."[32]

An administrator put it this way: "Lacking a coherent vision of why we are here, administration becomes the mere lunging into one crisis after another without anyone stepping back and asking, 'Why are we here?'" Surprising as it may sound to Enlightenment molded minds, their diagnosis is "Two decades of allegedly value-neutral education have taken a heavy toll on the academy."[33]

And they ask, "But why should we be surprised that alcohol abuse, careerism and an obsession with high technology pervade college campuses whose administrators and faculty boast of being value-neutral?"[34] Value-neutral, that is, on the fundamental questions of human existence.[35]

How do people become good people? Why are we here? Willimon and Naylor sense that students slide into drunkenness-as-meaninglessness in large part because institutions have given up on being places where those kinds of questions are at the "heart" of the institution's life. They have traded the inheritance of reasons-for-being such as "veritas et virtus" and "eruditio et religio" (Duke's motto) for "Teach me how to be a moneymaking machine." Always and everywhere, the chickens come home to roost.

To switch metaphors, ideas have legs. The Enlightenment vision so ably critiqued by MacIntyre, Bernstein, Steiner and Newbigin—with its debilitating facts/values dichotomy—is not only intellectually dishonest; it is educationally impoverishing. And it has consequence for students and societies.

Education for what purpose? Competence to what end? Boyer's questions still haunt, because they continue to press at the whys and wherefores of higher education.

WHAT IS THE POINT OF LIFE—AND OF EDUCATION?

What is it that really matters? And how is that sense of *what really matters*—moral meaning—formed during the critical years between adolescence and adulthood? For those whose pathway leads them into the world of the university, decisions are made during that time that are determinative for the rest of life. In the modern world, the years between eighteen and twenty-five are a time for the settling of one's convictions about meaning and morality: Why do I get up in the morning? What do I do after I get up in the morning? One then settles into life with those convictions as the shaping presuppositions and principles of one's entire life.

This notion is not new; in fact it is as old as our knowledge of education. The time span of these critical years has varied over the centuries, as our civilization has moved from a primarily agrarian culture to a primarily industrial culture. But the movement from childhood to adulthood has been worthy of every culture's greatest attention and perhaps its finest education.

From the *bet midrash*[36] (the "house of study" for the most advanced students) of the Hebrew culture to the Greek gymnasiums and museums[37] (early forums for higher education in the second and third century B.C.) to the Roman *collegia iuvenum*[38] ("where gilded youths could learn how to live" in the first century B.C.) on to the Christian *schola* of the sixth century[39] (the episcopal school founded by Gregory of Tours after the collapse of Rome), there has been a long history of understanding that there are in fact certain critical years in human life and learning. They are years of deciding how one will make sense of life over the course of life.

In our own time is there anyone among those whose intellectual contributions will take their names into the next century who has not reflected on the meaning of higher education? Even a short list includes Bertrand Russell's *Education and the Good Life*, Alfred North Whitehead's *The Aims of Education*, John Dewey's *Experience and Education*, C. S. Lewis's *The Abolition of Man*, Jacques Barzun's *The American University*, Charles Habib Malik's *A Christian Critique of the University*, Mortimer Adler's *Reforming Education*— they are each analyses of a civilization-long debate on what happens and should happen while a student is at the university.[40]

In a brilliant series of lectures given at the University of Chicago in 1950, T. S. Eliot offered his own answer to this perennial question. Published as "The Aims of Education," he wrote,

> But we can have no clear or useful idea of what education is, unless we have some notion of what this training is *for*. Thus we come to inquire what is the purpose of education, and here we get deeply into the area of conflict. . . . I do not suggest for a moment that we should abandon the attempt to define the purpose of education (and the definition of the purpose is an inevitable step from the definition of the word itself). If we see a new and mysterious machine, I think that the first question we ask is, "What is that machine for?" and afterwards we ask, "How does it do it?" But the moment we ask about the purpose of anything, we may be involving ourselves in asking about the purpose of everything. If we define education, we are led to ask "What is Man?"; and if we define the purpose of education, we are committed

to the question "What is Man for?" Every definition of the purpose of
education, therefore, implies some concealed, or rather implicit, philosophy or theology. In choosing one definition rather than another,
we are attracted to the one because it fits in better with our answer to
the question "What is Man for?"[41]

Eliot's point is that education, always and everywhere, is about the deepest questions of life and the world. The great tragedy is that in the twentieth
century, laboring under the myth of neutrality, education in the West attempted to offer a value-free answer to the questions "What is Man?" and
"What is Man for?"[42] Not only is it philosophically and pedagogically impossible to do so—which creates its own problems in terms of truthfulness
about what is actually happening in education—but its fruit is Postman's
technocrat's ideal: "a person with no commitment and no point of view but
with plenty of marketable skills."

One of the most perceptive examinations of this issue in the last generation is Sharon Parks's *The Critical Years*.[43] A professor in several different colleges and schools within Harvard University, she argues that the college experience is principally one of *meaning-making,* which is "the activity of
seeking pattern, order, form and significance. To be human is to seek coherence and correspondence in the disparate elements of existence. To be human is to want to make sense out of things."[44] She describes the university
experience in this way:

> Although there are other contexts for young adult formation (the mil-
> itary, work apprenticeships, marriage, programs like the Peace Corps,
> prisons, and sometimes travel), it may be said that higher education is
> the institution of preference for the formation of young adults in our
> culture. . . . Young adults in higher education (both undergraduate
> and graduate) quickly don the trappings of adulthood—an aura of in-
> dependence, a measure of responsibility for self, and cultural permis-
> sion for participation in the world of work. But the young adult is still
> in formation, still engaged in the activity of composing a self, world
> and "God" adequate to ground the responsibilities and commitments
> of full adulthood. The young adult is searching for a worthy faith.[45]

MAKING SENSE OF LIFE OVER THE COURSE OF LIFE

But lest we lose sight of what is at stake—not so long ago I was riding on Washington's Metro one afternoon, reading *The Book of Laughter and Forgetting* by Kundera.[46] One of the unspoken protocols of Metro riding is that one does not speak to strangers! How many times have I seen someone's eyes gaze away, rather than meet mine as a basis for conversation? Deep into my own little universe of an open book, I could hardly believe it when someone appeared to be speaking to me. As I came to consciousness, I heard him again say, "I read a novel by Kundera when I was in college."

I looked beside me to find a young man in his twenties, well-dressed, good-looking, athletic; he was like thousands who swarm into the nation's capital year after year from Minneapolis and Memphis, Boston and Baton Rouge, San Francisco and Savannah, wanting to do something important with the young years of their lives. Some are empowered by a vision of "a government of the people, by the people and for the people" and want to do their part. Others come, first and foremost, for themselves. They want to meet the right people and do the right things, then go home to Los Angeles to plan their return to Washington ten, twenty, thirty years later. Still others come for the sake of God and his kingdom, wanting to take up their responsibilities as salt and light in society. And some, of course, get it all mixed up and want to do something for democracy, for themselves and for God, all at the same time.

I asked him what he had read by Kundera and what he thought of it. As we talked, I asked him what had brought him to Washington and what he was doing. He had come several years earlier, had earned a much coveted position "on the Hill" and had worked very hard for two years. "But I just got worn out," he told me. "The bureaucracy is awful. For someone like me who really wanted to get something done . . . well, it just can't happen." My heart plummeted, as I know too well how hard it is—especially for those full of youthful energy and idealism. His face brightened almost immediately, though, and he went on, "I've now got the job of my dreams. I'm off the Hill and over in Georgetown, working for a sports marketing firm. The challenges are big," and he smiled, "and of course there's a lot of money to be made."

Not only was it obvious that he had not taken to heart his reading of Kundera, which in and of itself is not tragic, but it was also clear that whatever convictions about life and the world he had left the university with at age twenty-one, at age twenty-five he had given up on them as a way of making sense of his life. Like countless knights before him, he had charged into the world with lance raised, thinking, *Political responsibility, I take thee up.* But after a relatively short fight, he came off the Hill, lance shattered, shaking his head, muttering, "It's a dirty world, politics."

It is, of course. The world is dirty, which is another way of saying that "the devil laughs because God's world seems senseless to him." That is, he laughs because the human person as a responsible actor—in families, in businesses, in schools or in politics—seems senseless to him. And yet it is that challenge which education in our time has before it: to understand that meaningful education is possible only if questions of meaning are allowed in education.

Schools are of course only one institution among many which affect the formation of a society's young people; but they are "the institution of preference" in our culture, as Parks has reminded us. With characteristic insight, Peter Berger sees the dilemma in this way:

> Modern man almost inevitably, it seems, is ever in search of himself. If this is understood, it will also be clear why both the sense of "alienation" and the concomitant identity crisis are most vehement among the young today. Indeed, "youth" itself, which is a matter of social definition rather than biological fact, will be seen as an interstitial area vacated or "left over" by the largest institutional structures of modern society. For this reason it is, simultaneously, the locale of the most acute experiences of self-estrangement and of the most intensive quest for reliable identities.[47]

The question for us is this: In the face of the pressures of modernity, especially the morass and malaise which has settled over the world of the university, is it possible to so educate students that they are prepared for making sense of their lives over the course of their lives—developing a coherent vision of life, "a reliable identity"? In the next chapter we begin to answer this question, examining the pressures of modernity through the lenses of three disciplines—the history of ideas, the ethic of character and the sociology of knowledge—as a way of understanding why and how this crisis of moral meaning in the modern university affects students in the way that it does, its implications echoing across life.

Making Sense of It All

Modernity has accomplished many far-reaching transformations,
but it has not fundamentally changed the finitude, fragility and
mortality of the human condition.

PETER BERGER, *The Homeless Mind*[1]

Ith tears he said to me, "But what does this have to do with where I work?"

As we explored contemporary policy debates in the American Studies Program as a way of understanding the meaning of responsible public involvement, we worked hard to understand them in the light of biblical themes such as justice, idolatry, stewardship and *shalom*. I had just finished speaking to our students on the kingdom of God, and this young man came up afterward with a question that burns to the heart of those who care about meaningfully connecting personal convictions with public responsibility.

Like all of our students, he was daily walking between learning and life, spending half of his week in class and the other half in an internship. Given his interest in politics and economics, he chose to work in a major think tank. It is the kind of place where "experts" in a variety of disciplines beaver away at the bidding of corporations and governments on questions of international and strategic interest. A junior in college, he had come with a solid foundation of faith nurtured at both home and school, and he had the advantage of having lived many years overseas. A healthy family, a better-than-average education and an international perspective: all together they should have been enough to send him off to whatever challenges the modern world held.

AND YET, HE CRIED

His tears were tears of frustration and bewilderment. Desperately wanting his foundational commitments to make sense of his new experience, he wondered how this vision of a comprehensive faith—one that understood the kingdom of God as a now-but-not-yet reality addressing the whole of life—could still be true, given what he had seen at work. How could he connect the belief that Christ is Lord over every area and arena of human existence with the apparent reality of his work setting? All that he had been taught to believe as true now seemed in question as he went to work day by day in an institution funded by powerful people whose priorities and passions were a million miles from the faith of his family. The think tank seemed to function as if his most deeply held convictions were irrelevant.

As I looked into his face I could see the pain of a young man who was bearing the bruises of his first try at engaging the modern world. His experience, of course, is not unusual. Peter Berger has written with great understanding of the impact of "privatization" on the possibility of developing a meaning-system which can order one's life (his views are summarized in a report on young people's beliefs):

> Meaning systems, moreover, are not mere intellectual exercises, but must be lived collectively; constant interaction with other people who perceive and interpret reality in the same way as oneself is necessary if one's "nomos" is to be automatically effective in imbuing one's everyday experience with meaning. But modern societies have largely dissolved these supportive systems. . . . This happens when the individual in his multiple and fragmented role exists partly inside and partly at a tangent to so many institutions and associations that no one of them addresses itself to "meaning" throughout the whole range of his life experience, but only to snatches and fragments. So in the end the individual is in a certain sense alone with the task of making sense of the world and his own place in it out of scraps and oddments culled here and there in his differentiated life and contacts.[2]

Basil Mitchell, Nolloth Professor of the Philosophy of Religion at Oxford University, comments on this insight of Berger's:

I suggest that this represents the greatest "external" challenge to Christian apologetics in Western countries. . . . This, for the time being at any rate, leaves many ordinary people, particularly young people, quite happy to adopt a pragmatic, utilitarian attitude to society at large, and to meet the crises of personal life with odd and often inconsistent scraps of "philosophy" picked up from anywhere and claiming no universal truth or even relevance. . . . The very conditions which create the need for meaning also make it extremely difficult to meet it.[3]

Our current social condition—the maelstrom of modernity—makes it incredibly difficult for Christian students to form a life that integrally connects their personal and public worlds. Characteristically, it is not that they choose to disconnect; rather it is in the air they breathe as they grow up in America.

Few have had as keen an eye on life in these United States as Bill Watterson. For years his daily observations came to us in "Calvin and Hobbes," the mirrorlike comic strip report on our national sense of self. We are still missing him. As a professor, I often began a lecture with a reference to one or more conversations between the little boy and his tiger. Some of the best were taped on my office door, warning students that I took his insights seriously!

One day Calvin and Hobbes were contemplating their creation of a snowman, with Hobbes remarking, "This snowman doesn't look very happy." Calvin responds, "He's not." In the next frame he goes on, "He knows it's just a matter of time before he melts. The sun ignores his existence. He feels his existence is meaningless." In the final frame, Hobbes asks, "Is it?" And as usual, Calvin has the last word: "Nope. He's about to buy a big-screen TV."

BEARING THE BRUISES OF MODERN CONSCIOUSNESS

What does it mean to grow up in the first years of the twenty-first century? How does the cultural context affect the formation of consciousness, the way we make sense of and order our existence? Professor Mitchell's observation is worthy of more attention. He says that the spirit of the age has particular consequence for young people, leaving them with a philosophy of life marked by pragmatic utilitarianism, "picked up from anywhere and claiming no universal truth or even relevance."

And yet young people face choices about meaning and morality that last for life, affecting not only the particular individuals but communities and cultures as well.

In order to understand the weight of such choices, this chapter will explore theories within three disciplines that open important windows onto these questions and their answers. In their own distinct ways, *the history of ideas, the ethic of character* and *the sociology of knowledge* each illumine our understanding of the impact of modernity on the quest for human integrity.

The history of ideas assumes that belief and behavior are primarily a consequence of theories weighed and sifted over time. These cognitive convictions are internalized in each generation and are passed on, book by book, to the next generation. The study of history, then, either personal or political, is intellectual history. Within this framework of analysis we will look at the work of Thomas Oden.

The ethic of character is a centuries-old conversation about how we make sense of our lives and order our existence. Its vantage point is that it is in beliefs expressed and shaped by behavior, characteristically, that the moral life is formed, individually and collectively. And so the first questions of ethics have more to do with how one lives than what one believes. Within this discipline we will look at the work of Stanley Hauerwas.

The sociology of knowledge teaches us that what we see and how we understand what we see are a complex construction of our circumstances, our communities, our callings, our countries and our centuries. So in order to answer the questions we have taken up here we must faithfully study the social context in which students are learning to make sense of the world and their place in it. Within this discipline we will look at the work of Peter Berger. The three perspectives are distinct, representing the richness of their respective disciplines as they have asked and answered common questions.

Through it all, this is the question that threads its way through the tapestry of this chapter: Within the context of higher education under the impact of contemporary consciousness, how is it that students learn to consciously and coherently connect what they believe about life and the world with how they live in the world? Three theories, growing out of three disciplines, each in their own way contribute to our understanding of why growing up in the modern world makes it very difficult to acquire the habits of heart needed to live a life of integrity, personally and publicly.

THE FIRST LENS: THOMAS ODEN AND THE HISTORY OF IDEAS

My favorite poet is Steve Turner. British and brilliant, his poems are "for people who feel that poetry has forgotten them." One that I often read to students as I try to help them understand their world is called "Creed." It begins like this:

> We believe in Marxfreudanddarwin.
> We believe everything is OK
> as long as you don't hurt anyone,
> to the best of your definition of hurt,
> and to the best of your knowledge.

He continues his walk through contemporary belief and behavior—bright as a light, sharp as a razor—showing incredible insight into the modern creed of secularism. These are his last lines:

> We believe that each man must find the truth
> that is right for him.
> Reality will adapt accordingly.
> The universe will readjust. History will alter.
> We believe that there is no absolute truth
> excepting the truth that there is no absolute truth.
> We believe in the rejection of creeds.[4]

Turner's cultural criticism is rooted in a tradition of analysis that takes its primary cues from the history of ideas, for example, "We believe in Marxfreudanddarwin." Certainly anyone who is fluent in the intellectual history of the twentieth and twenty-first centuries understands the confluence in the contributions of Karl Marx, Sigmund Freud and Charles Darwin. Is there an academic discipline or a university faculty in the world that has not been seriously shaped by one or more of that famous troika? In critical ways their ideas about human nature and destiny have definitively affected the academic discourse of the modern world. Its mindset and metaphors are different because of Marxfreudanddarwin.

The question here is this: How do ideas influence the formation of moral meaning during the university years? In what sense do "ideas have legs" that carry one on into the rest of life? While it is too much to argue that the alienation of the African American adolescent on the streets of Washington, D.C. (or any large urban center), is a result of reading either Sartre or Malcolm X, both the French existentialist and the black liberationist have decisively affected the contemporary world. A few years ago I could not walk between my office on Capitol Hill and Union Station without seeing baseball caps and T-shirts with a black X emblazoned on them, worn by young people who had no idea what Malcolm X's ideas were. And yet somebody, somewhere, was reading his work, and it was filtering its way through the popular culture and consciousness.

The history of ideas is a lens for understanding why and how this happens. The particular phenomenon may be any of thousands of ordinary examples from ordinary lives—a Malcolm X baseball cap on a disenfranchised African American sixteen-year-old boy, or the riots in South Central Los Angeles (Marx), the screenplays of Woody Allen (Freud), the worldview implicit in the message on the billboard advertising a local radio station, "Evolve: Modern Rock" (Darwin).

Whether we read the theoreticians or not, their ideas are in the air we breathe. Consider Tom Wolfe's novel *I Am Charlotte Simmons,* one more finger-on-the-pulse of who and where we are in American culture. Sometimes explicitly, sometimes implicitly, the Marxfreudanddarwin worldview is at the heart of Dupont University, the fictional school imagined after Wolfe spent months on the campuses of Duke, Harvard and Stanford doing research for his tale of a young woman's first year in college. It is uncanny, even eerie, how much the intellectual ethos of Dupont reflects Turner's "creed." This perspective on why people believe what they believe argues that it is ideas passed from one generation to the next that are the primary carrier of contemporary consciousness.

One wise man who sees the world this way is Thomas Oden. Throughout the 1970s he was a rising star in the theological orbit, and he expected to make a name for himself by finding some "new" idea which would challenge and change the discussion within his discipline (his own self-description).

But then he was asked a simple question by Will Herberg, an older faculty friend from Yale, author of the groundbreaking study of American religion titled *Protestant, Catholic and Jew.* A Jew himself, Herberg one day asked Oden if he had ever read the church fathers, wondering how it would be possible to be a Christian theologian without having studied the earliest Christian theologians. Chagrined, Oden began to read Athanasius, Basil, Chrysostom, Ambrose and Augustine, and he discovered a whole new world of doctrine and discourse. Writing in many different theological disciplines, he has introduced an increasingly wide audience to "consensual, ancient classic Christianity, with its proximate continuity, catholicity and apostolicity."[5]

When the Soviet Union first opened its doors to the West under Gorbachev's glasnost, Oden was invited to teach at Moscow State University. He explains:

> I had agreed to lecture to undergraduate students on the theme of postmodern Christian consciousness, and to doctoral students on the structure of awareness in time. I intended to develop and interpret for a Soviet audience some of the basic arguments found in two of my books, *After Modernity . . . What?* and *The Structure of Awareness.* Actually much more developed . . .[6]

The story of his semester is told in *Two Worlds: Notes on the Death of Modernity in America and Russia,* a fascinating tale of his experience but also of his perspective on "the death of modernity." Implicit in his subtitle is the thesis that both America and Russia have lived under the pale of modern consciousness, which he characterizes as their experiments in autonomous individualism and autonomous collectivism respectively.

Oden traces this "mod rot," as he calls it, from its inception at the French Revolution to its demise with the fall of communism. In a vein not dissimilar to Alasdair MacIntyre's in *After Virtue,* Oden understands this as an ideological worldview grown out of the Enlightenment, which he argues "has been spiraling downward in a relentless disarray during the three decades from 1960 to 1990, the period of rapidly deteriorating modernity. The malaise is acute in the American setting and chronic in the Soviet setting."[7]

What are the faces of modern consciousness, as seen from Oden's history-of-ideas lens? "Four types of criticism, which formerly were dominant, having held sway in modernity, are now struggling with social failure at every hand: Nietzschean relativistic nihilism, Marxist social planning, Freudian therapy and Bultmannian historicism."[8] He then delineates what he sees to be the distinctive contributions of these four figures: Friedrich Nietzsche "furnished modernity with the sharp knife of a cynical, egoistic critique of all moral striving"; Karl Marx "offered a class location critique which assumed that every ideological view has its final explanation in one's position in the class struggle"; Sigmund Freud "offered modernity a psychoanalytical critique which imagined that all neurotic behavior is grounded in sexual repression"; and Rudolf Bultmann was "the epitome of that modern chauvinism which assumes that recent worldviews are intrinsically superior to ancient ones."[9]

"Mod rot" is Oden's diagnosis. In the words of a recent Harvard undergraduate, speaking at his own graduation: "Among my classmates, however, I believe that there is one idea, one sentiment, which we have all acquired at some point in our Harvard careers; and that, ladies and gentlemen, is, in a word, confusion." At the same commencement, a graduate student put it like this:

> They tell us that it is heresy to suggest the superiority of some value, fantasy to believe in moral argument, slavery to submit to a judgment sounder than your own. The freedom of our day is the freedom to devote ourselves to any values we please, on the mere condition that we do not believe them to be true.[10]

Latent in his lament is a frustration with the dichotomy between public truths and private values. It is of course public truths which are operative in the daily business of Harvard University, the White House and Wall Street. Private values are for dorm discussions and chapel exercises. Retired Harvard president Derek Bok said it simply: "Relativism and individualism have rewritten the rules of the game. They have extinguished the motive for education."[11]

They have, in effect, produced a generation of students who have "homeless minds."

We believe that each man must find the truth
that is right for him.
Reality will adapt accordingly.
The universe will readjust. History will alter.
We believe that there is no absolute truth
excepting the truth that there is no absolute truth.
We believe in the rejection of creeds.

Yes, we believe in Marxfreudanddarwin—at even the best universities.

THE SECOND LENS: STANLEY HAUERWAS AND THE ETHIC OF VIRTUE

Exposure to politics leads to disillusionment with politics. After having
worked on Capitol Hill for several years, I realize the political realism embedded in that aphorism is only too true. There are exceptions, but they are
exceptions.

Those who came to study with us were in Washington for one semester.
They were typically intelligent and industrious and had a history of interest
in the wider world. That third quality, more than anything else, brought
them here. From disparate backgrounds ethnically and academically, they
came to us wanting to learn how to connect learning with life. For a few, that
question was quickly and crassly answered by picking up on all the accou-
trements of "Vanity Fair," what in our day is called "the fast track." Their semester of study, with all of its opportunities for meeting people and ideas,
became merely a passport to privilege. But most were not so easily satisfied.
Instead, they wanted to understand the world and to discover their place of
responsibility and service within it. That can bring its own pains, as the story
of the student with tears always reminds me.

Washington is a city that lives and dies by partisan politics. In the 1992
presidential campaign, Bill Clinton promised that if elected he would "end
gridlock." Perhaps to his dismay, he discovered that the privileges of the
presidency do not extend that far. In every administration, the president, the
Congress and the interest groups create a brand new story in American political history, dancing to their own unique drumbeat. But the players are the
same; again and again the Democrats and the Republicans claw away at each

other, as if the future of the cosmos depended on one's party allegiance. And yet somehow in the midst of that turmoil and anguish, there is something in the air—locals call it "Potomac fever"—which causes individuals and institutions from all over the earth to want to be part of it. At least for a while.

But there is the rub. The vision of the American Studies Program is to give students some of the skills they will need to responsibly engage their society and world as a calling, a vocation—for a lifetime. And yet, like most everyone else, they find that exposure to politics leads to disillusionment with politics. They have seen Bismarck's proverbial sausage being made, and they want nothing more to do with it.

The messiness of *realpolitik* is only part of the problem, of course. At the deepest levels, their souls are stressed by the pressures of modernity—the sociological privatization and ideological pluralization seen so keenly by Berger and Oden—and they feel "lost in the cosmos." The apparent implications of the spiritual schizophrenia that seems implicit in entering into the public world is debilitating to students. They wonder whether participation in the public world requires that one make no meaningful connection between personal belief and public behavior. As I have listened semester by semester, teaching now in a variety of venues across the city and around the country, it is that dichotomy which is most deeply disturbing to the students who come here wanting to meaningfully connect learning with life, wanting a calling, not just a career. And as I have struggled to respond with lectures and readings that address their anxieties, I have been drawn to the wisdom of the ethic of character. What is it? And what is its stake in the formation of moral meaning during the university years?

No contemporary scholar has written so widely and so well about the ethic of character as has Stanley Hauerwas. He writes with equal ease about the intricacies of Fletcher's situation ethics and Aslan's "new morality" in his first volume, *Vision and Virtue,*[12] but it is the thesis that "we can only define choices within the world we can see"[13] which is the continuing passion of his scholarship—the relationship between "vision and virtue."

That first book proposed "the ethic of character" as a way of understanding the moral life, a way of seeing and choosing. In it he distinguished between "having character" and a "character trait."

To speak of a man "having character" is not to attribute to him any specific traits; rather the point is that, whatever activity he takes part in or trait he exhibits, there "will be some sort of control and constancy in the manner in which he exhibits them." We often speak of integrity of character, thereby closely identifying integrity and consistency with the meaning of having character.[14]

It is, of course, precisely at that point that his writing is relevant for students struggling to connect the personal and the public realms of their lives. Integrity and consistency are what they long for, as an expression of their humanness; and yet modernity seems to exact the price of integrity and consistency for those who want to participate in the public world.

In particular I have drawn on two of Hauerwas's essays which deal with the dichotomy between personal and public lives. Both are stories of public figures who wrestled with the possibility of achieving meaningful lives, of gaining personal integrity at the expense of public integrity.

The first, "Self-Deception and Autobiography: Reflections on Speer's *Inside the Third Reich*,"[15] is a negative example of someone whose meaning system was so corrupted—both by modern consciousness and by his own moral weakness, particularly vanity—that he was content to disconnect himself from his work. In his late twenties, Albert Speer was an aspiring young architect, very promising and yet largely untested. Adolf Hitler approached him and asked if he would be interested in designing buildings which would "last a millennium" for the Third Reich of Germany. Speer acknowledged that from the beginning he was not interested in Hitler's politics but was intrigued with the promise of being given such a large responsibility, with immediate acclaim. But he maintained, credibly, that he was apolitical: "My new political interests played a subsidiary part in my thinking. I was above all an architect."[16]

In his attempt to ground meaning exclusively in the personal—"I was above all an architect"—Speer's life is a tragic witness to the meaning of privatization. Hauerwas's essay is a profound analysis of self-deception and opens the window for understanding both its personal and its public implications. There is a cost to both the self and the society.

What is most troubling about Speer's involvement in the Nazi crimes is his seeming "ordinariness"; he was not a "crazed student" from Dostoyevsky but a "man in a gray flannel suit." An article in the British *Observer* (April 9, 1944) includes a description of Speer which is an eerie reminder of the reality that it is in the ordinary disciplines and decisions of life that modern consciousness has its most profound consequences.

> [For Speer] is very much the successful average man, well-dressed, civil, noncorrupt, very middle-class in his style of life, with a wife and six children. Much less than any of the other German leaders does he stand for anything particularly German or particularly Nazi. He rather symbolizes a type which is becoming increasingly important in all belligerent countries: the pure technician, the classless bright young man without background, with no other original aim than to make his way in the world and no other means than his technical and managerial ability. It is the lack of psychological and spiritual ballast, and the ease with which he handles the terrifying technical and organizational machinery of our age, which makes this slight type go extremely far nowadays. . . . This is their age; the Hitlers, the Himmlers we may get rid of, but the Speers, whatever happens to this particular special man, will long be with us.[17]

A technocrat's ideal, remembering Postman. And generation after generation they hurt and haunt us in ways which eat away at our societal soul. This propensity for self-deception growing into self-destruction, with society-wide consequences, has caused one commentator to ask, "Can a nation die of too many lies?"[18] The ordinary people—with "technical and managerial ability" but who lack "spiritual and psychological ballast"—are not very different, whether their success stories are known as Auschwitz, the Gulag, Watergate, the Challenger tragedy or Tiananmen Square. Hauerwas reflects:

> Love of country that once inspired noble deeds can lead us to commit the worst crimes when we have lost the skills to recognize how other loyalties must qualify that of patriotism. Rather than demand whether it was possible to avoid self-deception, we should rather try to assess

how effectively deceived we have become. Our ability to "step back" from our deceptions is dependent on the dominant story, the master image, that we have embodied in our character. Through our experience we constantly learn new lessons, we gain new insights, about the limit of our life story. But "insights are a dime a dozen" and even more useless unless we have the skills—the images and the stories—which can empower those insights to shape our lives. It is not enough to see nor is it enough to know; we must know how to say and give expression to what we come to see and know.[19]

Skills, images, stories—the shaping of life. This is the ethic of character, and vision and virtue are at its heart, because they address both seeing the world as it truthfully is and shaping one's life in relation to that truthful account of the world. But implicit in that vision of life and the world is a belief that it is possible to see *truthfully*. This not only has consequences for the possibility of avoiding self-deception—which is not a small thing—but it also has consequences for the recovery of a meaning system that provides coherence to the whole of one's existence. Simply said, truthfulness provides that possibility.

It is here that I have drawn on the second of Hauerwas's essays, "Hope Faces Power: Thomas More and the King of England."[20] Basing their assessment of More on Robert Bolt's play *A Man for All Seasons,* Hauerwas and Shaffer pursue the core question of the moral problem of power, that is, "how a virtuous person uses power, and lives close to power, without losing the sense of self that is necessary to negotiate the temptations of power."[21] In poignant contrast to Speer, this account tries "to show how More's hope involved moral and intellectual skill—skill in the use of power, skill in serving power in such a way that he was not consumed by it, and skill in knowing when to spurn power and to accept the consequences."[22] This understanding of "skill" is based on a centuries-old conversation about the virtues, where Hauerwas draws on the contributions of Aristotle and Aquinas, whose "understanding of virtue as habit is best understood in terms of the acquisition of skills for discrimination and action."[23] Again, vision and virtue.

After months of seeing "how the sausage is made," students need to acquire habits of heart which enable them to negotiate the horrible complexities of the bureaucratic state, whether they meet that in a think tank, the Senate, the judicial system or the Pentagon. We give them an essay on hope. But it is not hope in hope; rather, it is a deeply wrought vision of an alternative reality, of what might be, of how it could be different—if modern consciousness is not the last word on the reality of our existence. This kind of hope is a worldview away from optimism, as we have no desire to nurture starry-eyed idealists who will burn out when their dreams die. Hauerwas argues instead,

> Optimism is not hope as we mean to talk about hope. Optimism differs from hope in that optimism can exist without truth. Because it can exist without truth it is defeated and perverted by power. Hope, when seen as optimism, is, in the poetic phrase, dashed. An optimistic person whose "hopes are dashed" becomes a cynic. He becomes a cynic because he still needs some way to locate and protect "that little area in which I must rule myself." Cynicism gives him a way to do that without requiring that he worry about the truth. Cynicism thus promises a check against power, against the persons, institutions and roles that claim our lives. Both the hopeful person and the cynic have found a way to stand back from their engagements; but cynicism stills the imagination against the possible, and therefore protects the cynic without requiring that he be truthful. The price of cynical protection is self-deception. The cynic abandons the human burden of deciding what is true and what is not; he does this by refusing to believe in anything.[24]

Hauerwas pushes his point even further by insisting that "optimism leads to cynicism because it does not pay attention to truth. Hope, as we are talking about it, is based on truth and forces the imagination to look for alternatives."[25]

A few years ago a student came—remarkably, given the story of Speer— as apolitical and wanting to have a great internship experience in architecture which would enable him to get into the right graduate school. My first impression, watching him in class and hearing about his motivations, was, "How did he get through our admissions process?" But as I got to know him, I began to see that there was a depth to his questions that set him apart from the average student. He read the assignments carefully, listened to the lectures, always with an ear to making sense of it all. One responsibility we required of the students was a daily journal, which we hoped would weave together their reading, the lectures and briefings, and their internship. Toward the end of the semester he wrote:

> Reading the Hauerwas article on Speer's biography was a rather rude awakening to me. Speer's problem, it is said, could be traced back to his philosophy on life. This was "I am an architect, I'm not interested in politics." If one were to go back and look at my application for this program, one would read almost word for word this very sentiment. That is really scary considering where this philosophy led Speer. This is probably one the strongest forces that I have felt pulling me this semester toward a more politically aware life.
>
> I have had, for many years, a fairly well developed "telos"—to use terms from class today. My "teleios" or general path in life, however, has slowly been narrowing. Originally I wanted to serve God. Then I wanted to serve God and be a veterinarian, which later gave way to architecture. Finally I wanted to serve God in architecture. This meant for me trying to find a means of serving God from within architecture instead of being an architect and serving God in my free time. Now I see that I cannot merely concentrate on architecture, but I must remain aware of the state of the world around me.
>
> So I find myself, for the first time in a long time, enlarging my *teleios*, making room for political awareness so as to avoid becoming pulled into deception. Not that what happened to Speer is likely to happen to me, at least not on that scale. However, I can see the attraction that purely architectural pursuits hold for me.[26]

Wherever students study—whether in Washington, D.C., or in cities scattered across North America and all over the world—they must develop the skills they will need to take up their responsibilities in service to the world, facing head-on the impact of privatization in modern consciousness. For that to happen, the distinction between hope and optimism needs to be written into their vision. Then they can begin to distinguish between what is and what ought to be—because they believe in the possibility of *truthful* discrimination and action, and so they can begin to look for alternatives to the deceptions which are so deadly for persons and polities.

THE THIRD LENS: PETER BERGER AND THE SOCIOLOGY OF KNOWLEDGE

Few can compare with Peter Berger for his lucid commentary on the meaning of modernity. For forty years he has done pioneering scholarship on the relationship between belief and behavior in the light of modernity's power to shape how we see and live in the world. His voluminous writing could be drawn on at many points, but for our purposes here *The Homeless Mind: Modernization and Consciousness* will be sufficient. In it he and coauthors Brigitte Berger and Hansfried Kellner explore "the worldview of modernity."[27] Building on his thesis in *The Social Construction of Reality*[28] that the social experience of "ordinary people leading ordinary lives" is a pretheoretical means of constructing reality—more so than their exposure to the history of ideas or the history of philosophy—he advances that thesis by identifying what he understands are the primary agents of modernization and therefore of modern consciousness. Much of the book is taken up with explaining the impact of technological production and the bureaucratically organized state upon everyday life.

Lest we get lost here, remember Calvin and Hobbes. At issue is what people believe about the world and how they live in the world. That is a perennial question, and is asked and answered in every generation. Berger's unique contribution to that query is his lens shaped by the study of ordinary social experience and its effect on consciousness, on how people make sense of life.

For Berger, *consciousness* "is the web of meanings that allow the individual to navigate his way through the ordinary events and encounters of his life with others. . . . Consciousness in this context does not refer to ideas, theories or sophisticated constructions of meaning."[29] There is a passion in

Berger to connect his theoretical musings on the nature of the world with how people see and live in the world. Writing about "collisions of consciousness" in the modern world, which he argues is characterized by "the collective and individual loss of integrative meanings,"[30] he observes, "As the individual's apprehension of the social world is changed by modernization, so is his apprehension of his own identity. . . . At this point, all of reality becomes uncertain and threatened with meaninglessness—precisely the condition that sociologists commonly call anomie."[31] Anomie, literally "without law," is typically understood as a lack of purpose and identity, metaphysically and ethically, that is, homeless in the cosmos. Simply and sadly, it is the loss of moral meaning.

This philosophical and psychological crisis of "ordinary people leading ordinary lives" was captured brilliantly in the writings of Walker Percy, among them one actually titled *Lost in the Cosmos*. For one to understand Berger's insight, it is almost imperative that one read Percy, as his novels are the literary counterpoint to Berger's sociological analysis.[32] Both are deeply concerned about the effects of modernization on consciousness, but at the same time, both are explicitly writing about Everyman.

"For Percy, the typical alienated man is not some half-starving, half-crazed student out of a novel by Dostoyevsky or Sartre, but precisely the well-fed, successful, middle-class man or woman who seemingly 'has it all' and yet feels totally bored and empty."[33] As Percy himself put it, his great theme was "human sadness—specifically . . . the question of why man feels so sad in the twentieth century."[34] One writer, reviewing Percy's last novel, *The Thanatos Syndrome,* assessed his literary effort in this way:

> Three of author Walker Percy's five previous novels bear titles with implications of apocalypse: *The Last Gentleman, Love in the Ruins* and *The Second Coming.* The other two, *The Moviegoer* and *Lancelot,* are exceptions in name only. For all of Percy's fiction revolves around a central question: can humane, civilized life survive this murderous, mechanized century?[35]

That central question, full as it is of Percy's own prophetic passion, is the central question that Berger has raised in his discussion of "the homeless

mind"—a twentieth-century consciousness shaped by the social consequences of modern technology and bureaucracy. One of its most poignant
and painful faces is the dichotomization of private and public life, which,
when all is said and done, was the reason for my student's tears.[36] More than
anything else, he wanted to connect those two worlds in a meaningful way.
And quite apart from having read Nietzsche or Sartre who persuaded him
otherwise, his Everyman experience of life in the city was that that connection was both impossible and irrelevant. And yet, he cried—because his aspirations and expectations were for something more.

Princeton sociologist Robert Wuthnow, a keen observer of American social experience, put it like this:

> Modernity engenders very real "discontents" for those who are part of it.
> The aggregate effects of these discontents is summarized by the notion of
> a metaphysical sense of homelessness. Modernity erodes precisely that
> which man's psychological and organismic constitution requires.[37]

That "something more" which my student desired was "precisely that
which man's psychological and organismic constitution requires"—nothing
less than the quest for integrity, personal and public, individual and institutional. There is something in our humanness which recoils at the schizophrenia seemingly forced on us by the modern world. To settle for a split in
one's consciousness—the dichotomy between the private and the public—
is to settle for two realities, a private world with no meaningful connection
to the public world.

As the little boy says to his friend the tiger: "Look, Hobbes, this world is
kind of like TV. A casual observer might even confuse the two. But if you
notice, here the colors are less intense and the people are uglier. Also, I see
that several minutes can go by without a single car chase, explosion, murder
or pat personal exchange." Hobbes leans over the chair and asks, "Why settle for less, hmm?" With eyes transfixed on the TV, Calvin says, "Shh. This is
my favorite deodorant commercial."

THE NECESSITY OF INTERWOVEN INSIGHTS
If the bumper sticker is right—THE ONE WHO DIES WITH THE MOST

TOYS WINS—then the graduate students at Carnegie-Mellon University must take the prize. Several years ago I met regularly with a group of unusual students, all of whom were pursuing Ph.D.s in engineering disciplines. Week by week we studied in a seminar-style setting in the Robotics Institute, a high-high-tech section of one of the best engineering schools in the world. Contrary to caricature, these were not "nerds" in any sense of the word. In all my years of teaching, I have never met a group so "Renaissance" in their backgrounds and aspirations. They read widely in history, literature, philosophy and theology—and yet were bright enough in their own fields to have earned coveted places in a very competitive graduate program. Most were doing work in artificial intelligence, and because of the promise that field holds, a large amount of funding was available to assist them in their studies. One of them graduated and took a position at IBM's think tank, and he remarked that he had had better equipment—that is, more toys(!)—while a graduate student at CMU.

Over the years that we spent together, we worked hard at understanding the world through the perspective of our faith-formed vision. We read books on the philosophy of technology, on the nature of progress and on theological ethics, as well as studying the Scriptures. Through it all we emphasized the importance of learning to "think Christianly" about technology and about vocations within the technological society.

But easily the most persistent discussion we had was about "the meaning of it all." Here in the midst of a veritable technological wonderland, where it seemed that all things were possible, this question was raised again and again: But does it really matter?

Though I always took the question seriously, it seemed terribly ironic, given the setting in which it was asked. In effect these very gifted students wondered whether is was possible to meaningfully connect their personal convictions about God, human nature and the meaning of history with the apparent reality of life on modernity's cutting edge. No one dropped out in despair, but the question was asked and asked and asked again.

Mod rot, cynicism, the homeless mind—is the critique too harsh? We do not have to stay within the academy, lest it seem that the view from the ivory tower is skewed and out of touch with "ordinary people leading ordinary lives." For years Mike Royko had as keen an eye and as attentive an ear as anyone, and he wrote about the heartbeat of America from Chicago, capital of the Midwest. In one column he reflected on an article in the *Wall Street Journal,* which focused on the social phenomena known as "Generation X." The term comes from a bestselling book by Doug Coupland, who described his generation as "cocked to conquer the world . . . uncertain if the world is worth the trouble."[38] Royko wrote:

> "Sometimes I wonder why we haven't all committed mass suicide, because we don't have a hell of a lot to look forward to." That is a quote from a page 1 story of a recent Wall Street Journal. Let us have a multiple-choice guessing game. Who said it and why?
>
> 1. A patient in a hospital wing filled with people who are terminally ill and suffering terrible pain.
>
> 2. A very old and feeble person in a crowded and understaffed nursing home, whose relatives never come to visit.
>
> 3. A fifty-one-year-old employee of a defense industry company who was laid off from his job several months ago and has a mortgage, two children in college and is attending a support group of other jobless middle-aged people who can't find work.
>
> 4. A black woman living in Chicago's public housing whose youngest child was killed by gang crossfire, talking to another woman whose oldest son is in jail for selling drugs.
>
> 5. A bent-backed factory assembly line worker whose house, dog and all worldly possessions have been swept away by the Mississippi River.
>
> 6. A forty-year-old illegal immigrant who hoped to get a job chopping the heads off chickens but has been nabbed and is about to be shipped back to his Third-World homeland.
>
> 7. A healthy, attractive twenty-three-year-old college graduate who is sitting nude in a hot tub with her handsome boyfriend and eight

other naked friends, complaining about how difficult it is for a young person to find a good job these days.

Your time is up. Okay, take a few more seconds if you wish and check it again. Done? If you guessed 1 through 6, sorry, but you are wrong. Such people might be justified in feeling hopeless, but they aren't the ones quoted by the Wall Street Journal.

No, the answer is number 7, the healthy, attractive one. She was featured in a fascinating story about those members of what is called "Generation X"—people in their 20s—who are having a hard time finding jobs that suit their educational backgrounds. This young woman had been working as a nanny, a job she loathed. Her boyfriend was also doing something unsatisfying. Their hot tub friends had similar problems.[39]

Some hyperbole, yes. In these voices from the hot tub there are neither tears nor thoughtful questions; and yet there is still a longing to feel meaningfully connected to life. For a tapestry of reasons—explained in part by theories drawn from the history of ideas, the ethic of character and the sociology of knowledge—young people are finding it increasingly difficult to make sense of the world and their place in it.

And yet some do. There are students who make their way through their university experience with a vision of responsible involvement in the world, formed in indelible ways by their deepest convictions about meaning and morality. But even more than that, there are people who develop lives of integrity—spanning the spectrum of human responsibilities, from family to neighborhood to work to politics to church—with those university experiences significantly shaping their lives for the rest of life. Who are they? Is their experience critically different from the experience of those who do not achieve integrity? How does it happen that so many fall by the way?

Some are deeply affected by modernity, without ever knowing it, and they suffer all the pains of those moral visions marked by mod rot, cynicism and homelessness. They never see beyond education as a passport to privilege, and we all live with the effects of that sort of self-absorbed individualism. Mike Royko even writes about it. On the other hand, others seem to transcend that myopia for a time—their university years—but do not make it into mature adulthood with their convictions intact, and they discard rather than deepen the worldview which they came to prize as their own while students. Sometimes that results in a privatizing of convictions, which is a form of relativism; sometimes its consequence is more virulent, causing a disintegration of the meaning system itself.

How is it that some form habits of heart that enable them to negotiate and navigate their way through the complexities and crises of life with their integrity intact—and some do not? In the crucible of those critical years between adolescence and adulthood, what happens to those who make it through and are still making it, twenty years later? In this next chapter we will study the stories of people who live like this, who continue on into the diverse responsibilities of adulthood with an integrity that connects the whole of life, from the most personal disciplines to the most public duties.

As these stories are told, listen for how it is the students learned to connect their lives in a coherent way, particularly the way in which they talk about the formation of their convictions, the place of their teachers in how they came to those convictions, and the role of friendships and larger communities as they began to take those convictions into adulthood.

A Worldview, a Way of Life

In an age of relativity the practice *of truth when it is costly*
is the only way to cause the world to take seriously
our protestations concerning truth.

FRANCIS SCHAEFFER, *The God Who Is There*[1]

The first time I saw the film *Howards End,* I thought as I walked out, *This*
is what film could be! A well-told story, true to the way the world really is, and
beautiful cinematography—what more can we ask for? I decided that it would
be a good one to discuss with my children and their friends.[2]

So one day after school we went to Georgetown and made an evening of
it. Afterward we walked around the corner to get pizza and to talk. Amid the
music and general clatter, I asked my usual question: "Well, what did you
think?"

Lots of different opinions were offered, and we followed up on several interesting ideas. One thoughtful sixth-grader commented on the inconsisten-
cies in the life of Mr. Wilcox, the wealthy industrialist who with his wife
owned the country home called Howards End. Even to the children, the
contradictions were obvious—and yet Mr. Wilcox was seemingly unbur-
dened by those contradictions. At critical points and places in his life, touch-
ing both the most public and the most personal areas—his understanding
of national and international economic life as well as his most intimate family relationships—Mr. Wilcox failed to see what was so plain to others: at a
fundamental level he lacked integrity.

At one point a young friend of the family, worried about economic trends and their effect on his career, asked Mr. Wilcox his opinion. "How could Mr. Wilcox *not* be responsible for the advice he gave to Leonard Bast, who then lost his job?" my children and their friends asked.

Later in the film, at a family wedding, a former flame of Mr. Wilcox's inexplicably shows up and in her drunkenness boisterously identifies herself as an intimate acquaintance of his. Deeply shamed, he slinks down into despair, assuming that his wife will not be able to forgive him. And yet with great grace she does. Then, toward the end of the story, Mrs. Wilcox asks her husband to give grace to her sister, who has become pregnant out of wedlock. With amazing obstinance, he refuses. The children wondered, "How could he *not* forgive his wife's sister, when his wife had forgiven him?"

At evening's end, I was pleased with the willingness of these little ones to think, aloud and together, about ideas that matter.

ONLY CONNECT

Some time later, when I picked up a copy of the novel by E. M. Forster on which the movie was based, I was stopped in my tracks to find on the dedication page these two words, standing starkly on their own: "Only connect." And I immediately thought back to our conversation over pizza and the disconnections that my children and their friends had seen.

Few if any films can match a book for development of character and plot, and even with their unusual abilities, Merchant and Ivory fell short of Forster in their effort at *Howards End*. It is the musings, the inner world of thoughts and feelings, which is so hard to capture cinematically. After disaster strikes the Wilcox clan—a son is accused of manslaughter—and their privilege and power prove to be no protection against prison, Margaret (the teller of the tale as the second Mrs. Wilcox) reflects on a very difficult conversation she has had with her husband over his moral blindness.

> Now that she had time to think over her own tragedy, she was unrepentant. She neither forgave him for his behavior nor wished to forgive him. Her speech to him seemed perfect. She would not have altered a word. It had to be uttered once in a life, to adjust the lopsid-

edness of the world. It was spoken not only to her husband but to thousands of men like him—a protest against the inner darkness in high places that comes with a commercial age. Though he would build up his life without hers, she could not apologize. He had refused to connect, on the clearest issue that can be laid before a man, and their love must take the consequences.[3]

And what is that clearest of issues? To "only connect" what he says he believes about the world with how he lives in the world.

Throughout the pages and chapters thus far we have analyzed the issue of connecting belief to behavior, exploring why it is so difficult for students—and for every one of us. In these next three chapters we take the next step, listening to representative accounts of those who continue to connect, who still believe that the gospel of the kingdom makes sense of the whole of life—twenty years after their university experience.

The theoretical constructs provided by the three disciplines of the history of ideas, the ethic of character and the sociology of knowledge are a deductive lens through which we have asked questions about modern consciousness and its effects on the formation of moral meaning during the university years. Now we will look at the same questions through an inductive lens, hearing individuals reflect on their experiences as students and the ways in which those experiences affect their lives twenty years later.

Why do you get up in the morning? What happened during your college years to shape your understanding of the world and your place in it? What do you care about and why? Over the course of hours of listening to people who still believe in the vision of a coherent faith, one that meaningfully connects personal disciplines with public duties, again and again I saw that they were people (1) who had formed a worldview sufficient for the challenges of the modern world, (2) who had found a teacher who incarnated that worldview and (3) who had forged friendships with folk whose common life was embedded in that worldview. There were no exceptions.

How is it possible, under the impact of modern and postmodern consciousness, for young adults in this century to hear Qoheleth's admonition, as Ellul interprets him for us: "You must take sides earlier—when you can actually make choices, when you have many paths opening at your feet, before the weight of necessity overwhelms you."[4] Our answers to the cosmic questions—beliefs about God, human nature, history—form the pretheoretical framework for how we understand and interpret the world around us. With them and from them we make sense of what we see and hear. As a constellation of cares and commitments, they become a tapestry which connects the disparate strands of our lives; because this is true for every person under the sun, we can understand Iris Murdoch's assertion that "at crucial moments of choice most of the business of choosing is already over."[5]

Belief and behavior are braided in the very deepest places of the human heart. Qoheleth's warning takes on its own urgency in a time in human history when, as Basil Mitchell noted about modernity's effects on young people, "the very conditions which create the need for meaning also make it extremely difficult to meet it."[6]

As those interviewed answered questions about how they make sense of life and the world, two factors stood out: their desire for coherence and their belief in truth. No other issues seemed as central to their articulation of their worldviews as these two; together they are woven into the fabric of faith of those who still believe and who act on what they believe. In this section we will look at what these factors meant for several folk—and what they mean in the context of the challenge facing human beings in the modern-becoming-postmodern world.

A Longing for Coherence

The story of Mr. Wilcox in *Howards End* reveals a dichotomy that debilitates, rather than a sense of self that stimulates connecting belief with behavior. And yet, Forster's early twentieth-century warning is for "thousands . . . like him—a protest against the inner darkness in high places that comes with a commercial age." Surely in the confluence of industrialization and bureaucratization he saw something about modern consciousness and its potential effects on character and culture, something that drew out of him a novel dedicated to the end "Only connect."

The college years need to help students develop ways of thinking and living that are coherent, that make sense of the whole of life. It is the difference between a worldview which brings integration to the whole of one's existence and one which brings disintegration. In those who were interviewed, simply said, it was the integrity between what they believed about the world and how they lived in the world that marked them as so deeply different.

One of these was John John, formerly the director of industrial policy in the Ministry of Trade and Commerce in Malaysia, and now involved in various business efforts throughout his country. Chosen as a boy to attend a school for his nation's next generation of leaders, he was sent to the U.S. after university training in his own country to do graduate study in management theory. When asked about his own deepest reasons for being, he openheartedly said,

> I get up in the morning to live my life for the glory of God . . . a vision of life that comes from a long, long, long time ago. It is in my blood. My parents live like this and taught me to live like this. . . . I summarize it into three aspects: the private, personal; the public, relational; and the lived life, which is distinctive because I think it is in our actions that we communicate the first two. So it is wholly related, but very often the first and the second are not related, and therefore we live disintegrated lives.
>
> I have always been impressed by people who live integrated lives; the epitome of that comes in seeing the life of Christ in someone. Living a life of glory to God is living a life of integrity, a life that speaks louder than words. The private, personal aspects we develop over many, many years through thinking about things and testing our espoused theories about how to live life. The public, relational aspect is theories in use (using language of the Theory of Action). My lived-out life has been a struggle to keep the integrity of the first two. Very often good friends give feedback by telling you certain things don't match up with how you say you live. The more friends you have like that, the more you are held accountable for your own actions. Very often in life people don't want to tell you the not-so-good thing. It is important to develop a community of people who are honest to keep you straight.

For those with ears to hear, his own account of the whys and wherefores of his life reflects the reality of what was heard again and again. He went on to connect this vision to his vocation.

I chose to go into public service twenty-two years ago by the influence of my father. It was like any other bureaucracy, yet I felt called to it and I had occasions when I felt God confirmed my calling. In fact, the calling was put to the test about six weeks after I joined the civil service when a friend offered me a job in the private sector with one-and-a-half times the salary, a better title and better perks. I told him that I wanted to be more responsible and involved in contributing to people's lives in some meaningful way through public service, rather than making people's houses look better. I wanted to be a part of defining the reality of the society through contributing my ideas. I started out in the prime minister's department, and there we were doing evaluation of public policies and projects, which gave me a very good sense of national direction. I got a vision of life intended by the party in power, then I went on to do teaching, volunteering at a teaching institute to further educate myself and share my experience with those who were learning. I was there quite a few years. Now I am with the Ministry of Trade and Commerce in Malaysia. I am able to say that this is all I want to do every day in life. When I go home, look in the mirror and ask myself if I have done an honest day's job, I can say yes—that is all I want to do. In continuing to answer yes, I feel as though I have lived my life, to the best of my definition, working to the glory of God.

When asked, "What qualities do you draw from this vision of life to the glory of God that have any kind of influence on the Ministry of Trade and Commerce?" he answered,

The first quality is integrity—this applies to all areas of life. In a world of greater pluralism and globalism where people will recognize their roots and belief systems more, and the lack of universality of these, and so then will cry for commonality—since we need to conduct life with some notion of decency—we are going to be faced with the question, "What is our theory of change, and what is its basis?"

I have come to the conclusion that the only valuable theory of change is one of integrity. Whoever espouses such a theory needs to live by it, and when you do that you have set up a model for moral leadership where people will begin to trust what you say, buy into your vision, get excited with the vision and make it their own. They too become agents of change. The Christian vision is the only vision of change I have seen to work. I believe that the issue of integrity will be the key in the next decade, and we will come at it from every direction, including the sciences. Other qualities are honesty, trustworthiness, respect of others. Integrity, though, is the bridge between word and deed—the only valid theory of action.

The longing for coherence, connecting the cords of one's life, is at the heart of the task of constructing a worldview which can sustain one for life. John spoke of it as an integrity which "applies to all areas of life." How can this be nurtured in students during the critical years in which they are forming a vision of meaning and morality which will last a lifetime? There is no issue more critical than this one for students and for those who care for them, as well as for men and women who are finding their way into vocations that will sustain them for the rest of life. The fragmenting forces in contemporary culture make it incredibly hard to hold together belief and behavior, as the pressures of the modern world bear down on discipleship in ways that disintegrate rather than integrate.

ON TRUTH, WOODY ALLEN AND THE TRIUMPH OF THE THERAPEUTIC

I remember a student who asked wonderful questions about important ideas. Week after week we would talk after class, as he seemed able to understand more than most the complexity of belief in general—and belief in truth in particular—in a pluralist society. And I took his questions seriously, until I began to see that he did not ever come to any conclusions. He kept asking the same questions, again and again. I found myself doubting that he really understood the difference of truth and the difference it makes. His immaturity, intellectually and experientially, finally pushed me over the edge.

One day we met for lunch in the café underneath the National Gallery of Art. As the water cascaded down the wall nearby, we talked one more time about the very same issues. Finally I said to him, "I am not going to talk with you again about this until you pack your bags and travel the world, talking with people who believe differently than you—I want you to see the alternatives to believing in transcendence and truth, to see alternatives to the Christian worldview lived out and to wonder what it means. Or you could watch all of Woody Allen's films, from *Annie Hall* on.[7] You do one of those of two things, and we'll talk again."

Why Woody Allen's films? When the conversation took place there was no American filmmaker who so consistently raised the hardest questions in his films. For years I celebrated the announcement of a new film by Allen, eagerly anticipating the fruit of his honest, humorous mind and heart at work. He seemed to be willing, on the whole, to see the world more truthfully than most. Movie by movie, he raised the stakes on the small choices, the trifles, which are the substance of our daily existence. In *The Purple Rose of Cairo,* an incredibly creative look at the question of reality on and off the screen, Mia Farrow's character asks, "You do believe in God, don't you?"

"Meaning?"

"You know, the reason for everything."[8]

Hannah and Her Sisters is one more story set in Manhattan, full of folk who struggle for some measure of happiness. Allen directs and acts in this one, portraying a TV producer whose hypochondria takes him to a hospital for tests. After finding out, one more time, that he is healthy, he acknowledges, "In a godless universe, I didn't want to go on living." And why is it so stark? At another point in the film, he confesses, "The only absolute knowledge attainable by man is that life is meaningless."[9]

In the end, though, his films always "blinked." That is, he did not push the presuppositions he argued for to their logical conclusions. His stories have typically had happy endings where, against cosmic meaninglessness, his characters find their measure of happiness in the arms of someone to love and be loved by.

That history is terribly ironic now, of course. With his choice to leave his long-time companion and mother of his child, Mia Farrow, and to take as his lover Mia's adopted daughter, he seems to have become a parody of his own filmmaking. On a certain level he understands, as perhaps no other American filmmaker does, the reality of Steiner's argument that "the wager on the meaning of meaning . . . is a wager on transcendence." And yet, against the force of that logic—with all of its implications for what one understands to be real and true and right—he fell into the arms of a teenager, and in so doing has offered deeply mixed messages about his own insight into moral meaning.

Boston Globe columnist Ellen Goodman is one voice that reflects that confusion. Like many Americans she spent the spring of 1993 increasingly saddened by the news accounts of the horribly troubled Allen-Farrow household. "It is notable that the dearest, maybe even the sanest words heard at the Woody and Mia custody trial so far were offered up by Moses, 'Everyone knows not to have an affair with your son's sister.'"

> This searing, flat-out judgment did not come from *the* Moses. It came from fourteen-year-old Moses Farrow Allen. This phrase was not inscribed on a stone tablet. It was written in a letter to somebody he once called Dad. Nevertheless, the boy's vision was as unclouded as his pain when he wrote, "You have done a horrible, unforgivable, nerdy, ugly, stupid thing." It stands in stark contrast to the rest of this bizarre trial being conducted in a dreary New York courtroom under the strictures of the law and in the language of "Shrink-ese."[10]

Goodman goes on to lament the "triumph of the therapeutic," as Phillip Rieff has called it,[11] wherein the psychologists, psychotherapists and psychiatrists have become the high priests of contemporary culture. "Under the linguistic rules of Shrink-ese, good and evil are now translated into 'appropriate' and 'inappropriate.' Right and wrong have become 'good and bad judgment.'" She confesses,

> I rarely side with people who want to put good and evil stickers on every piece of human behavior. . . . But there are times, and this is one of them, when I wonder whether our adoption of Shrink-ese as a second language, the move from religious phrases of judgment to secular

words of acceptance, hasn't also produced a moral lobotomy. In the re-
luctance, the aversion—dare I say the phobia—to being judgmental,
are we disabled from making any judgments at all?[12]

Through a glass darkly, Goodman has seen what others have seen. It is not
a substantially different assessment from that of Kundera in *The Unbearable
Lightness of Being*, when he laments our "profound moral perversity . . . everything is pardoned in advance, and so everything is cynically permitted."[13] But
it is precisely this point that I labored over with my young student friend. I
wanted him to see, to understand in the deep parts of his being, that there
are not many alternatives when it comes to the meaning of truth.

Because I see so much of this in people young and old—men and women
who have not thought deeply about the perennial questions of God, human
nature and history, and who are affected largely unawares by the subtle seductions of the contemporary world—I have committed myself to taking a
more active role in my children's education.

At Rivendell School, parents are encouraged to be a part of the school life,
from playgrounds to plays, from curriculum development to the classroom.
This last year I spent several mornings with the seventh and eighth graders
while they studied World War II. One day we watched a film, *The Scarlet and
the Black,* a story about an Irish priest in Rome whose sense of responsibility
led him to provide protection for thousands of Jews and others via his Vatican office.[14] A few days later, after their visit to the Holocaust Museum, we
had a discussion about what they thought about what they saw. I brought in
a small section from C. S. Lewis's *That Hideous Strength.* A "fairy tale for
grown-ups," Lewis called it. Written in 1946, it is both a reflection on what
Walker Percy, a generation later, called "the mechanized, murderous century"—epitomized by the war then just completed—and a prescient reading
of the next half-century, forty years before the terms *postmodernism* and *deconstructionism* were even used. Lewis critiques them as the "legs" of ideas
being proposed in his own day.

In Lewis's story Mark Studdock, a professor who has been taken in by the
blandishments of prestige and power of the N.I.C.E. (National Institute of
Co-ordinated Experiments), after much pain to himself and others, begins

to see through the external, formal "niceness" to the horrible hollowness of its moral vision for Britain and the world. In his cell, piece by slow piece he starts to see where the scientific naturalism of N.I.C.E. has led him and will lead his nation.

> He saw clearly that the motives on which most men act, and which they dignify by the names of patriotism or duty to humanity, were mere products of the animal organism, varying according to the behaviour pattern of different communities. But he did not yet see what was to be substituted for these irrational motives. On what ground henceforward were actions to be justified or condemned?[15]

THE DIFFERENCE OF TRUTH AND THE DIFFERENCE IT MAKES

It was this dilemma, of course, that led MacIntyre and Bernstein to their critiques of contemporary culture. And it was the existential wrestling with the questions of meaning and morality that grow out of this soil, particularly as understood by modern prophets such as Sartre and Camus, that led Bob Kramer to drop out of Harvard: "When he saw the disjunction, he dropped out"—stubbornly insisting on some kind of integrity between what he said he believed and how he lived. How could he reject right and wrong as a meaningful distinction and then argue the injustice of rent controls in Cambridge?[16]

What he believed about the world and how he lived in the world produced a profound tension in Bob—and it broke him. The disjunction between worldview and way of life was resolved by coming to a knowledge of the truth about himself and the world, like Raskolnikov, Nekhlyudov and Volodin before him. Their stories are different; each of the Russians found their repentance and redemption as prisoners or the friend of prisoners.[17] In a different century and culture, Bob went to Europe, and after months of traveling ended up in a small village in the Swiss Alps, where he met a community of people who called themselves L'Abri.

> I began to see that there was a sufficient foundation for justice. The challenge of L'Abri was not the positive message, but their critique and consistency. First of all their critique, which put more systematically my own critique, the lack of answers to be found in other places. But

then it was their consistency. These people lived what they believed. I might enjoy wine, women and song—while believing in absurdity. That was contrasted with people who lived the life of faith and prayer—and lived what they believed. I told them they took a leap of faith but they forced me to the logic of my own presuppositions; or you might even say my own conclusions, in terms of what alternative there was if there was not a God and a world that God created.

Yet I did not live a life consistent with my beliefs. In other words, I embraced absurdity with my head but not with my life—by the grace of God. Many people, many of my colleagues—including a good friend from college who committed suicide—really did try to make an all-out effort to embrace absurdity, and in some sense succeeded. And it really did destroy them. I tried, and God didn't let me. It was only the grace of God; it had nothing to do with me. When I went over the edge, God didn't let me fall off; he pulled me back. I saw other friends go over the edge. I was reading R. D. Laing, Allen Watts . . . insanity is where it's at, and all of that. Samuel Beckett was my favorite playwright, and I carried his plays all over Europe.

But L'Abri really put that to the test; they really called my bluff. Their negative critique and their consistency were compelling. So then I read the New Testament for the first time, and read C. S. Lewis, particularly *The Great Divorce* and *The Screwtape Letters,* which had a great effect on me. Many of my non-Christian friends were most helpful to me on my path to Christ. A very prominent Maoist student leader in Stockholm, whom I went to visit after being at L'Abri the first time, said to me that my problem was—he said this just out of the blue— he said my problem was I wasn't looking to discover Jesus Christ, I was looking to *be* Jesus Christ. God used that statement to unveil to me that I had to be willing to make a commitment, to step inside the circle of Christian truth. Someone couldn't taste and experience from outside and then commit. In that case, you would be god, not God. That realization was incredibly important to me because I was trying to know it from outside.

I think that in becoming a Christian, the key thing for me was that

this was really the most radical thing I could do—because I was getting to the root of what was really true about myself and the world. I
was owning up to the truth, not running from the truth. But at the moment when I came to Christ, it was with a sense: "God, only you can
enable me to know that what I'm doing is genuine, and not because
I've flipped out, and not because of some wish-fulfillment or whatever. At the same time, only you can give me the strength to keep this
commitment. I'm being asked to make a commitment. I know I can't
keep that. But dear God, you can enable me to. Finally, I don't know
what it would take to convince me, but surely God, you do—and you
surely could do that."

I prayed that prayer with Edith Schaeffer. Part of me was saying, "It's
the craziest thing I've ever done, I've freaked out"—thinking I'd never
get out of this room with this crazy lady if I didn't pray. The other part
of me was sensing that this room was the only place in the world, that
there was no place to go outside that door. I could not go outside that
door. The whole world was shrunk to the size of this room. When I
prayed that prayer, no bells went off, and there was no handwriting on
the wall; but I knew that God was there and that he was trustworthy.
And I felt I had a promise at that moment, that if I would try him I
would indeed find holy truth and that he would never let me down.
I've never doubted the existence of God, or the truthfulness of God,
or the goodness of God, since then. I've doubted myself lots of times,
and I've decried my own inability to keep faith, to be consistent, to be
obedient.

For those who keep faith over the course of life, answering the question
"In an increasingly secular and pluralist world, is anything true and right?"
becomes a critical component of a worldview which is sufficient for the crises and questions which come to all who make their way through the valley
of the diapers and on into the responsibilities of mature adulthood—spanning the spectrum of concerns, from the most personal to the most public.
After his extracurricular education at L'Abri, Bob returned to finish his undergraduate degree at Harvard, then did theological study at Oxford Univer-

sity and Westminster Theological Seminary, moved to Annapolis with his young family, and has been involved in local and state politics ever since, sometimes in elected positions, other times as a citizen. Seeing the impact of his official role on his young family, he eventually stepped away from elective office and began a consulting firm which works between the private and public sectors on issues of health care and the environment.

Though the social dynamics are different, the maelstrom of the years between adolescence and adulthood made Dan Heimbach's experience similar to Bob's. A Naval Academy graduate who had a deep sense of calling to public responsibility since he was a young boy, he decided to pursue a Ph.D. in social ethics so that he might be prepared to take up his vocation in the public square. After working on the staff of a senator with strong foreign affairs interests, Dan served in the early 1990s on President George Bush's Domestic Policy Council. At the time of the interview he was working at the Pentagon with responsibility for all education and training within the Department of the Navy; he has since gone into the academy, working in North Carolina as a professor. He comments on this decisive development in his own life, of making the choice to believe in truth, with all that it implied for the whole of his life.

> It was in my last year of high school, after being raised in a Christian family and accepting the truths of Christianity as early as I can remember, that I came to a time when I needed to take my faith apart and start from the beginning—because I was profoundly struck by the need to be authentic. I didn't want to just go along with the Christian thing I had always known; I wanted to be convinced that it was in fact true. I was willing at that point to give the whole thing up if it turned out to be a charade.

He describes his wrestling with questions like "Is God real? Is he the God who is revealed in the Bible? Is the Bible really the Word of God? Is the Bible reliable?" As he told the story of the years immediately following the Naval Academy, as a commissioned officer serving in the combat zone of Vietnam, the question of convictions came up again: "Could I really live with them?"

I was in an environment where I knew no other Christians, had no fellowship, accountability or encouragement—except what I brought with me and what I could gain in my own prayer life and study of the Bible. Everyone had overwhelmingly different value systems. While there I once asked myself why I had to be so different. With a sense of tremendous internal challenge I could say that the one thing keeping me from being like the others was that deep down I was convinced of the truth of my faith; this moment highlighted what truth meant to me, and I couldn't turn my back on what I knew to be true. This caused me to put the roots down.

I couldn't turn my back on what I knew to be true. In different ways, because they are different people with different backgrounds and different vocations, each person in the study group made peace with the notion of truth in a pluralist world. And yet that peace is very hard won, given the nature of the pressures facing folk who seriously take up the challenge of life in the modern world.

If people are to understand the world and their place in it, then at some point they must deal with the questions raised by MacIntyre and Bernstein, Steiner and Newbigin: Is anything true and right? And on what basis do we decide? A common characteristic of those interviewed was that they believed that the worldview shaped by historic Christian orthodoxy was *true;* in Newbigin's language, not simply the truth of "private belief" but of "public truth," for all peoples and in all times. With a variety of vocations and from diverse theological traditions, each person interviewed had wrestled with relativism and had come through believing in a transcendent truth.

As a counterpoint to these stories, I sought out a series of conversations with someone who got lost, who did not make his way through the valley of the diapers. I knew enough of his earlier history to know that through his college years he was one who seemed to have rooted himself in a consciously formed worldview—and was even teaching it to others. And yet he foundered over this very issue—the relation of transcendence to truth. He entered graduate school with the intention of beginning a vocation as an apologist for the Christian faith. In his years of study he read widely, finding friends who shared his concerns and teachers who opened their lives to him. But in that period of time, in his mid-twenties, he stumbled over the truthfulness of the worldview he had embraced.

As I listened, it seemed that he was caught in what Bernstein has called "the Cartesian Anxiety." His early training as a Christian persuaded him of an objectivity about the truthfulness of his convictions—what Newbigin has characterized as the promise of an "indubitable certainty"[18]—which led him eventually, through many tears, to the collapse of his belief and to skepticism. Newbigin's own work in understanding the souring of the Enlightenment Project and the Cartesian Anxiety would have been grace to this young man, particularly as Newbigin skillfully weaves the contributions of Polanyi, Kuhn and Berger to uncover the possibility of truth—even a certainty of faith—in a pluralist world.[19]

That is the question at the heart of this exploration of the forming of a worldview: Is truth a possibility, even a reality? And is it a truth that has the possibility of providing coherence for the whole of life? Against forces both overt and covert, those who continue to strive for coherence, years after their days of early idealism, are those who have worked through the difference of truth and the difference it makes.

Bill Waterson has seen into that difference and allows us to smile as we ponder its significance. Calvin says to Hobbes, "Whenever I need to do some serious thinking, I go for a walk in the woods." Looking under a rock, he adds, "There are always a million distractions out here." Seemingly out of the blue, he blurts out, "I don't believe in ethics any more. As far as I'm concerned, the ends justify the means. Get what you can while the getting's good—that's what I say! Might makes right! The winners write the history books!"

They continue on through the woods, Hobbes still listening to his friend. "It's a dog-eat-dog world, so I'll do whatever I have to, and let others argue about whether it's 'right' or not."

Suddenly, Hobbes comes out of his stupor and shoves Calvin into a mud puddle. Calvin cries, "Hey! Why'd you do THAT?!?"

With a smile, Hobbes explains, "You were in my way. Now you're not. The ends justify the means."

Full of frustration, and covered with mud, Calvin protests, "I didn't mean for *everyone,* you dolt! Just *me!*"

Hobbes walks away, musing over the meaning of it all and saying, "Ahh . . ."

The challenge for the contemporary person—especially the Christian student whose creedal commitments are rooted in the possibility and reality of truth—is to form a worldview that will be coherent across the whole of life because it addresses the whole of life: from sexuality to politics to economics to the arts, from local commitments to global responsibilities. In a word, it is the challenge of developing convictions which do not, by their own inner logic, require one to "blink."[20]

Masters, Mentors and Moral Meaning

We can know better what we already know in outline. Moral "learning"
is all the time "thinking." It is the intellectual penetration and
exploration of a reality which we can grasp from the beginning in a
schematic and abstract way, but which contains depths of meaning and
experience into which we must reach.

OLIVER O'DONOVAN, *Resurrection and Moral Order*[1]

Doesn't sound much like pedagogy, does it?" lamented a young professor at a state university. As we talked I could hear him struggling to maintain his excitement over having a teaching job, after years of schooling; at the same time I knew that so much of what he had deeply committed himself to in terms of a vision for teaching was compromised by the university's understanding of the meaning of education, namely, one professor and scores of students meeting three times a week to study comparative religions.

As he told me of his course outline, of the original sources he planned for them to read plus the novels and films he intended to draw on, I found myself sharing in his enthusiasm. I have watched him as he has moved on through his early years in graduate education, to the choice of a subdiscipline, to frustrations with faculty, to various honors given for the excellence of his labor, on to his hard work in developing a dissertation on a question that really matters. And as I have watched him become a scholar in his own right, I have also watched his vocational vision deepen. Simply said, he wants to walk along with students in the task of learning. His wide reading in history and his theological and philosophical reflection have persuaded him that the best education is done where there is more accountability built into the relationship between faculty and student; something more like the master/apprentice relationship than the lecturer/audience setting which characterizes much of contemporary higher education.

LEARNING WHAT LEARNING IS ALL ABOUT

And yet, the structural demands of his university—from the outset—deny him the opportunity to do much more than what he calls "crowd control." Two cries come from his heart, at the same time, together: "I want to teach!" with "What can I teach in this setting?"

As I listened, I pondered the evolution of higher education in America, remembering decisions made in the nineteenth century—innocently and without malice—to shift from the British college and tutorial method to the new German research university model.[2] Could anyone have foreseen what it would mean a century later? Clearly, its efficiency and accessibility were virtues commending it to the industrializing world. Hundreds of thousands have been educated who would have been blocked from entering the smaller, more collegial American institutions patterned after Oxford and Cambridge—places such as Harvard, Yale, Princeton. Plainly, there has been no plot to undermine undergraduate education in the Western world; at the same time, the sociology of knowledge helps us understand that social factors such as industrialization have deeply affected Berger's "ordinary people leading ordinary lives," so that higher education means something dramatically different for people in our contemporary context than it did for their forebears going into colleges and universities in earlier centuries.

With efficiency has come a pragmatism that thinks bigness is usually better—deans across the country carefully counting faculty/student ratios, introducing an enervating cost/benefit analysis into the educational equation. With accessibility has come a lack of accountability that allows a debilitating anonymity into the relationship of faculty to student—teachers do not have time to thoughtfully evaluate, and students think that their reason for being in school is to pass the next test. Sadly, the situation in American higher education is too close to the cartoon caricature in "Non Sequitur," where two older men are studying a graduation diploma which is situated behind a parrot on his stand. One man says to the other, "He earned it fair and square. And as long as he's able to repeat what he hears, he can earn a degree from any college in the country."

In a very perceptive study called *Teaching Values in College,* Richard Morrill asks several large questions about the meaning of higher education: Does the study of ethics improve one's moral character? Is it possible to teach values without indoctrinating students? What are the best methods for developing moral awareness in the classroom and other settings? How does the campus environment influence student values? Aware of both its history and its present challenges, Morrill probes the possibility of reconnecting intellect and conscience, thought and action, within the modern academy. He understands that

> recent developments in college life provide a difficult setting in which to pursue, extend and deepen the educational task of the analysis, awareness and criticism of values. Values press claims that go beyond the minimal and the contractual, that require a depth of self-questioning into which the student as a consumer might prefer not to enter.[3]

And yet he also sees that it is in the relationship of faculty to student, within the context of an educational community that has committed itself to common ends, that the recovery of a deeper vision of education is possible.

Many of the perspectives we are suggesting can be summed up in the idea of the teacher as model or mentor. One learns best the values required for good scholarship—patience, tolerance, rigor, fairness, precision—by seeing them in action, by experiencing their authority with and through another person. But we would like to emphasize another potential feature of the relationship, the claim that the self experiences to strive for its own fulfillment, to reach its utmost possibilities. Teachers, and others, can effectively require students to face themselves, to become responsible for their own learning, to take themselves seriously as independent thinkers and agents, and to unearth the best that is in them.[4]

I remember two conversations with students who have asked questions which reflect both their own dissatisfaction with the "parroting paradigm" implicit in so much of contemporary education and their desire to stand against this quenching of the spirit of an older, deeper vision of education.

One was a young woman who excelled in her scholarship. "It took me a month to figure out what you [American Studies Program] were expecting of me. I've been going to school for a long time, and I do well. If I don't get A's, it's a problem. After three years of college, I have learned that the way to get good grades is to take good notes, read the assignments, and then give back to the prof what he has given to me. This semester I discovered that you wanted me to be responsible for my own learning, that you didn't want me to just hand it back to you. Instead you wanted me to think it through for myself. How could I have gone to school all these years and never learned what learning was all about?"

After our final class one semester, another student asked if she could talk with me about the afternoon's lecture. In my office, she said, "I think I am finally understanding what this program is all about . . . but I wonder, is it too late? You see, I know how to get good grades, and I get them. For years now, that's what has motivated me—the next exam, the next paper. I've done them and then gone on. But you are asking me to reflect on what this means for my life. In fact, I have begun to see that this is my life! Is it too late? Can I still make something of my college education?"

Many students discover along the way the relation of education to life— hoping against hope that "it's not too late." They want their work to be taken seriously, they want their work to be about something that matters—and they want their educations to give them tools for living in the world, not only "for getting a good job" but for "having a good life."[5] It is that question of "the good life" that causes all of us to pause, as our answer to it determines how we think about the meaning of life and of education.

THE GOOD LIFE AND GOOD EDUCATION

As I listened to the voices of those who still believe in a coherent world and the possibility of a coherent life, another characteristic—after the forming of a worldview—was that they found a mentor during their university years whose wisdom and experience gave flesh and bone to the notion of "the good life" which was developing in the student's heart and mind. Professors, professionals, pastors all served as older friends whose cares and commitments incarnated the substance of the worldview which the student was learning to embrace.

Rick Wellock now works as a "calling" consultant, with particular expertise in helping people within corporations understand the fabric of their lives as a means of deepening their vocational vision. With wife and children, he now lives in Ligonier, a community in a farming valley in the foothills of Pennsylvania's Allegheny Mountains. While an undergraduate at Geneva College, a liberal arts institution in the Presbyterian tradition, he remembers having three teachers who were different: rather than distancing themselves from students, as he had come to expect from years of education, they each engaged him. "They were peers who were also professors."

Again and again, it is that dynamic relationship of a faculty member opening his life up to a student which enables young people to understand that their worldview can also become a way of life.

Grace Tazelaar's story is told from within the context of Wheaton College (near Chicago), another school like Geneva with a serious commitment to thoughtful learning within the contours of Christian faith. In her years as an undergraduate she chose the vocation of nursing; later she taught in the U.S. before deciding to use her gifts in the reconstruction of Uganda, after Idi Amin's reign of terror. They were very difficult years, as she poured out her life in service to a broken nation. "In one year's time, all of our leadership was wiped out by death. One was killed in an ambush, another in an auto accident, and yet another by AIDS, as the result of a blood transfusion. The bishop of our diocese also died." When asked about her formative years as a student and how they shaped her understanding of pain and suffering, especially her response to it in the vocation of nursing, she said:

> I encountered death and dying in nursing school, and so early on began wondering about the question of a good God and evil. That question has intrigued me and permeated my whole life.
>
> My college years were also a developmental stage for friendships and

for thinking about issues like the Vietnam war and racial prejudice. As I pondered these things, I found support from the Christians around me, friends and faculty. A course on apologetics taught by Dr. [Alan] Johnson centered around the book of Job, which gave answers to my questions and provided a whole new way of thinking about suffering. Over the years there the pieces of the puzzle began fitting together, as I remembered Bible stories and studied history, philosophy, science and math in a curriculum that made connections. I was involved in a small-group Bible study in which we pursued themes of love, unity and Christian community. We had fantastic speakers like John Stott and Francis Schaeffer, who challenged me about what I believed and how it would affect my life. At graduation, Dr. [Hudson] Armerding talked about our responsibility to use our developed minds, and to this day the Wheaton motto, "For Christ and His Kingdom," is my motto.

When she described her growth into the vocation of nursing, understanding her own deepest desires and thinking through the needs of the world, she remembered asking a former teacher to be her spiritual mentor. This woman, who had spent years in South Africa, gave herself to Grace as she was beginning to explore her own place of responsible service. At the core of her teacher's life, Grace recalls, "I saw much love amidst trauma." Those lessons cannot be taught from a textbook; they have to be learned from a life. Twenty-five years after her course on God and human suffering and her choice to see her life given "for Christ and His Kingdom," Grace is now back in the States. After serving as a nurse in a rural health clinic in Cary, Mississippi, she has now taken up a position as community health program director for the Luke Society, attempting to establish health clinics in medically underserved areas all over the United States, in rural settings as well as urban areas.

Born belonging to Virginia, Larry Adams chose the University of Richmond for his undergraduate studies. Ten years later he was deep into a dissertation at the University of Virginia in political science, which was a launching pad for a move to Washington, D.C., and a position on a Senate committee. From there he moved to the position of senior policy analyst for a think tank dealing with national and international questions of religion and democracy; he then spent several years teaching politics at an undergraduate institution. Some years later he has come back to Charlottesville and has taught in a variety of settings, including the University of Virginia and his local Anglican church.

Larry remembers how the forming of his worldview was virtually synonymous with finding a mentor.

I first went to college with an autonomous, individualistic view of life, and became quite bewildered in a tough freshman year. The key change in my attitude and direction began to come about at my first invitation to an InterVarsity Christian Fellowship meeting. The people there were serious in growing in their faith and doing campus ministry. It seems providential in retrospect that our InterVarsity core group of ten or so went on to serve all over the world, in places like West Africa, Singapore and Latin America. Through this group I met deeply committed Christians who attempted to live under Christ's lordship. My relationship with Christ had been only a small compartmentalized part of my life.

I was singled out by the leaders because they perceived my leadership abilities, and I was drawn into relationship with the faculty advisor, Dr. [Richard] Chewning, a professor of economics. Because of my great respect for the way he struggled hard to be a godly husband, church leader, father and citizen, as an older Christian man, I decided to attach myself so as to watch his life. The whole role model concept was one I couldn't identify with at the time. I see a distinct break in the patterns and ways of my life from the first eighteen years to the second. The changing point occurred in the later years, and in some ways I see the former years in a suppressive light, because I don't remember them so well. I don't remember role models from those days, although I had a great relationship with my dad. Dr. Chewning became a surrogate father for a few years, and without my relationship to him my life as a father would be tougher. I learned from the way he opened up himself to many people.

An intellectual awakening occurred within my college experience through sitting under some fine teachers who were disciplined in mind to be thinking Christians. The InterVarsity meetings had stimulating Bible teaching. Before, it had never occurred to me that the Bible could be understood, explained, examined and found to have integrity. Had it not been for teachers who perceived my intelligence and who were of great ability, I am certain that I wouldn't have pursued a Ph.D. My liberal arts college emphasized teaching as opposed to research. This model of education provided old, classical concepts for instruction in its curriculum. There was an emphasis on Latin, Greek, language in general, history and literature. I was drawn to political science because it was taught with a theoretical and philosophical approach, and also by my desire to develop a Christian understanding of the political realm. I ended up understanding how to research, comprehend and assimilate ideas.

Byron Borger, now a husband and a father and an owner of Hearts and Minds Bookstore in central Pennsylvania, is still involved with students, teaching and writing in forums that affect undergraduates throughout his region. In the last few years he has poured himself into the care of Chinese refugees who have been imprisoned in his community after having fled China's forced abortion policy—a complex story involving years of Sunday-evening prayer vigils outside the prison as well as participation in Capitol Hill hearings.

Byron remembers his own student days at a state university, those who opened their lives to him and what effect they had on the nature and direction of his convictions.

I struggled as a new college freshman as I dove in with the little bit of left-wing movement there was on campus that worked against the CIA, the tiger cages of the human rights abuses in South Vietnam, the bombing policies and so on. I met some of the politicos who were student radicals left over from the sixties. These acquaintances could not believe that I was a Christian and a part of a very vibrant, growing Christian fellowship of which Pete Steen and the Coalition for Christian Outreach [a ministry to university students within a two-hundred-mile radius of Pittsburgh] were a part. . . . I went to Bible studies with folks who could not understand how I could associate with the left-wing peace people. Students from the Bible studies would chide and harangue me for not really being committed to Christ, so I ping-ponged back and forth, and sometimes I wouldn't go to any of the Christian meetings because they didn't have eyes to see that they should be involved in some kind of basic human decencies in this world. I would pray about these things and then dive into social change.

That November Pete Steen [a professor "without portfolio" who gave seminars rooted in Dutch Reformed philosophy on college campuses throughout western Pennsylvania in the 1970s] gave an address on the election, and he said that the Democrats and the Republicans were two different sides of the same bad coin; thus Christians shouldn't vote for either of them. We began to talk about Christians who were truly radical in Canada and other places, where they had Christian Farmer's Federations, alternative Christian schools and new magazines.

I identified with these things and was enthused. Without any idea what this guy was talking about, something intriguing was going on, and it began my pilgrimage into understanding the Dutch Reformed worldview: third parties and third ways of doing things that rejected both the left and the right of secularism, giving a much more radical critique of the radicals by exposing the roots of Western culture—capitalism, progress and so on. He fleshed it out by way of tracing the history of philosophy, the history of ideas. Since I was very impatient with that, I was never one of Pete's best students. . . .

I was involved with Cesar Chavez and the Farm Worker's Union, which Pete thought was just ridiculous. The Roman Catholic Church sent me to the first annual Right to Life convention, shortly after *Roe v. Wade,* because they knew then that if they were to win the battle for the respect of life they would need to involve the evangelicals too. There I saw the formation of the prolife movement, which was a remarkably life-changing event.

The Coalition friends yelled at me for going over to the Catholics, and Pete Steen yelled at me for going with the radical social change people who were doing the antihunger fast. But I endured. I took some of Steen's philosophy class, which said to understand poverty you need to also understand Plato. For some reason I knew he was right, even though I was always groused by it. Though not academically bright, I followed him, tracing the roots of Western culture and how the Greeks divided life into sacred and secular, consequently ruining everything. I realized that if I were to ever get people involved in peace and justice, my burning passions, I would have to get rid of the dualism of the sacred and the secular. Pete was doing that, providing a whole new horizon to change my life forever.

When asked, "Why did you endure?" Byron responded:

I knew he was right. I left those meetings and went back to Coalition staff, who gave systematic explanations, using the Bible. The fundamentalists were narrow and restricted in their personalistic way of reading the Bible. The Coalition attracted me by their relevance and timeliness, and also their orthodox doctrine, which I studied in Romans. I trusted them. I mostly hung around the liberal campus ministries through my world hunger work, but I realized that ultimately they didn't have the real answers. I sensed that the Dutch Reformed worldview that Steen taught was more substantial and biblically orthodox, and also ultimately more radical in terms of wanting to redirect Western culture. It wasn't just Band-aiding over things (of which I was accused) or being a little pea shooter by going after this or that problem—he wanted to change the whole world, and I was attracted to that.

Some of it was playing with my youthful zeal for a big vision, but that comes back to the meaning question. I want my life to be full of meaning! I want even the little stuff to count—everything has to count. My wife makes fun of me sometimes, in a good way, because everything has to be so darn meaningful! I can't blow my nose without it being like a worship service. I have this angst if things aren't meaningful enough. There is a connection between small acts, as the feminists used to say, and one's personal and political views—how we live our lives affects the big picture. The meaning of our lives is that we are part of God's movement to bring restoration and healing to the whole wide world. Somehow, in my little ways, I see that my lifestyle, the way I shop, the way I vote, and whatever, plays a big role in the restoration and redirection of the whole world.

In Byron we hear several themes that were repeated over and over again by those interviewed: (1) early struggles as a young student to make sense of life as he faced the challenge of new ideas and new relationships, (2) beginning to choose which ideas and relationships "made sense" given his developing understanding of the world and of his place in it, and (3) finding a few significant relationships with older friends—a professor and campus pastors—who both stimulated and nourished him in the meaning system he was beginning to call "mine."

EDUCATION AS FORMATION

It is that last thread that binds the others together, as it points us in the direction of understanding what the wisest of the ancients have always understood about the relation of the mentor to the formation of moral meaning. Even the words themselves teach us. MacIntyre in *After Virtue* offers a brief etymology of the word *moral*:

> In Latin, as in ancient Greek, there is *no* word until our word *moral* is translated back into Latin. Certainly *moral* is the etymological descendant of *moralis*. But *moralis*, like its Greek predecessor *ethikos*—Cicero invented "moralis" to translate the Greek word in the *De Fato*—means "pertaining to character," where a man's character is nothing other than his set dispositions to behave systematically in one way rather than another, to lead one particular kind of life.[6]

And so *moral* is itself about the formation of character, about developing dispositions "to behave systematically in one way rather than another." For centuries, education was character formation, and not just in the small sense of nurturing private virtues of kindness and temperance, as central as those are to human happiness. Werner Jaeger's monumental *Paideia: The Formation of Man*[7] continues to instruct us; visions of character formation are always integrally a part of every vision of culture formation.

Augustine understood this pedagogical principle in a most profound way. From what can be learned implicitly from his *Confessions* to what is made explicit in *On Christian Doctrine,* we see that his life as a professor and a bishop was lived within this vision of education. In Book IV of the latter, he takes up the task of offering his own *paideia,* arguing that teaching is incarnational at its heart. Moving beyond Cicero, who had emphasized that the mere study of rules is insufficient for the education of the orator, Augustine goes further, maintaining that the rules are not necessary at all. "For boys do not need the art of grammar which teaches correct speech if they have the opportunity to grow up and live among men who speak correctly."

A fascinating look into this principle comes in his letter "To Dioscorus, a Student."[8] A young Greek who had traveled to Carthage to be educated in Latin literature—in Cicero's *Tusculan Disputations*—Dioscorus wrote Augustine about some questions which had come up in his studies.

Perhaps remembering his own student days in Carthage where he had also studied Cicero and been converted by him and to him, Augustine wrote a lengthy reply, taking the student very seriously. He understood that the young man was making sense of life for life, that his definitions of meaning and morality were being formed; his "set dispositions to behave systematically in one way rather than another" were being decided. Even while playfully chiding Dioscorus for the number and complexity of his questions ("You must have intended to wall me in, or even bury me completely, with your countless multitude of questions . . . the length of time involved would exhaust my attention and wear out my fingers"), Augustine asks, "Tell me, what good has the reading of all these dialogues done if it hasn't helped you define and attain the goal of all your actions?"

He is asking the young student, "What is the point of your life? How are your studies in Cicero contributing to your end as a human being, particularly your end as a young Christian?" Remembering the transformation of consciousness brought about by his own study of Cicero and the years of vanity to which it led him, he warns Dioscorus to be on his guard: "They can so easily impose on you by being cloaked with some semblance of virtue and with the name of liberal studies."[9] He then goes into pages of thoughtful,

critical interaction with Dioscorus's questions, showing an amazing familiar-
ity with the intricacies of Cicero's arguments—all the while reminding the
student that mastery of Cicero and the Latin literature is not a worthy end,
not sufficient to help him "define and attain the goal of all your actions." Obviously engaged in heart and mind, Augustine writes,

> Finally, suppose that, when you've been asked all the questions you've
> sent to me, you've been able to respond. Lo, people now call you su-
> premely learned and acute! Lo, Greek breath lifts you to heaven on its
> praises! But remember your own worth, and your reason for wanting
> to deserve this praise: to teach something supremely important and
> wholesome to the people you have so easily impressed with your tri-
> fling talk, and who are now hanging on your words with such great
> eagerness and goodwill.
>
> What I would like to know is whether you possess and can accu-
> rately impart to others anything supremely important and whole-
> some. It's ridiculous if, after you've learned a lot of unnecessary things
> in order to prepare people to listen to you tell them what is indispens-
> able, you yourself don't possess it; and if, while you are busy learning
> how to get their attention, you refuse to learn what to teach them
> when you've gained it. But if you say that you already know, and an-
> swer that it's Christian doctrine (I know that you prefer this to every-
> thing else and entrust your hope of eternal salvation to this alone), you
> don't need to be familiar with the dialogues of Cicero and a collection
> of the beggarly and divided opinions of other people to win an audi-
> ence. Attract them by your way of life if you want them to receive such
> a teaching from you.[10]

Attract them by your way of life. One cannot listen to Augustine—whose
vision of "the formation of man" shaped Western civilization for a thousand
years—without being deeply impressed that he understood what learning
was all about: teachers opening their lives to students, allowing an apprenticeship in what is *supremely important.* It is nothing less that the formation
of moral meaning.

In our own time, Stanley Hauerwas's wide-ranging writing in the ethic of character has made him a voice worth hearing, particularly when he roots his reflection in the best teachers of the past, as he does here: "Becoming virtuous requires long training, as it is an esoteric achievement not accomplished by many. In particular, it requires apprenticeship to a master who can initiate another into the painful process of becoming a person of character—that is, someone capable of becoming virtuous."[11] In a footnote to his essay "Hope Faces Power: Thomas More and the King of England," Hauerwas develops this view more fully.

> Our claim is this: Not only does hope employ and give the basis for certain skills, but it is a skill. It is a skill which one learns. We do not learn to lay bricks without guidance from masters; neither do we learn how to hope without guidance from masters. The acquisition of a skill involves, usually, an initiation into a way of life. A master, who has gone before, usually presides over the initiation. . . . We need a narrative display in order to understand how it is we should hope. From this perspective, the traditional theological virtues—faith, hope, love—are best understood as reminders of the narrative of the master Jesus, a narrative that schools the self to serve God rightly. Such virtues become distorted if they are treated as independent norms for behavior. If the moral life is inseparable from the life of wisdom, then, in spite of modern philosophy's attempt to secure an independent status for "morality," our moral lives as lived continue to depend on the existence of masters.[12]

Few have written as well about what this perspective on moral education means for higher education as Mark Schwehn in *Exiles from Eden: Religion and the Academic Vocation in America*. He weaves together insights from theology, philosophy, sociology and literature; the heart of his argument is that there is an integral relationship between transcendence and teaching.

> My major aim here is to ponder the significance for us academics today of Weber's achievement in basing his conception of our task upon religious views of life even as he at the same time insisted that we must and do live in a world without God. Like much of Nietzsche's work,

Weber's analysis of the academic vocation demonstrated the impossibly exacting, even absurd, psychological consequences of attempting to live out a Christian ethic absent any belief in the God of Christianity. But whereas Nietzsche proceeded from this demonstration to urge us to abandon the Christian *ethos* altogether, Weber urged us to retain the Protestant ethic while abandoning the system of religious beliefs that made such an ethic bearable. Indeed, Weber's account of our calling as academics can seem, for these reasons, alternatively ennobling and devastating.[13]

His critique is strong, though it is characteristically fair. But the thrust of his work is constructive, as he articulates a vision of the academic vocation which attempts "to change its Weberian character by redirecting its moral trajectory." He writes,

This reorientation of academic life entails at least three radical revisions of the Weberian conception of the academic calling.

- First, teaching, not *Wissenschaft* [the making of fact-oriented knowledge, as in the Enlightenment's "facts/values" dualism], becomes the activity in terms of which all others—publication, collegiality, research, consultation, advising—are to be understood, interpreted and appraised.

- Second, the cultivation of those spiritual virtues that make genuine teaching and learning possible becomes a vitally important aspect of pedagogy.

- Finally, both charity and *philia* [a multidimensional understanding of friendship, addressing interpersonal relations as well as the possibility of an emotional bond to what is known in and of the world], the loves that Weber banished from the academy, become once again central to its self-conception and to its overall mission in the world.[14]

As he develops these revisions with an unusual wisdom, he gracefully notes that "Cardinal Newman certainly made these points, as he made so

many others, more eloquently than anyone else before or since." In Newman's words:

> The personal influence of the teacher is able in some sort to dispense
> with an academical system, but that system cannot in any sort dis-
> pense with personal influence. With influence there is life, without it
> there is none; if influence is deprived of its due position, it will not by
> those means be got rid of, it will only break out irregularly, danger-
> ously. An academic system without the personal influence of teachers
> upon pupils is an arctic winter; it will create an ice-bound, petrified,
> cast-iron University and nothing else.[15]

Schwehn then comments:

> It is an eerie coincidence perhaps that Weber's last works were filled
> with similar images of cold, darkening loneliness: the future of Ger-
> man politics in the immediate aftermath of World War I he called a
> "polar night of icy darkness"; the modern university in the twentieth
> century, an outpost of exiles, not unlike the ancient Hebrews, inquir-
> ing of and in the night; the dwelling place of the "specialists without
> spirit," an iron cage of their own making.[16]

The contemporary university student is caught between the pedagogical visions of Newman and Weber; their humanness requires the relationship in order for the ideas to become real, and yet their culture so shapes their experience that becoming "specialists without spirit" seems the only possibility.[17]

Few films better capture this dynamic tension than Akira Kurosawa's *Red
Beard,* the story of a young medical student whose moral vision is transformed in a rural health clinic.[18] Throughout his medical school years Yasumoto works hard, showing such excellence that he is chosen to intern in the
royal palace of the emperor. Then, to his great surprise, his graduation papers instruct him to go into the country, a million miles from where his passport to privilege was supposed to take him. With great resentment and re-
luctance he goes, all the while expecting that a mistake has been made, and
that as soon as it is rectified he will find his way to fame and fortune as a
court physician. For several weeks he pouts, letting everyone know that

someone with his talent does not belong in a place as unimportant as the clinic.

Slowly, very slowly, he begins to see his setting with new eyes. The senior physician, Red Beard, is a wise and experienced man whose skill and compassion draw patients with many different needs. The awakening of Yasumoto's heart comes in a bedside vigil over a speechless sufferer. After the patient dies, Red Beard explains his own interest in the man and why he has cared for him in the way he has. A candle has been lit, and Yasumoto's calling is gradually transformed as he begins to offer his gifts of healing to those who find their way to Red Beard's clinic.

Kurosawa sees deeply into the meaning of life and education in this story of the apprentice and his master. In an interview after the film's release, Japan's most celebrated filmmaker acknowledged, "With all my heart I want this kind of man to stand as an example. Red Beard is an imaginary person, but in creating him I represented the ideal of a being of good will."[19]

I want this kind of man to stand as an example. One thing is clear: for those who learn the deepest lessons—ones in which visions of one's world and of one's place in it are transformed—there is always a teacher whose purposes and passions ignite a student's moral imagination. But it is also clear that, in the end, it is the students who choose to learn from their teachers who experience this metamorphosis of moral meaning.

The Context of a Common Life

A man's morality is his religion enacted in social experience.

LANGDON GILKEY, *Shantung Compound: The Story of Men and Women Under Pressure*[1]

Scribbling on a subway wall, one recent poet simply, sadly observed: "Disenchanted, disenfranchised, disconnected, disgruntled."

Reality Bites, whose title itself speaks volumes, was the quintessential film for what was called "Generation X." Not surprisingly, as is always true of the best stories, its perspective is remarkably perennial, its sadness echoing across the centuries and cultures: "There's no point to anything . . . it's all just a random lottery of meaningless tragedy in a series of near escapes."[2] It is not so profound as it is poignant.

A more scholarly attempt to understand the incoherence implicit in contemporary consciousness, "How the World Lost Its Story" by Robert Jenson, professor at St. Olaf College, is an assessment of the modern and postmodern experience. Analyzing where it has come from and what it means for Christian discipleship, Jenson argues that the self-destruction of modernism is reflected in the loss of "realistic narrative"—a loss that is particularly damaging to human life in our time. This "realistic narrative" has two characteristics: (1) "sequential events are understood jointly to make a certain kind of sense—a dramatic kind of sense," and (2) "sequential dramatic coherence is of a sort that could 'really' happen, i.e., happen in a presumed factual world 'out there,' external to the text." Pressing the implications, he writes that the assumption of coherence presumes that it is "the *appropriate* way to understand our human task and possibility."[3] (Making the same criticism, Newbigin starkly states: "If there is no point in the story as a whole, there is no point in my own action. If the story is meaningless, any action of mine is meaningless."[4])

WHAT DO WE LOSE IF WE LOSE THE STORY?

Jenson looks at the arts as a window into what this means for our century, pondering portrayals in literature, painting and the theater, expecting them as works of art to reflect something about the meaning of human life under the sun. Writing that "modernity was defined by the attempt to live in a universal story without a universal storyteller," like Kundera and Steiner before him he sees the alternatives quite plainly. "The experiment has failed. It is, after the fact, obvious that it had to: if there is no universal storyteller, then the universe can have no story line. . . . If there is no God, or if there is some other God than the God of the Bible, there is no narratable world."

He then presses the point home, to the streets of our cities and suburbs:

> Modernity has added a new genre of the theater to the classic tragedy and comedy: the absurdist drama that displays precisely an absence of dramatic coherence. Sometimes such drama depicts a long sequence of events with no turning points or denouement; sometimes it displays the absence of any events at all. . . . The arts are good for diagnosis, both because they offer a controlled experience and because they always anticipate what will come later in the general culture. But the general culture has now caught up with postmodernism, and for experience of the *fact,* we should turn from elite art to the streets of our cities and the classrooms of our suburbs, to our congregations and churchly institutions, and to the culture gaps that rend them. There we will find folk who simply do not apprehend or inhabit a narratable world.[5]

MacIntyre makes a critical connection to Jenson's critique in his examination of the fundamental failure of the emotivist "social content and social context," when he argues that the loss of a credible *telos* creates a severe crisis of identity for human beings. Jenson's "narratable world" makes sense only in the light of a credible *telos* which has both a social content and social context.

The self is now thought of as lacking any necessary social identity, because the kind of social identity that it once enjoyed is no longer available; the self is now thought of as criterionless, because the kind of *telos* in terms of which it once judged and acted is no longer thought to be credible. What kind of identity and what kind of *telos* were they? In many premodern, traditional societies it is through his or her membership in a variety of social groups that the individual identifies himself or herself and is identified by others. I am brother, cousin and grandson, member of this household, that village, this tribe. These are not characteristics that belong to human beings accidentally, to be stripped away in order to discover "the real me." They are part of my substance, defining partially at least and sometimes wholly my obligations and my duties. Individuals inherit a particular space within an interlocking set of social relationships; lacking that space, they are nobody, or at best a stranger or an outcast. To know oneself as such a social person is however not to occupy a static and fixed position. It is to find oneself placed at a certain point on a journey with set goals; to move through life is to make progress—or to fail to make progress—toward a given end.[6]

He adds another lens to that of Jenson: that with the loss of a sense of being "on a journey with set goals . . . toward a given end"—a narratable world—the modern person has also lost the sense of "an interlocking set of social relationships . . . that define my obligations and my duties." The consequence? A fraying social fabric that gnaws away at our feeling of responsibility to and for each other, and that nurtures cynicism about anyone and everything at the highest levels of public responsibility.

The way that we resolve this dilemma is a matter of immense importance to our democratic experiment, to the future of our culture.[7] The scholars whose study became *Habits of the Heart: Individualism and Commitment in American Life* (which is both an inductive and a deductive examination of our national character—particularly the conflict between a deeply bred, fiercely defended individualism and our urgent need for meaningful, sustainable commitments to one another) fear that the "individualism may have grown cancerous."[8]

> Those most trapped in the language of the isolated self ("In the end you're really alone") are troubled by the nihilism they sense there and are eager to find a way of overcoming the emptiness of purely arbitrary "values." We believe that much of the thinking about the self of educated Americans, thinking that has become almost hegemonic in our universities and much of the middle class, is based on inadequate social science, impoverished philosophy and vacuous theology. There are truths we do not see when we adopt the language of radical individualism. We find ourselves not independently of other people and institutions but through them. We never get to the bottom of our selves on our own. We discover who we are face to face and side by side with others in work, love and learning. . . . We are parts of a larger whole that we can neither forget nor imagine in our own image without paying a high price.[9]

From the most sophisticated cultural critiques to the street-level despair of the "dissed" generation, the evidence seems conclusive: for individuals to flourish they need to be part of a community of character, one which has a reason for being that can provide meaning and coherence between the personal and the public worlds. It is this final characteristic that we will explore here.

For students to stand against the acidic effects of the contemporary world, they must become people who understand the meaning of Berger's contention that "the availability of an effective plausibility structure, that is, a social base serving as the 'laboratory' of transformation" is the most important social condition for successfully establishing a counter-identity to that imposed by the culture—namely, in our time, a fragmented, incoherent life.[10]

WE DISCOVER WHO WE ARE, FACE TO FACE AND SIDE BY SIDE

Community is the context for the growth of convictions and character. What we believe about life and the world becomes plausible as we see it lived out all around us. This is not an abstraction, though. Its reality is seen in time and space, in the histories and circumstances of real people living real lives.

Hauerwas has written for nearly three decades now on the narrative nature of Christian social ethics, his central contention being that the church is, rather than has, a social ethic. In *The Community of Character* he writes,

> The story of God does not offer a resolution of life's difficulties, but it offers us something better—an adventure and struggle, for we are possessors of the happy news that God has called people together to live faithful to the reality that he is the Lord of this world. . . . Moreover, through initiation into such a story I learn to regard others and their difference from me as a gift. Only through their existence do I learn what I am, can or should be.[11]

Those whose stories are told on these pages have understood this, at least in retrospect. That qualification is an important one, as it allows for young people to make stumbling and fumbling choices toward a *telos* whose character is not altogether known at the time; it also allows for grace, which is always a surprise.

Long a gifted administrator, Donald Guthrie has moved from college to seminary to the university, spending several years at the University of Georgia studying adult learning. A husband and father, he has made a life of decisions that have taken his responsibility to his family into the calculus of his calling—sometimes at what seemed a cost to his career. For many years the vice president for academic affairs at Covenant Theological Seminary in St. Louis, Missouri, he does what he does for the sake of people, people with names and faces he comes to learn and love. And while he loves to teach, more often he is the one standing behind the scenes who has made it all happen.

Those who know Donald, young and old, respect him and have affection for him. When asked, "What are the pressures that have made it hard to keep connecting what you believe about life and the world with how you live in the world?" he very succinctly answers, "The cynical nature of our culture, as it permeates the lives of people around me—and me. And only community can stand against that." In his own words he has restated the thesis of Bellah et al.: we discover who we are—and who we are meant to be—face to face and side by side with others in work, love and learning. His story and statement were not unique.

In interview after interview, it was uncanny how similar the stories were in terms of the importance of finding a community of like-minded and like-hearted folk, as a crucial context for learning to connect belief with behavior. Though the vocational visions, the geographical settings and educational experiences were different, in their differences they each told a story of community as the place where their convictions and character began to make sense. Bob Kramer's account of his wrestling through existentialism as a politically interested undergraduate (chapter two), and coming to believe in the Christ of historic orthodoxy (chapter five), continues to instruct us as he reflects on his understanding of his calling in light of the choices he made after finishing his years of schooling. He and his wife chose where to live on the basis of the priority of community, finding a people and a place where their own deepening worldview could become a way of life.

Bob was asked, *Were there other influences shaping your sense of what was important?*

That's a complicated question, with a lot of different threads and strands. When I first came to Harvard, it was people like Daniel Patrick Moynihan and others who were just beginning to develop the urban studies program, applying political theory to the urban setting. It was a combination of people; for instance, when I heard the tapes of Camus and Sartre, I could really relate to that. I loved Camus. I thought Sartre was more honest, but I really identified with Camus. As a new Christian, I read Schaeffer, Guinness, Stott and Packer. I read them all, absorbed them all, and at the same time was trying to integrate or apply much of their thinking to the field of political theory and urban studies. That was my concentration as an undergraduate. At Westminster [Theological Seminary] I greatly increased my understanding of biblical theology.

But what has always excited me has been a sense of worldview. And a worldview in this sense: because God is trustworthy and Scripture is true, therefore it speaks into all areas of life. And it not only speaks, but it orders them and interprets them. It enables us as God's stewards to be able to understand, to be able to make discoveries and connections. I have had the sense that in following Christ, one has the unique opportunity to be creative in his thinking and actions under God, in a way no one else does. But they do it without being able to give credit, without knowing why the connections they discover are there. I continue to be motivated by the desire to see change—to look at social problems and figure out new ways of thinking about them. But not just to think, but making changes in structures and in society.

What happened to keep that connection alive in you (not only the importance of change, but being part of making the changes)?

That had as much to do with the people that I was surrounding myself with as with the ideas. We—Diane and I together—sought out people and wanted to spend time with people who had the same commitment to make these connections, to see their lives demonstrate the impact of Christ upon our lives, and by extension of our lives, our families, our careers and upon our society. So I think whether it was the discipleship group we started in 1974 at Westminster (with people we still meet with today—getting together with twice a year for twenty years), or whether it's the friendships from L'Abri . . . everywhere we went, my wife and I sought out such folks because we felt we were challenged and exhorted by being in that kind of fellowship. Not just to pray out loud for each other or study Scripture, but to encourage and exhort one another. What does it mean to live for Christ? What does it mean to live out the truth? How do we live persuasively? How do we make our lives persuasive?

It was very difficult for us making the cultural change, much tougher for my wife than myself because I at least had a purpose for being at Westminster. I wanted to study Scripture. For my wife it was coming to a one hundred percent alien culture, and that was very tough. Her culture was one part hippie/counterculture, the other part private girls' college, Long Island, Nantucket. . . . Both of our fathers are educators. Both of them put a premium on being caring and sensitive, very liberal and publicly involved. It is a culture in which Christianity means kissing your brains goodbye.

As I have gotten involved in politics and business, I am more and more convinced that the people you choose to have around you have more to do with how you act upon what you believe than what you read or the ideas that influence you. The influence of ideas has to be there, but the application is something it's very hard to work out by yourself. You work it out in the context of friends—just as you work it out with your spouse, so you work it out with a group of friends. What does it mean, when you're trying to think through new structures or new ways of living, when you don't see models around you?

We chose the place that we went after seminary on the basis of looking for people who were raising second-generation Christians and who we thought were doing a good job. The reason we came to Annapolis had nothing to do with a job opportunity, really. It came down to the fact that we met families whose teenagers were excited about Christ, and we said, *This is the place we want to be.* The other communities we looked at were all communities that offered me a job, but we chose the one that we thought was the best place for us as new Christians who did not have Christian parents as models, in terms of raising our kids. We chose a place where we could see some living examples to talk to, e.g., what does it mean to raise your kids so they are not immediately turned off but are excited about living for Christ? They were excited about the opportunity of living as Christians—not feeling it's a burden that they carry.

The influence of ideas has to be there, but the application is something it's very hard to work out by yourself. You work it out in the context of friends . . .

A similar note is sounded in the conversation with Ron Stegall, who has a photo of an Amish barn-raising on his wall, picturing something of his deep convictions about the place of community in Christian discipleship. A teacher, pastor and social worker, he has lived with his wife, Kathy, and children between Cyprus and Kansas throughout his adult life. The commitment to community has been the source of the happiest experiences of their life, and some of the saddest.

How has your answer to the question "What is most important to you?" changed over the last twenty-five years?

From the time that I started to have some understanding of this, primarily in the sixties and through a lot of struggles, the idea that our citizenship is in heaven has been very important to me as a way of holding everything together. I would say my understanding of it has grown and matured, and has gone through all the trials and tribulations that one has in life. It's knocked the sharp edges off of it in some ways, I suppose, but it's made it far deeper and a more mature faith.

What kind of "sharp edges"?

From the first rush of enthusiasm and the kind of black-and-whiteness of it all, to contact with the real world in which we live, understanding that it is God's timing and God's will and God's work. We can't usher in the kingdom ourselves. It requires a deeper dependence in some ways, a stronger faith to see all the pain and struggles—and still understand Christ bringing it about in his own time.

When you talk about meeting up with the trials and tribulations of the years between, what are you thinking of?

Of a certain kind of disillusionment, having a certain kind of expectation and not seeing it fulfilled. But I think there are deeper ones too. More personal. Lots of people you know who have struggled, ended up in pain. Good friends who have died, been killed; marriages that you thought were good that have dissolved; leaders who have taught, yet at the same time have betrayed their own teachings by their actions. And certainly the trial of knowing your own heart, knowing that you're not such a great guy inside and that if anybody looked inside they wouldn't like you so much. So it's just a reality check, that's what it is. It's just a realization that Christ calls us to himself and his kingdom but doesn't promise an easy way. In fact the disciples he called all ended up dead.

Of course that's all kind of one-sided. There's also a huge amount of joy and happiness and satisfaction, actually experiencing the benefits of the kingdom as well. It's all just mixed in there together.

What happened in your college years that shaped your sense of what is most important?

I was trying to figure out what it meant to be a Christian in the sixties. The culture in chaos, and the issues that confronted us out of which that chaos came, like Vietnam and the civil rights movement, were all influencing how I saw myself in the world. I was very sympathetic to what the counterculture was saying and the criticisms that were being made, such as their evaluations of the society and the church. But I also knew that I wasn't in favor of their general alternatives. I had a very good group of friends my junior year in college, about seven to ten of us who did everything together. They supported me not only in my intellectual struggles, but really in every part of my life.

I was struggling with Vietnam at the time, with what I would have to do and all the rest. At a profound level I wondered about *Just who are we as a people? What does it mean to live in this world? What does justice mean? What does fairness mean?* The real basic issues of humanity were being explored. At that same time I discovered Romans 12:1, about not being conformed but being transformed, and that really made a whole lot of difference to me as I struggled about how to be a citizen in that age and that world. I think the Holy Spirit opened my eyes to see not only the truth of God's Word but how the truth fits together and applies to the world.

What has kept you "in this" for the long haul?

I could answer on many levels. That vision of the kingdom and of my part in it, is obviously very critical. But clearly, over those years, my best teachers were my best friends. We were all trying to figure this out together.

My best teachers were my best friends. We were all trying to figure this out together. Face to face and side by side.

Michelle Clark is an artist with a social conscience. To see her and hear her is quick confirmation: so full of life, from the obvious aesthetic sensibilities behind her choice of clothes to the artistry of her words, she is an artist. But she also feels the pains of the world quite profoundly. After years of Washington's world, moving from educational institutes to human rights organizations, she spent several years in Israel working among Russian immigrants and then returned to lead the Protection Project at Johns Hopkins University's School for Advanced International Studies. Michelle now lives in Vienna, Austria, where she directs an international effort to address human trafficking, working under the Organization for Security and Cooperation in Europe (OSCE).

She told about her university years—the window between ages eighteen and twenty-five—and what happened in those years to shape her sense of what is most important, in other words, the good life. As she walked through her years from adolescence on into adulthood, what was impressive was her own deepening sense of what was important. One thread which is increasingly visible in the tapestry of her life is that of community—her choice to live her life amid people who were also on "a journey with set goals . . . toward a given end."

Michelle, what matters most to you? And how did your university years affect the way you answer that question today?

My mother died when I was seventeen, and I fell apart. In a foreign service family, we had two constants: family and faith. We were a very devout Catholic family. I prayed to God that my mother wouldn't die, and when she did I lost both God and the family.

I went off to college—this was in 1970—right after Kent State. The counterculture was in its heyday, and I was ripe. So I became an actress in the college theater and embraced all of the related lifestyles. At the end of two years I realized I was in big trouble. I had no focus. I was doing too many drugs and I was losing control. At Carleton College we were very liberal. It was one of the first schools to drop *in loco parentis*. The school was wide open. What I did know was that I was so alienated. Now I would use the word, though we didn't speak that way then. I didn't know how to connect with people. I was just living in this great stage of tremendous alienation and felt so much distance from other people. And I was pretty nasty and pretty bitter—because I was very volatile and would lash out at a moment's notice when something offended me or if I disagreed or if someone tried to cross me. I was smart enough to be fairly good with words. I was not an easy person to get along with, and I wasn't usually very straight. Through it all I recognized that I was in trouble and that I was out of control.

My father said he would let me study in Paris for a year. So I took him up on his offer, not for reasons that he intended. I needed to get out. In Paris I met a Frenchman—dashing, handsome, a wonderful craggy face, dancer, actor, intellectual, university student. We began this wonderful, idyllic, impassioned, every-American-girl-dreams-about affair. He was older that I was, and he was much more thoughtful. After a few months he came to visit me, and he said I'd never really thought about or made decisions for myself in life. Because of the emotions involved and because he was the sum and substance of my existence at that point, I was devastated. It was as if someone had taken a wet dishrag and slapped it across my face.

Well, it was absolutely true. I decided very specifically that whatever was true in the world, I would find it. I had to find the meaning of life. It was as conscious and as naive as that. Simultaneously a very good friend, a woman who still is my friend, was studying art. We made an agreement that she would never preach to me. I said, "Nancy, I really like you, but if you preach to me, then we're history." Because even though I thought I could do this truth thing, I immediately excluded any notion of Christian truth. I saw that it had failed me, and I was going to move on.

During the course of the year I read everything from the French literary writers to the philosophers. I read Eastern religions, and I read old Egyptian religion. I read anything, talked to anybody I could. Essentially, slowly during the year, I came to realize somewhere along the line I had to make some kind of concession to Christianity. It was too big and too intellectually valid for me to dismiss it completely. I was trying to be a thinking person at the time, and you can't dismiss Aquinas and the church writers and deem that completely unacceptable. Because I was trying to be intellectually honest, as a student I had to revisit my initial stand of completely dismissing Christianity as viable and begin to consider it as one option among many options. That gradually narrowed down.

I went with my friend Nancy and six thousand others on a pilgrimage to the Cathedral of Chartres, and we marched across the flat countryside to that part of France. Everywhere you looked on the horizon we were in groups of thirty, and the leader of each group carried a cross. It was very medieval and pageantrylike, and there was something very stirring about it. It's really marvelous that God gives so much attention to the need of the individual. I needed drama, basically, and God gave me drama.

We got to Chartres. I who have the constitution of an ox got terribly ill and had to go to the Red Cross tent. I could not even stand. I tried to go into the cathedral for communion. As hostile as I was toward Christianity, I wanted to be there for communion, as the mystical wonder of what I experienced as a child had never left me. I couldn't do it and had to be taken out of the church. I remember collapsing against this stone wall, looking at the cathedral and just crying and crying. I was no dummy. I was denied access. I couldn't go into that place where I wanted to go.

Well, as if that were not symbolic enough, at the time of communion my friend mentioned to the priest that there was a very sick girl outside, and they came out of the church and brought communion to me. Pursued by the hound of heaven. It was a month of probably the greatest unhappiness in my life. I wanted to believe, but I didn't. This business of cost—that this God wanted all of me—was so frightening to me. My mother had died, so I wasn't going to give away all of me to anybody.

One day, May 24, 1973, I was walking along the Seine River, of course thinking about all of this. Why did it have to be the kind of God who required all—and not just some? I understood what that cost. I felt encompassed by the most incredible peace very suddenly. It stopped time, motion and history. God revealed himself to me. For the first time I could see what it all meant, and the cost became very small. It was a very small price to pay. I don't know if you can do that on your own. In all of my thinking I could never analyze it into a place of accepting. I had to be in the presence of God to see that the cost was so small. So I just didn't know what to say . . . I just remember saying "yes yes yes," over and over again.

What happened after that?

I went back to college, and it was real difficult. The Christians on the Carleton campus didn't know much what to do with me. I was still a theater person. I smoked. I drank. I liked Catholicism. The fact that many of us survived the early days of the Jesus movement was the grace of God. After that I finished college, graduated, moved to Washington, met the people who still are my closest friends, very quickly. I got involved with them, so I had a little bit of a sense of community. My first year was very lonely. The second year was a combination of people, this little community, the work we were doing on GW [George Washington University], and God's continuing to woo me and bring me closer.

In many ways my first years as a Christian were unhappy years. It was a difficult time, circumstantially, in life. I'd never lived in this country before. I'd never worked before. I was working for the first time in my life. In college my father was gracious enough to make sure I didn't have to work. So now I managed money for the first time. I was trying to develop my own sense of relationships. I came to Washington, and I realized I didn't have the first sense of how to become affiliated with the community. I was always a loner, and in college it was easy because I was never alone. But here if I chose to be alone, I was alone. So they were really dark and unhappy years for a long time. That I had made this commitment of faith was really important, and I sort of kept nurturing that.

Of all that happened in those years that continues to shape your life—what stands out as "most important"?

I used to read all the time . . . a lot of [Francis] Schaeffer, history, novels, lots and lots of classical literature. The most important, though, in the way I think about the world, was moving in with my little community of friends. Ultimately that's what really made the biggest difference. That, more than what I read. That was the first time that what I believed and thought was put to the test. Before I graduated from college, I was all set to join a cloistered convent. For me and my frame of reference, once you get this tremendously intense faith, you go off and become a nun. With me, if I was going to be a nun I was going to be a cloistered nun. So what made a difference was meeting this exceptional young family. They were working as campus ministers, bought a house and asked me to move in with them. So then all of a sudden there was a larger picture to this.

When you keep deciding to keep at this, what metaphors, images or ideas do you draw on to know it's still worth the cost?

There's one: there's no place else to go. If I were to throw in the towel, where would I throw it? I have seen, felt and experienced the wonder of God. It's a memory that forces my heart to remember. So when there's no telling that it's alive at the given moment, I remember that nothing ever compares with being in the presence of God. Dogged obedience. I went through about six or seven years I refer to as my sabbatical, where I really shelved faith. I quit going to church. I quit hanging out with Christians. I just put a lot of it on hold, and I got shaken up pretty badly at the end of that time. The metaphor I used then is that there's a train that's leaving, and this is my last chance to be on it. In my bones, I know that nothing else is real.

What do you mean by "real"?

Nothing else that will stand under adversity, that will provide any kind of ultimate sense of permanence or value. God is the only thing that

ultimately is true, that ultimately is good, that ultimately is beautiful—that will stand the test of time.

One more question: When you think about your efforts to live a life of connecting,
in a coherent way, your personal beliefs with how you live in the world . . .

Great struggle. None of it is easy. I remember when the whole Woody
Allen/Mia Farrow thing was going and how slimy and disgusting the
whole thing was. Woody Allen's very glib, horrible response at the end
of a *Newsweek* or *Time* article was "The heart wants what it wants." My
heart wants a million things . . . but look what happens to our culture,
our lives, our children and the children of others, the climate we live
in, if that becomes the justification for everything. I've developed
crushes on married men, on nonbelievers, I've lusted for unlimited
charging privileges at Neiman Marcus, and on and on. I have a ten-
year-old little car that's paid for. I'd love to drive a Lexus. From the enticements of the mind to the enticements of the flesh to the enticements of the eyes, I fall under all of them.

One of my prayers materially is the Proverbs 30 prayer: "Lord, give
me enough that I shall not want and cry against you—but don't give
me so much so that I am full and forget you." I pray that for myself
because I know my limitations. God, don't make me wealthy because
I might forget you. So before we even get to that point, why don't we
head it off at the pass. It's a scriptural prayer. So I consciously try to
not aspire to wealth. It's a struggle to not let the heart get what it
wants. But God is a shield to those who walk in integrity. My life is
safe. I'm a single woman. I'm vulnerable to a lot of things. But I know
that I am safe when I am obedient, and I feel insecure if I step out.
That is a set of internal boundaries that I know and I walk within,
sometimes better than others.

There are certain struggles that become easier with time. In discipline—it's easier to pay off credit cards, save money, develop certain
attitudes of temper over time. Other things are less easy for me, especially for me emotionally, because I'd like to be married. I'd like to
have a family—I don't. My heart wants it and doesn't have it.

I do not want to grow old and be a bitter person, so sometimes I have to choose acceptance just out of fear of what a bitter old lady looks like. Not that I want to accept. I want to be really angry and cry out to God, *Why in the world did you do this to me? I didn't want any of this professional stuff, literary stuff, art stuff. I'm doing it because I don't want an ordinary life. But what I really want, you've never given me.* I see bitter people, and that scares me. So if I continue to hope and strive and work to accomplish the service to another person and creation of something beautiful, sometimes that's out of fear of the alternative; the fear of what bitterness and giving in to resentment looks like. That's ugly. I'm vain enough that I don't want to be cragged and gnarled and pouting even at ninety. You get the face you deserve. I don't want that kind of face.

So the reasons for keeping on and for making choices range from the positive enticement to running from the fear of the alternative. I'd have to say that at different points I've been in both, one or the other. It'd be nice if I lived my life in total response to God all the time—I can't, you know.

One thing I have learned is that it is the people you surround yourself with that is one of the most important choices you make. I chose my employer. She hired me. But you have to serve somebody, and it's who you serve that is the choice. I choose my friends, and they do respond to my overtures and affections, but the people I surround myself with on a regular basis—even on an irregular basis—are people who in many ways are more than I am. That is absolutely essential, because they always cause me to go back and wonder what else I need to do. Do I guard my friends' reputations, do I care for my friends in the way that they demonstrate so marvelously and consistently? The people I consider my wise counselors and the pillars of my life are people who in many ways are more than I am.

One thing I have learned is that it is the people you surround yourself with that is one of the most important choices you make.

I have chosen this more extensive selection from Michelle's interview because it tells with unusual grace the story of her journey through the critical years of deciding what she would believe and how she would live. As eloquent and honest as her story is, it is one among many which tell the same story. Those who keep on pursuing the vision of a coherent life—one that meaningfully connects the disparate strands of one's existence—are people who have made the choice to live their lives out among folk who share their vision of the good life.

On the other hand, those who seek a self apart from social content and social context, in the end, find themselves disenchanted, disenfranchised, disconnected, disgruntled. This is true to the way the world really is: premodern, modern and postmodern, north, south, east and west.

COMMUNITY AS A MORAL IMPERATIVE

For those who have pledged themselves to live within "the plausibility structure" of historic Christian orthodoxy, this decision to become a part of the lives of others is a moral imperative—with all the pleasures and pains implicit in that decision. And as a moral imperative it is situated within a worldview founded on coherence and truth and learned in relationship to those whose own commitments are embedded in that worldview. Berger puts it very plainly: "To have a conversion experience is nothing much. The real thing is to be able to keep taking it seriously; to retain a sense of its plausibility. This is where the religious community comes in."[12]

From the beginning of this study, we have explored the challenge of facing up to modernity, particularly as it is experienced by the contemporary college student. In attempting to understand the nature of the challenge, we have looked at a variety of factors that bear down on the formation of moral meaning in the modern world. Some are written into our social context, such as industrialization, and all that that has meant in terms of urbanization, mass communication and education. Some are argued on an intellectual plane, such as the dualism of facts and values, a debilitating moral vision which drives the way we converse about anything and everything in the public square. The end of it all, though, for "ordinary people living ordinary lives," is a profound loss of coherence.

And yet some have held on. We have told the stories of those who have not only survived but thrived. In contrast to every expectation, they still believe in the vision of a coherent life—personally as well as publicly—having made choices about the meaning of their lives which have sustained them in the more complex responsibilities of adulthood. What is it that so marks their lives, that gives them the skills to stand? As their stories were told, during the critical years between adolescence and adulthood they were people who (1) formed a worldview that could account for truth amidst the challenge of relativism in a culture increasingly marked by secularization and pluralization; (2) found a mentor whose life "pictured" the possibility of living with and in that worldview; and (3) forged friendships with folk whose common life offered a context for those convictions to be embodied. In different areas of the world and in different arenas of life, they are people who have woven together a fabric of faithfulness.

Convictions, Character,
Community Incarnate

I can only choose within the world I can see, in the moral
sense of "see" which implies that clear vision is
a result of moral imagination and moral effort. . . . The moral
life, on this view, is something that goes on continually,
not something that is switched off in between the
occurrence of explicit moral choices. What happens in
between such choices is indeed what is crucial

IRIS MURDOCH, *The Sovereignty of Good*[1]

To spend a day walking through the Holocaust Memorial, standing gray and granite between the mall and the Jefferson Memorial, is to suspend one's sense of time and space and to step back into an era in the last century which is both horrible and historical. Since it opened in the spring of 1993, I have taken and sent groups of students and faculty there to try to make sense of what happened in those years of injustice and suffering. Each time I have asked this question: What would you have to believe about life and the world to have seen Nazism as evil during the Holocaust itself? It is a question of one's worldview, of presuppositions and perceptions, of understanding and interpreting. But it is also a question of one's way of life, of practice, of action.

As the elevator opens onto the fourth floor and immerses us in the social and political climate of the decades preceding the Holocaust; as we descend into the terrors of the Wahnsee Conference and the decision to exterminate the Jews; as we come face to face with the reality of Auschwitz and Dachau, seeing and hearing the unimaginable; and finally as we are confronted with the stories of those who chose to stand against the evil, the question presses itself onto our consciousness: What kind of persons were they, who could see it for what it was and had the courage to act?

One of the stories told in the last section of the Memorial is a story of students. Made into a film in 1982, *The White Rose* won Germany's award for "film of the year."[2] For many years I have shown it to students as a way of understanding the meaning of education—trying to help my students understand, as Schwehn has argued in *Exiles from Eden,* that "epistemologies have ethical implications . . . ways of knowing are not morally neutral, but morally directive."[3]

The story is set in 1942. A literal handful of friends at university began to tell each other of letters and conversations, from brothers and cousins, which simply do not make sense, given the patriotic public face of Nazism. The news keeps coming, though, and they find themselves having to reevaluate their understanding of what is happening in Germany. It is *not* an agonizing, drawn-out decision. With a profound simplicity they decide: "We are Christians, and we are Germans; therefore we are responsible for Germany!" With great conviction and courage they choose to publish their news in a periodical leaflet which they call *The White Rose.* At first they circulate it secretly at their university, but as their understanding of the society-wide implications of their knowledge grows, they decide—at great personal risk—to deliver *The White Rose* to universities across Germany.

From the very beginning there is a sense of the responsibility of knowledge. Some more than others see the implications of their choices. But before the Holocaust is unmasked in all of its totalitarian terror, each of the students is confronted—at the most profound level—with the cost of discipleship. Where does that kind of moral vision come from? How was it formed in the painful face of modernity's technological and bureaucratic world, so perversely personified in Hitler and the Nazis?

Two generations later, these students offer us deep insight into the formation of moral meaning in the university years. Their brutal deaths at the hands of the Nazis stopped short their witness to the reality of what and why they believed, and therefore our ability to understand where their beliefs and choices might have taken them as they moved from adolescence into adulthood is limited. And yet their journey through the critical years is an important study of students who formed a worldview complex enough to make sense of their own moment, who found teachers whose own lives incarnated the students' deepening convictions about the nature of the good life, and who forged friendships with others whose common life nurtured their own developing understanding of meaning and morality.

The most poignant window into this story is *At the Heart of the White Rose: The Letters and Diaries of Hans and Sophie Scholl*. Brother and sister, Hans and Sophie grew up in a home that nurtured a love of life and learning; their impulses and eloquence are clear testimony to that. They also grew up politically conscious; their father was imprisoned for several months for being overheard referring to Hitler as "the scourge of God."[4] From all that is written here and elsewhere, it appears that their family's religious commitments were nominally Protestant; not hostile to the gospel, but not nourishing of live orthodoxy either. In the late 1930s, they went off to study at the University of Munich, Hans preceding Sophie by several years.

Like many young men away from home, Hans found a special friend in Rose Naegele. It is obvious that as he tried to make sense of his life in the world, he was forced to the most foundational of questions. On May 2, 1941, he wrote her:

> Even though May came in accompanied by rain, all the fields were bright with the loveliest green imaginable. A sunbeam pierced a little gap in the dark sea of cloud, and the world laughed and glittered in the light of heaven. I stood there marveling and thought, Does God take us for fools, that he should light up the world for us with such consummate beauty in the radiance of his glory, in his honor? And nothing, on the other hand, but rapine and murder? Where does the truth lie? Should one go off and build a little house with flowers outside the windows and a garden outside the door and extol and thank

God and turn one's back on the world and its filth? Isn't seclusion a form of treachery—of desertion? Things are tolerable in succession— the youthful spirit emerges from the ruins and soars toward the light—but simultaneities are antithetical, ruins and light at the same time. I'm weak and puny, but I want to do what is right.[5]

And yet Hans struggled to know what was right. Seemingly across the whole of his society the wall between right and wrong was crumbling. Frustrated, deeply disenchanted by the national socialist political vision but not knowing where and how to find a place to stand, he wrote in his diary, "My pessimism gets worse every day. Skepticism is poisoning my soul."[6]

But then, along with his closest friends, he met Carl Muth, a theologian and the editor of the Nazi-banned *Hochland.* An elderly man, Muth had a Christian faith that deeply shaped his understanding of his citizenship in those troubled years between the wars. This relationship between Muth and Hans offers rich insight into the interwovenness of the influence of a teacher upon the development of a student's vision and virtues; in critical yet mysterious ways, they nourish each other. Inge Jens, editor of *At the Heart of the White Rose,* describes this time in Hans's life:

> Hans's "conversion" process is more intellectual than Sophie's, his spiritual growth being nurtured in large part by books. Many of these are by French Catholics, among them Leon Bloy, Paul Claudel, Georges Bernanos and Etienne Gilson. . . . For both Hans and Sophie another strong Catholic influence comes from their friendship with the elderly writer and editor, Carl Muth, and from Theodor Haecker, whose books had been banned but who would read from them to members of the White Rose.[7]

Both Hans and Sophie began to explore the worldview opened up to them by Muth and Haecker. And by amazing grace, a candle was lit in their minds and hearts which gave light to the dark times. On December 7, 1941—the day of Pearl Harbor—Hans wrote to Rose, "I'm thinking of you on this second Sunday of Advent, which I'm experiencing as a wholehearted Christian for the first time in my life."[8] Yet this new understanding of his life and the world had to be worked out in the context of the social setting in which he found himself. Hitler remained in power, and Hans's pilgrimage within the university seemed very lonely. Some months later he wrote in his diary, "O God of love, help me to overcome my doubts. I see the Creation, your handiwork, which is good. But I also see man's handiwork, our handiwork, which is cruel."[9]

The formation of Sophie's character and convictions followed many of the paths that Hans had walked ahead of her. Yet she had her own questions and concerns. Jens writes:

> Sophie is more intuitive, less schooled; full of a self-doubt which strikes me as the rarest kind of humility, she struggles with anguished hope toward a point of affirmation and peace. "I'd so much like to believe that I can acquire strength through prayer," she writes in her diary. "I can't achieve anything by myself." And in another entry: "I've decided to pray in church every day, so God won't forsake me. Although I don't yet know God and feel sure my conception of him is utterly false, he'll forgive me if I ask him." And then in the loveliest of self-effacing gestures she writes: "I pray for a compassionate heart, for how else could I love?"[10]

As she began her own journey of faith through her student years, reading deeply and widely in philosophy at the time, she wrestled with the cosmic questions too. For everyone under the sun, at some point in time questions about God, human nature and the meaning of history must be addressed. Inarticulate and unconscious as the question may be, everyone is pressed at some point to answer, "What does this life mean?" Perhaps it was through the lectures of Professor Kurt Huber that Sophie was formally faced with this. She introduced Hans and his fellow medical students to her philosophy professor, who was described as "the best thing at the whole university." Students throughout the university attended his lectures; to find a seat one had to get there early.

The professor's lectures on Leibniz and his theodicy were excellent. Theodicy—the vindication of the justice of God, an important and complex area of philosophy—was of course particularly difficult in time of war. For how does one trace out the work of God in a world where killing and suffering are raging?[11]

Sophie wrestled with this on a profound level, digging into the Bible to understand her own responsibility in the midst of the social and political turmoil all around. How is it possible that God is sovereign, that Christ is Lord, if there is so much injustice and pain?

In a letter to Fritz Hartnagle on October 28, 1942, she records her meditations on Romans 8 and its light on the striving between the "now but not yet" nature of her time in history. Gracefully, she applies this text to her relationships with the unbelievers around—throughout her country and in her university—arguing for more compassion. "Aren't they terribly, terribly poor, the people who neither know nor believe that? Their poverty ought to make us eternally patient with them (that, and the knowledge of our own weakness, for what would we amount to by ourselves?), even if their stupid arrogance tends to infuriate us."[12]

"WE ARE RESPONSIBLE FOR GERMANY!"

Brother and sister began to find a place to stand. Reading the Scriptures in the light of the challenge presented by their culture, having conversations with friends about the world and their place in it, meeting older, wiser people who offered them their time and their books—together they molded a vision about what was real and true and right. In particular, Hans, Sophie and friends pursued a relationship with Carl Muth, for in him they found someone who

> represented more than just the center of a circle in which opponents of National Socialism could, without fear of denunciation, discuss political issues and current events as well as aspects of theology, literature and philosophy. On a very personal level, his function was that of an older, more experienced friend and Socratic mentor who opened up new worlds for them by suggestion and example. . . . Under Carl Muth's influence, Hans and Sophie's religious perceptions—as their letters bear witness—acquired greater intensity and firmer definition:

The Christian Gospel became the criterion of their thoughts and actions.[13]

We learn more about Muth and his interest in students from Franz Joseph Schoningh, who at Muth's death wrote his obituary:

> He was able, throughout his life, not only to understand the concerns of the younger generation, but to share them in a loving manner. This was especially evident in the septuagenarian's frequent endeavors to make the acquaintance of young men, explore their ideas and aspirations, and enlighten and encourage them by dint of serious conversation and correspondence. Even after *Hochland* [*Highland,* the journal Muth edited] had been suppressed, Muth still had his young "associates" just as he used, when still editing it, to lavish solicitude and encouragement on all the gifted young people who came his way, even more for their own sake than for that of *Hochland.*[14]

As Hans and Sophie continued on in their studies—both formally at the university and informally with their mentors—they began to see that they were responsible for Germany. Hans put it plainly, as he began to understand Nazism through the eyes of Muth and the German resistance: "Where are the Christians?"

More softly but with equal strength, Sophie wrote, "I want to share the suffering of these days. Sympathy becomes hollow if one feels no pain."[15]

One evening Hans was the only student invited to a social gathering in the home of Frau Doktor Mertens, where a reading was to take place, with conversation following. Professor Huber was also in attendance.

> After discussing the literary theme that had been read aloud, the talk, to the chagrin of the hostess, turned to politics. No one present knew each other well; the subject was dangerous.
>
> There was general consensus that German culture was decaying. Someone ventured the opinion that the only way to cope with the situation—the Nazis—was not through protest but simply by hanging on, tending to one's cultural obligations and tasks as scholars and just waiting out the nightmare.

At that point a medical student broke in with a caustic remark. A dark and scowling Hans Scholl said, "Why don't we rent ourselves an island in the Aegean and offer courses on worldviews?" Considering his lowly status in relation to the academics and professionals who were present, one gets a glimmer of Hans's enormous self-assurance and also of the passion that made him break out of the usual docile-student role required in traditional German society.

The atmosphere must have turned glacial after such an impertinence. But Kurt Huber was becoming flushed. He was not offended by what Hans said; on the contrary, he was suddenly galvanized. He spoke loudly: *"Something must be done, and it must be done now!"*[16]

The professor began to help the students of *The White Rose* in their writing. Over the next two years they produced and distributed a number of editions, first for their own university and later for universities all across Germany. The stories of those experiences are both exciting and horrifying, as they tell of unusual insight and courage on the part of a literal handful of friends who together identified a great social ill and chose to do something about it. As *The Altruistic Personality: Rescuers of Jews in Nazi Europe* notes, with a simplicity that is profound, "The step from inclination to action is a large one."[17]

But act they did. As they faced the consequences of their convictions they had to address the indifference not only of the university community but of Germany itself. Keeping their sense of responsibility alive—"We are Christians, and we are Germans; therefore we are responsible for Germany"—was a daily task. And yet against every obstacle, external as well as internal, their moral imagination grew.

Inge Scholl, sister of Hans and Sophie, in her own thoughtful remembering of that time, *The White Rose: Munich 1942-43,* describes the growing loneliness of those who were "the White Rose."

The yearning just for once to shake off these risks and dangers, to be free and unencumbered, seized them at times with great force. There were moments and hours when life simply seemed to be getting too difficult; when the uncertainties and the anxiety surged over them and engulfed their courage. Then there was no help but to descend deep within themselves, where a voice assured them that they were doing the right thing, that they would have to continue, even if they were all alone in the world. I believe that at such times the students were able to converse freely with God, with that Being whom they gropingly sought in their youth, whom they tried to find at the end point of all study, action and work. At this time Christ became for them in a strange way the elder brother who was always there, closer even than death. He was their path which allowed no return, the truth which gave answer to so many questions, and life itself, the whole splendid life.[18]

This spiritual dynamic gave them vision and energy to keep going, connecting belief and behavior, knowing and doing, at the deepest level of human consciousness. Their protest grew out of their most profound presuppositions about God, human nature and history. And because it was rooted so deeply, it was neither short-lived nor misdirected. As "The Fourth Leaflet" (the fourth issue of *The White Rose*) stated, "Though we know that National Socialist power must be broken by military means, we are trying to achieve a renewal from within of the severely wounded German spirit."[19]

The day finally came when that "severely wounded German spirit" rejected their commitments and cares. The students were caught in the act of distributing *The White Rose* at the University of Munich. After their arrest and imprisonment, the wider circle of folk throughout Germany whose convictions had led them to an active resistance of the systemic evil grieved the loss of these courageous, compassionate Christian students.

It was only a matter of days before Hans, Sophie, their friends and their professor were beheaded. One older friend in the underground movement waited and waited for Hans that night, planning to take him to meet Dietrich Bonhoeffer—not knowing that Hans had been executed.[20] Upon hearing the horrible news, Carl Muth "was distressed less by the house searches he had to endure and the fears he had to entertain for his own safety than by the news of the young man's death. . . . He spoke of him and his sister . . . with the sorrow of a bereaved father."[21]

To the end, Professor Huber was the only member of the faculty at the

University of Munich to support the students. In papers published after his death, there is one soberly titled "Final Statement of the Accused." It was reported that these remarks were given in court.

> You have stripped from me the rank and privileges of the professorship and the doctoral degree *summa cum laude* which I earned, and you have set me at the level of the lowest criminal. The inner dignity of the university teacher, of the frank, courageous protestor of his philosophical and political views—no trial for treason can rob me of that. My actions and my intentions will be justified in the inevitable course of history; such is my firm faith. I hope to God that the inner strength that will vindicate my deeds will in good time spring forth from my own people. I have done as I had to do on the prompting of an inner voice. I take the consequences upon myself in the way expressed in the beautiful words of Johann Gottlieb Fichte:
> "And thou shalt act as if
> On thee and on thy deed
> Depended the fate of all Germany
> And thou alone must answer for it."[22]

ON LEARNING TO CARE

"Somebody, after all, had to make a start."[23]

Sophie's simple statement before the chief justice of the People's Court of Germany captures the character of conviction in the moral vision that lit the lives of these students. When most of Germany "blinked"—including countless other students who chose to see their education as a passport to privilege and therefore were indifferent to the evil and injustice of their time—what enabled them to care? Why did they see themselves as responsible? In the tapestry of their experiences, developing convictions about moral meaning, character-forming relationships with mentors, and membership in a community of like-minded folk were woven together at one and the same time for Hans and Sophie. To read their letters and diaries, to become familiar with their families and friendships, is to be drawn into an unusual account of students learning to connect what they believed with how they lived.

But growing out of this story of students are still more questions, questions for contemporary students but also for those who care for students in other times and places, like the Muths and Hubers did for the Scholls and their friends at the University of Munich. How do we learn that the Christian vision of life and the world is always both character-forming and culture-forming, that it is always concerned for both the personal and the political, both the individual and the institutional? How do we learn to live wisely and bravely in a broken world? How self-conscious are we about the ways of knowing which give shape and substance to our educational efforts? Do we in fact see them as morally directive, in and of themselves? Does our teaching so integrally connect a worldview with a way of life, vision with implicit virtues, that our students are able to understand the ideas and issues of our time with the same clarity and conviction of those whose faithfulness in their time led them to publish *The White Rose?* And of course the questions have their own relevance for the many who are no longer students, who are now living life in light of their university years, who are working to meaningfully connect their educations with their vocations.

The questions are complex, as are the answers. At our best we see and live through a glass darkly, understanding a little bit—sometimes—of what it will take to grow and sustain our hopes and dreams. But our thesis is this: during the critical years in which moral meaning is being formed in ways that last, students need to be people who

- develop a worldview that can make sense of life, facing the challenge of truth and coherence in an increasingly pluralist world;

- pursue a relationship with a teacher whose life incarnates the worldview the student is learning to embrace;

- commit themselves to others who have chosen to live their lives embedded in that same worldview, journeying together in truth after the vision of a coherent and meaningful life.

Is this a guarantee of the good life? We can never engineer human happiness, of course. And yet we can listen and learn, doing our best to understand the world that God has made and our place in it. But when the day is done, every truly good life is always, first and last, a story of grace.

And yet grace, as it is known in time and space, is embodied in flesh-and-blood history. It is always set amid the struggles between *telos* and *praxis,* between one's dreams, aspirations and hopes and one's concrete experience in the ordinary demands of daily life. In the face of the tensions which are there for students in every time and every place, we have explored what is involved in helping them learn to see and act responsibly.

Interacting with literature and film as well as in academic conversations within the disciplines of philosophy, theology and sociology, we have attempted to understand how moral meaning can be formed against the pressures implicit within the modern world and the modern university. The retrospective interviews have made clear that there are certain habits of heart which characteristically direct people toward an integrity between belief and behavior. But we have also argued that there are several interpretative lenses which together provide a more adequate understanding of the complexity concerning the formation of what one sees and how one acts.

These two strands are critically dependent on each other. The more inductive conclusions about the framing of a worldview, the finding of a mentor and the forming of lifelong relationships echo off of the more deductive conclusions about the necessity of listening in on the disciplines of the history of ideas, the ethic of character and the sociology of knowledge.

Though a worldview is always more than a set of ideas, it is never less than a constellation of convictions which have a prepositional dimension. To understand the character of someone's convictions, at some point, requires an understanding of that person's intellectual history, not only the books they have read and the settings in which they have studied, but also the books and settings of their teachers, and their teachers' teachers. And on and on. Ideas do have a history.

But their history is never abstracted—it always has a "blood-stained face," as Camus put it so poignantly.[24] Ideas inherently have legs, human legs. And so we must understand that finding a mentor who incarnates the worldview is one side of a reality whose other side is that the ethic of character teaches that beliefs are most clearly seen in behavior. For a student to truly understand the content of his convictions he must see them lived. Both the history of reflection on the nature of pedagogy and the analysis of the interviews indicate that students need to see their worldview incarnated in the lives of their teachers, if it is to be grasped in a way that can make sense of life for life.

But our study also shows that teachers and mentors, on their own, are insufficient models. As crucial as they are, their role is to act as a bridge into a larger, more communal embodiment of the convictions the student is learning to live with. For those who take their university-framed ideas about what is real and true and right and deepen rather than discard them as they move into the responsibilities of adulthood, they have seen a social construction of their beliefs in the life of communities along the way. Often more stumbling than strategic, they have time and again found themselves among like-minded people whose own deepest beliefs are incarnated in a common life.

How does someone decide which cares and commitments will give shape and substance to life, for life? These bifocal lenses—developing a worldview, set alongside the history of ideas; being drawn into relationship with a teacher who incarnates that worldview, set alongside the ethic of character; seeing one's worldview embedded in a community of character, set alongside the sociology of knowledge—provide depth and breadth as we continue to ask and answer that question which has wound its way through the book from beginning to end.

LEARNING TO MAKE SENSE OF LIFE, FOR LIFE

In his delightful story of the beginning of Narnia, *The Magician's Nephew,* C. S. Lewis steps away from his narrative account of its first day and tries to explain why the magician, Uncle Andrew, and his nephew, Digory, see the new world so differently. The magician wants to flee from it, seeing it as a cacaphony of confusion and chaos, while the nephew is drawn into it more and more deeply, seeing it as a wonder of wonders. Lewis maintains, "For what you see and hear depends a good deal on where you are standing; it also depends on what sort of person you are."[25] A worldview and a way of life together shape cares and commitments.

Less imaginatively, and yet with penetrating insight into the nature of the imagination, Dykstra argues:

The imagination's possibility and potency are rooted in images. An image is "an internalized, essentially private, pattern of symbols, pictures, sounds and sensations of all varieties." As human beings, we are bombarded constantly by sensations of light, touch, smell, sound and taste. But these do not come to us nakedly. We receive them as beings who sense our own internal bodily movements in relation to them, and as beings who respond to these stimuli in the light of our memories, expectations and affections. The work of the imagination is to compose all of these external and internal stimuli into meaningful and apprehensible wholes-in sum, into images.

Our very consciousness rests on an unceasing flow of such images, which are constantly being related to one another in particular moments and over extended periods of time. The configurations of images that constitute the shape of each person's imagination determine what we can and do see, think and feel, and hence, how we act.[26]

Seeing, thinking, feeling and acting—they are what makes us human, in both our glory and our shame. From Augustine's anguished move from adolescence to adulthood, to Solzhenitsyn's story of a young man's wrestling with his worldview, on to Kurosawa's portrayal of a young doctor finally finding a calling rather than merely a career, we have explored the ways in which the integral connection between what we believe about the world and how we live in the world is given shape and substance. Somewhere, deep in the mysteries of how we learn to see and hear, and what we learn to care for and about, there is a place where presupposition meets practice, where belief becomes behavior. The reality of Iris Murdoch's insight is there for all of us to ponder: "At crucial moments of choice most of the business of choosing is already over."[27]

Worldviews do become ways of life, always and everywhere. Hans Scholl's too-truthful taunt "Why don't we rent ourselves an island in the Aegean and offer courses on woridviews?" and his sister Sophie's plain, yet plaintive, "Somebody, after all, had to make a start" reflect beliefs about meaning and morality ground out in the bloody face of history. Their beliefs were never an abstraction. Instead, in their simplicity there is a strength which teaches all of us about the formation of moral meaning during the university years—they are a time for negotiating the issues and ideas of life, of deciding what matters most and what difference it will make. Choices about meaning, reality and truth, about God, human nature and history are being made which, more often than not, last for the rest of life.

Learning to make sense of life, for life, is what the years between adolescence and adulthood are all about.

ONE MORE STORY OF STUDENTS

One fall, not so long ago, I was asked to speak at the College Weekend at Windy Gap, a wonderful Young Life training facility set in a beautiful little valley in the mountains of North Carolina. Some four hundred students gathered from universities and colleges, large and small, all over the Southeast. I can hardly think of a school that was not there. From the University of Virginia in the north, to the University of Florida in the south, to Louisiana State University in the west, students from Davidson, University of North Carolina, Duke, Wake Forest, Clemson, University of South Carolina, Erskine, Florida State, Emory, Georgia Tech, Covenant, Mississippi State, Tulane, and on and on, came "home" to Windy Gap, for a weekend in memory of their best high-school times.

I have friends who are "Young Life personalities," and I treasure them for it; I am not. I suppose that gave me the greatest nervousness in preparing for the weekend's talks. But I did my best to bring a variety of resources to bear on the task at hand: stories, music, film—even a few jokes! I wanted to walk between the Word and the world, offering them a vision of life in the kingdom, particularly reflecting on its requisite virtues.

I started off with a look at "how *not* to get all A's and flunk life," setting up a weekend of focus on those who grow up and into their faith with an integrity of heart and mind that can still make sense of a Young Life weekend— with its opportunity to "laugh your way into the most serious things of life"— forty years later. That night I introduced them to some of the themes from the first half of this book—the challenge of the cultural context for college students who want a life of integrity (drawing on themes from *Reality Bites*, U2's *Zooropa*, Beavis and Butthead). We looked at the parable of the sower, seed and soils (Mt 13). I asked the question "What kind of soil are you?"

Over the next three talks I offered them the substance of what I have
learned in this study, setting out the habits of heart of those who keep on
keeping on, whose love for Christ makes sense of life over the course of life.
"Gimme Some Truth" (a song by Sam Phillips on her album *Martinis & Bikinis*)[28] took us into "Habits of Heart #1: Framing a Worldview." From
Solzhenitsyn's story of a student to Calvin Klein's soft-porn ads, we looked
at the difficulty of *really* being in the world, but not being of it, especially
over the matter of truth and truthfulness. I wanted them to understand that
Christian convictions, shaped as they are by the Hebrew worldview—particularly its understanding of *knowing*—explicitly and implicitly connect
what we believe with how we live. And so truth cannot be something we
hold to "theoretically" with no real-life consequence. Knowing and doing,
hearing and obeying are integrally connected for people whose convictions
are truly and deeply Christian. Studying the Beatitudes together that morning gave us a window into that reality, as Jesus presents a picture of doctrine
and discipleship woven together in the lives of those who are blessed and
who are a blessing.

That night we looked at "Habits of Heart #2: Finding Teachers," asking
in a variety of ways Augustine's question, "What do you love?" After looking
at what Joe Montana and Steve Young, two of the greatest quarterbacks ever,
had in common—the same coach, Bill Walsh—we even spent some time examining the "Young Life personality," wondering out loud how "it" gets
passed on so well, generation after generation of staff and students. As we
looked at several stories of Jesus with people, each a different picture of
"where your treasure is, there your heart will be also," we finished by thinking about the reality that "most of who you will be, in terms of your commitments and convictions about what really matters—what you love—will
be in direct relation to who your teachers are."

And finally, Sunday morning we examined "Habits of Heart #3: Forming
Friendships." The previous weekend I had taken my older children to the
best movie theater in Washington—a 1920s ambiance, with a balcony, a 70
mm screen and Dolby sound—to see *Apollo 13*. Its themes of dependence
and providence are captured in part by the grateful greeting of astronaut Jim
Lovell (played by Tom Hanks): "It's great to see you again. . . . I'm thinking

of the thousands of people who worked to get us home." The film portrays something of our profound need for community *to get us home*. After looking at the friendship of Jonathan and David, and the call in Hebrews 10—11 to persevere in community, I asked, "Who are your friends? What kind of friend are you? What is your relationship to the church? Do you see it as a sustaining institution, a fellowship of friends, which is critical in helping you keep your commitments and convictions?" I finished with the story of the White Rose, telling the tale of Hans and Sophie Scholl as an incarnation of convictions, character and community. Together we reflected on how "the Christian gospel became the criterion of their thoughts and actions."

Before the weekend was over, one student—the editor of the newspaper at University of North Carolina at Chapel Hill—told me that she and her roommates had been talking late the night before about the weekend, and about my talks. I was nervous, feeling sure I had not told enough jokes! But then she said, "We all concluded, 'This isn't typical Young Life . . . but that's okay.'" She did not hear my "thanks be to God" as I smiled back, relieved that she had heard something worth hearing. (Of course, I had no desire to be "untypical" Young Life; it is simply that I am dispositionally unable! In the strangeness of history, several years later I was eating at a sidewalk café on Capitol Hill, and a young woman walked up to me, identifying herself as my breakfast companion from that morning, saying that "our conversation at Windy Gap is the reason I'm in Washington"—and I smiled, completely surprised.)

Through it all, one message came clear: these students were just like other students I have known—they want a faith that is coherent. In the conversations I had that weekend, and in the correspondence and conversations I have had since then, time and again students have asked me about the development of habits of heart and mind which will nurture a life of integrity between what they believe and how they live. Human beings as human beings, made in the image of God, long for that, in every generation and culture, anywhere and everywhere. These students were no different. As they talked to me about their studies, for example, there was a consistent desire to connect the reality of their personal faith in Christ with the challenges and complexities of their course work—and yet so many had no idea where and how to begin. As one student wrote me afterward:

> I'm a junior at the University of North Carolina . . . and have just ar-
> rived back from the college weekend you spoke at. Listening to your
> message this weekend has sent my mind reeling into new directions
> with my walk with Christ. Sharing stories of your students as they
> struggle to understand their role in the world touched me. . . . Your
> questions probed my mind and heart simultaneously and created
> great excitement. Now that I know that there is education that really
> educates, I am hopeful. During the middle of my sophomore year I
> found myself disconnected from my studies. I feel that my academic
> life is removed from the life Jesus has given me, and that the two don't
> meet. The questions you asked this weekend are not easily answered,
> but I would like to try.

This young man also came to Washington, and I watched him "try," answering the questions with a deepening sense of vocation that eventually
took him to graduate school at St. John's College in Annapolis, to a school
in the slums of Nairobi for two years and into marriage. He is now a teacher
himself, helping students to think and to care about the way the world is and
ought to be.

I meet students like this everywhere I go. It is for them, and for those who
care for them, that this book is written. But it is also for those whose pilgrim-
ages have taken them beyond their college years, who are scattered all over
the face of the earth, in worship and work learning about God's world and
discovering their place in it.

Epilogue

The Vocation of Healed Healers

Why is it that when we pray together, as the people of God gathered for worship on Sunday, we regularly pray for our missionaries in Kenya and Kazakhstan, but not for our attorneys on K Street?

A number of years ago I joined several friends for a conversation about the relation of the church's ministry to the callings of God's people. While wide-ranging, we eventually got to that question.

In the vocational geography of Washington, D.C., K Street represents Lord Bismarck's hard-won wisdom: "If you want to respect sausage or law, then don't watch either being made." It is a long avenue running east and west across the city, just a couple of blocks away from the White House at one point. With high-rise buildings, and full of cars and people, it is sometimes more crassly referred to as "Gucci Gulch" because of the shoes-of-choice characteristic of the highly paid lawyers and lobbyists employed there.

It seemed to those of us at lunch that day that the butchers and bakers and candlestick-makers of the kingdom needed to understand their work as blessed by God and prayed for by God's people just as much as did those whose callings take them to the far places of the earth as Bible translators, church planters, evangelists and pastors. So, while we said aloud "Yes!" to the importance of praying for Kenya and Kazakhstan, we pleaded for K Street too.

Now written into our weekly liturgy is a time of simple, heart-felt prayer for a handful of people, by name and by vocation. So-and-so, a journalist. So-and-so, a businessman. So-and-so, an attorney. So-and-so, a builder. So-and-so, a teacher. So-and-so, a politician. So-and-so, a homemaker. So-and-so, a social worker. And on and on and on. It is a good discipline because it reminds us that we are in this together, that we are a congregation taking up the ministry of truth and grace in our terribly fallen world, through our callings creating what Walker Percy called "signposts in a strange world"— even and especially signposts of the world that is to come.

Reflecting on this history, I said yes a few weeks ago to an invitation to speak to a gathering of attorneys on K Street. Month by month they meet under the banner of the Christian Legal Society for a lunch conversation over some aspect of the vocation of law. Men and women, older and younger, private and public—about thirty lawyers from across the city sat around a beautiful conference room with spacious views of the city to consider one more time the challenge of thinking and acting Christianly in the world of work.

I began with a story of a recent conversation. At the end of a weekend retreat where I had spoken on the dynamic relationship between faith, vocation and culture, a man came up to talk. An Englishman living in the New York City area, he said that "for twenty-five years I have prayed for God to be present in my work, and I think he has been. But doing what I have done, the business of technology and computers, I have had the aching sense that my work is a bit less than what it might be if I was a more serious Christian, that somehow business as a vocation is 'second-class' for a devoted follower of Christ. But I want you to know that during this weekend a wound in my heart has been healed." He smiled, and I smiled back, breathing in my heart *thanks be to God.*

And I wondered aloud to these attorneys: "What is the wound about? Where does it come from? What does it mean?"

Various ones offered insights, knowing as little about the man as they did, but all together a picture began to develop of someone whose understanding of his calling had been misshaped by things said and not said, prayed for and not prayed for, as the people of God come together to worship, to preach and to pray, to sing and to be silent.

Situating the story of the man whose wound had been healed within the larger vision of The Washington Institute, with our commitment to developing a coherent understanding of the way that faith forms vocation, and, in turn, that vocation forms culture, I set forth this thesis: what we believe about the most important things in life affects the way that we live in the world; but the reverse is also true: the way that we live and the world in which we live affect what we believe. So culture does shape faith, just as it does vocation. We are more whole people than we know, because of the mysterious and profound twining together of belief and behavior, of world-view and way of life, in ways that shape our very souls.

This is true whether we are lawyers or architects, builders or bankers, musicians or journalists, physicians or educators, teachers or politicians, whether our work takes us to the church building or to the corporate office, whether our passions are for human rights or the arts, for little children or for senior citizens, for the complexities of our local communities or of the continents of Asia or Africa. Day after day our work puts us right in the middle of these kinds of people, drawing them together into "conversations of consequence," listening as we think through a wider, richer understanding of the ways that belief and behavior echo across the whole of life, everywhere for everyone.

I then began to tell the stories of our two "patron saints" at The Washington Institute for Faith, Vocation & Culture—George Washington and William Wilberforce; I had brought books by and about both, and I explained that pictures of them and their work adorn our walls. We have been intrigued by these men, but even more we have been formed by them. In unique and remarkable ways, they offer windows into the faith/vocation/culture dynamic that is the heart of our work. Perhaps most important for us is that both saw themselves as implicated in history, as responsible for history, for the way the world is and ought to be—and that commitment plainly grew out of a thoughtfully framed understanding of faith and vocation, of creed and calling.

Acknowledging that while I had long honored Washington's military and political leadership at the most critical point in our nation's history, for years I had dismissed him as "another deist" among the founding fathers. I explained why over the last few years I have revisited the question of his faith. I do live in Washington, and his life and story shape the city. I am a member of The Falls Church, an almost-three-hundred-year-old Anglican congregation that at one point counted Washington as a member of the vestry; our historic church building was planned while he served in that role. I have listened to my rector, a holy and thoughtful man, every once in a while weave Washington into his sermons, helping his congregation understand the honest faith of this man whose name graces our city and whose gifts graced our church.

We see through a glass darkly—even when it comes to patron saints! But we are able to listen and learn, even from those who have long-ago lived and died. From what I have read, I offered some account of Washington's life, of the way that his Anglican beliefs formed his understanding of what he was to do and why he was to do it, all with an unnaturally keen eye to the meaning of his calling for the future history of the United States. *Faith. Vocation. Culture.*

One resource in particular that I drew upon is the recent biography *Washington's God* by Michael and Jana Novak, which tells the tale of Washington's life through the prism of his Anglican heritage and the landscape of faith in eighteenth-century Virginia. The central story is that Washington was shaped by both, not surprisingly. His understanding of God, human nature and history reflected the years of creedal and liturgical formation that was plainly part of life for someone who kept making the choice to worship God as Anglicans did and still do. But he was also a Virginian and a gentleman at that, and so the enthusiasm for faith that characterized Anglicans in England—such as Wilberforce—under the influence of the "methodism" of the Wesleys and Whitefield was foreign to his experience.

The Novaks take great care to understand the deism of eighteenth-century America, and especially the ways that Washington's God was decidedly different than Jefferson's. A deep, sustained, articulate understanding of providence is evident in the worldview of Washington, whereas a God who knows and cares, a God who sees and hears and feels—and expects his people to do so as well—was anathema to Jefferson. Against tremendous obstacles, from the most personal to the most political, Washington continued to believe that God was in heaven and that his purposes were being worked out on earth through the responsible and irresponsible choices of human beings.

The painting of Washington on our wall is by Gilbert Stuart, and shows the great man's head and shoulders, but below that his portrait is incomplete. We like that, as it is a visual metaphor for the incomplete character of Washington's connecting of faith to vocation to culture. Some ideas and issues he understood with unusual insight; he had an uncanny ability to understand his moment, and his responsibility in it. His calling kept calling him. Perhaps most important of all was his perseverance, the steadfast grace and courage that kept him going when the world, the flesh and the devil stared him and history in the face. A true hero who was extruded by God and history to step into his time and offer crucial leadership when no one else could have done so, he was also a man who saw through a glass darkly—like each of us.

At that point I introduced the paradigm that is the core curriculum of The Washington Institute. Articulated most clearly in *The Fabric of Faithfulness,* we believe that there are habits of heart that develop and sustain visions of faith and the vocations that grow out of them. Because we find ourselves face-to-face with Lord Bismarck's insight about sausage and law, sausage and business, sausage and education, sausage and the arts, sausage and medicine, sausage and international development, sausage and architecture, and feel the weight of the world upon bearing down upon us, we believe that over time our convictions can deepen and our callings can become clarified, rather than the more common experience of a discarded faith and a misdirected vocation,. It is not inevitable that growing up makes us cynical about the very possibility of a coherent life.

What are these habits of heart? Forming a worldview that can make sense of my life in the ever-secularizing, ever-pluralizing world, of my beliefs about God and truth, the human condition, good and evil, joy and sorrow; finding a mentor who embodies these convictions, as the truest truths are taught and learned only as we look over the shoulder and through the heart of someone who shows that the words can be made flesh, that the ideas can have legs; and making the choice time and again to link up, heart and mind, with a community of kindred spirits, people who together are committed to a coherent life where liturgy, life, learning and labor is understood as seamless.

Wilberforce's worldview offers another vision of the ways that faith, vocation and culture affect each other. In sum, of course, this is what every worldview is and does: it provides a way to understand the meaning of faith, vocation and culture—from the most secular understanding of life and the world to the most transcendent.

Born into a home much like Washington's, the merchant and landed class of the eighteenth-century British empire, he was raised in an Anglican world. Among those he met as a young man was the former slave captain and now pastor, John Newton, who was a friend of Wilberforce's family. He was sent off to Cambridge and lived a fairly dissolute life during his university years: drinking, playing and sometimes studying. Upon graduation he entered the House of Commons, representing his home district. A few years later he did a European tour and employed Isaac Milner, a Cambridge don, as a traveling companion. Over the miles of travel they talked long and hard about all sorts of topics, religious faith among them. Milner was a devout follower of Christ; he was "awakened" in his Anglican faith and was what today might be called an evangelical.

By amazing grace Wilberforce found his way to faith, and his first inclination was to leave politics—ungodly, unholy mess as it was (and is). *How can I, now a serious Christian, be involved in something as dirty as politics?* he wondered. Perplexed, he sought out his old friend, knocking on the door of Newton, asking what he should do. The old and wise man pleaded with him to stay engaged in his vocation, but to do so fired by his new faith, Queen Esther-like—for just such a moment as this— "to take up the abolition of slavery."

It is a long story, well-told in several books, but for us, the way that Wilberforce so purposefully pursued the formation of a Christian mind is instructive: reading and reflecting over many years, learning to think critically and carefully as a Christian whose vocation was public justice, the work of politics. Quite deliberately he apprenticed himself to Milner and to Newton, opening his heart and hopes to these godly teachers who walked along with him as he was learning to live within the contours of Christian faith. And finally—and this was crucial—he also gave his life to a community of like-minded, like-hearted companions, fellow pilgrims of diverse vocations (business, banking, education, the clergy, politics) who determined to live near each other in a neighborhood called Clapham, day by day eating, talking, praying, playing, thinking together.

To what end? They had two great objects: the reformation of manners and the abolition of slavery. The first is what we would call the renewal of the social fabric. They understood that there would be no political address of slavery without the culture believing that it was no longer acceptable for human beings to buy and sell other human beings. Among my friends here in Washington we put it this way, paying careful attention to the Clapham community: culture is "upstream" from politics. And so Washington matters. Bono does have to come here to plead for Africa—and yet there are countless families and neighborhoods, cities and schools, churches, synagogues, and mosques, that are culture-forming too. And in a moment when, economically speaking, the largest export of the United States to the rest of the world is popular culture, the cities of New York, Nashville and Los Angeles matter immensely. The second of the great objects was a huge undertaking, as the slave trade and its related enterprises were the primary economic engine of the British empire. Everyone and everything—politically, economically, socially—was connected to the slave trade. And so it was no small thing to take up its abolition.

In the story of Wilberforce do you hear the habits of heart that give us the skills to keep at our posts over a lifetime, deepening convictions and commitments as we live into the meaning of our vocations and occupations? Simply said, for Wilberforce as for each of us, they are *a worldview, a mentor* and *a community.*

Comparing and contrasting our two patron saints at these three decisive points, Wilberforce's life was more coherent than Washington's—even while we deeply honor both. For example, ponder their respective communities. The Mount Vernon setting of Washington's life, the beautiful plantation along the Potomac that is now a national treasure, is a very different place from Wilberforce's Clapham neighborhood, now subsumed in the suburb we know as Wimbledon. While Washington's table had regular visitors, he had no friends and neighbors, no men and women thinking, praying, working together on the founding of a nation. (It gives us heartache, even as we realize the historical context, that his local community was made up of his slaves.) Adams was in Boston and Jefferson was at Monticello, hours and days away from Mount Vernon; but even more sadly, they were not kindred spirits, caring for each other as they together cared for their culture.

Well, the story goes on, and we find ourselves telling it again and again. My colleague Ray Blunt is especially good at doing so in public sector settings, in courses and conferences across the country, creatively and winsomely engaging people in consideration of these two lives and what we can still learn from them.

As the lunchtime came to a conclusion, I finished with the lawyers by acknowledging that "few of us will be a Washington or a Wilberforce"—even as we learn and listen to the ways that they held together Christian faith, a strong sense of vocation and a compelling understanding of their responsibility for culture. And we do not need to be. Our callings will take us to different places, to different relationships and different responsibilities. Our lives feel more ordinary, and that is the way it ought to be. Sausage-making, after all, is pretty ordinary business, messy as it is.

Kenya, Kazakhstan and K Street too? Yes . . . that all of God's people might love and serve him with gladness and singleness of heart, in our various vocations taking the wounds of the world into our hearts—the heartaches and longings, sorrows and disappointments, and sometimes evil—and finding in that calling that our own hearts are healed too. In N. T. Wright's theologically rich image, becoming *healed healers*. May it be so.

Notes

Introduction

[1]The notion of "moral meaning" is central to this study, as it captures the dynamic interrelation between one's convictions about meaning and morality, about what one believes and how one lives. In a collection of readings intended to "continue the conversation" which the seminal work *Habits of the Heart: Individualism and Commitment in American Life* began, Steven Tipton, one of the four authors, argues: "Styles of ethical evaluation by themselves are empty analytical categories. They take on substance only when they are applied in turn to the different layers of moral meaning that make up social life. These include (1) cultural historical patterns of morality like biblical religion, which support (2) the norms of social institutions like the family, and underlie (3) the formal ethics of ideological organizations like *est*, which inform (4) the ethical outlook of persons in a particular place in society at a particular time in their own lives and in history, like middle-class sixties youth. Only when styles of ethical evaluation link the other elements that make up moral understanding—that is, perceptions of facts, loyalties to others and axial assumptions about the nature of reality—do these analytical categories reveal a living ethic by which persons make particular judgments." Robert Bellah et al., *Habits of the Heart: Individualism and Commitment in American Life* (San Francisco: Harper & Row, 1986), pp. 359-60.

[2]Augustine, *Confessions,* trans. F. J. Sheed (New York: Sheed & Ward, 1943), pp. 22-23.

[3]Erik Erikson, *Insight and Responsibility: Lectures on the Ethical Implications of Psychoanalytic Insight* (New York: W. W. Norton, 1964), p. 138.

[4]Augustine, *Confessions,* p. 105.

[5]Ibid., pp. 105-6.

[6]Ibid., p. 139.

[7]Ibid.

[8]Andre Jardine, *Tocqueville: A Biography,* trans. Lydia Davis and Robert Hemenway (New York: Farrar, Straus & Giroux, 1988), p. 61.

[9]Ibid.

[10]David Fricke, "Smashing Pumpkins: The *Rolling Stone* Interview with Billy Corgan," *Rolling Stone,* 16 November 1995, p. 52. I am indebted to my son David for working with me to help me understand the music of his generation.

[11]Smashing Pumpkins, "Zero," *Mellon Collie and the Infinite Sadness* (Virgin Records, 1995).

[12]Augustine, *The Enchiridion on Faith, Hope and Love* (Chicago: Regnery Gateway, 1961), p. xi.

Chapter 1: Learning to Care

[1]Jacques Ellul, *Reason for Being: A Meditation on Ecclesiastes* (Grand Rapids: Eerdmans, 1990), pp. 282-83. For an introduction to the thought of Ellul, see the book-length interview in Ellul's *In Season, Out of Season* (San Francisco: Harper & Row, 1982). Among his forty other books in the areas of theology and social criticism, *The Technological Society* (New York: Vintage Books, 1964) is perhaps his best known.

[2]Philip Kaufman, director, *The Unbearable Lightness of Being,* with Daniel Day-Lewis, Juliette Binoche and Lena Olin (Saul Zaentz, 1987).

[3]Milan Kundera, *The Unbearable Lightness of Being* (New York: Harper & Row, 1991), p. 4.

[4]Ibid., p. 193.

[5]Uri Barbash, director, *Beyond the Walls,* with Arnon Zadok, Muhamad Bakri and Assi Dayan (Israel, 1984).

[6]Sharon Parks, *The Critical Years: Young Adults and the Search for Meaning, Faith and Commitment* (San Francisco: Harper & Row, 1986). See also William Perry, *Forms of Intellectual and Ethical Development in the College Years: A Scheme* (New York: Rinehart & Winston, 1968); Erik Erikson, "Human Strength and the Cycle of Generations," in *Insight and Responsibility: Lectures on the Ethical Implications of Psychoanalytic Insight* (New York: W. W. Norton, 1964); Daniel Levinson, *The Seasons of a Man's Life* (New York: Knopf, 1978).

[7]George Steiner, *Real Presences* (Chicago: University of Chicago Press, 1989), p. 6.

[8]Jerram Barrs's theological insight and tutorial care were a great encouragement to me. His thinking on these questions eventually grew into a book done with a L'Abri colaborer: Ranald Macaulay and Jerram Barrs, *Being Human: The Nature of Spiritual Experience* (Downers Grove, Ill.: InterVarsity Press, 1978).

[9]Francis Schaeffer, *The God Who Is There* (Downers Grove, Ill.: InterVarsity Press, 1968); *He Is There and He Is Not Silent* (Wheaton, Ill.: Tyndale, 1972); *True Spirituality* (Wheaton, Ill.: Tyndale,1971); and *Escape from Reason* (Downers Grove, Ill.: InterVarsity Press, 1968); Donald Drew, *Images of Man: A Critique of the Contemporary Cinema* (Downers Grove, Ill.: InterVarsity Press, 1974); Os Guinness, *The Dust*

of Death (Downers Grove, Ill.: InterVarsity Press, 1973); Hans Rookmaaker, *Modern Art and the Death of a Culture* (Downers Grove, Ill.: InterVarsity Press, 1970).

[10]"Thinking christianly" was first articulated by a student of C. S. Lewis, Harry Blamires, whose work on the need for a distinctly Christian mind opened a generation-long discussion. Harry Blamires, *The Christian Mind* (London: SPCK, 1963).

[11]Paulo Friere, *Pedagogy of the Oppressed* (New York: Herder & Herder, 1972), p. 19.

[12]Craig Dykstra and Sharon Parks, eds., *Faith Development and Fowler* (Birmingham: Religious Education Press, 1986), p. 61.

[13]*Faith Development and Fowler* is a critical study of the discipline of faith development, edited by two of its most thoughtful scholars, Dykstra and Parks.

[14]James Fowler, *Stages of Faith: The Psychology of Human Development and the Quest for Meaning* (San Francisco: Harper & Row, 1981); *Becoming Adult, Becoming Christian: Adult Development and Christian Faith* (New York: Harper & Row, 1984); and *Weaving the New Creation: Stages of Faith and the Public Church* (New York: Harper-Collins, 1991); and James Fowler and Sam Keen, *Life-Maps: Conversations on the Journey of Faith* (Waco, Tex.: Word Books, 1978).

[15]In a penetrating critique of Fowler's understanding of "faith," Harry Fernhout of Toronto's Institute for Christian Studies argues that faith comes to mean too much for Fowler and therefore that it is conceptually difficult to distinguish faith development from human development. See Fernhout, "Where Is Faith? Searching for the Core of the Cube," in *Faith Development and Fowler,* pp. 65-89.

[16]Fowler, *Becoming Adult, Becoming Christian,* pp. 71-75. See also Dykstra, "Faith Development and Religious Education," in *Faith Development and Fowler,* pp. 253-54.

[17]Fowler, *Stages of Faith,* p. 201.

[18]In their introduction, Dykstra and Parks write, "The combination of a powerful nurturing in a particular faith community and subculture together with an introduction in young adulthood to the many ways there are of seeing and being in the world often leads to a kind of 'vertigo of relativity.'. . . A kind of skepticism develops when one encounters one system of meaning after another and they all seem plausible. It is the very plausibility of them all that seems to undermine each in turn" (*Faith Development and Fowler,* p. 4).

[19]In Levinson, it is the "settling down" stage, which often has as its underlying task "settling for" what is going to be important: the cares and commitments which will give shape and substance to one's life, for life. See Levinson, *The Seasons of a Man's Life,* pp. 139-65.

[20]With characteristic thoughtful insight, Sharon Parks observes, "The journey of faith can take us to new vistas of knowing, to deepened realms of trust and to ever-widening circles of belonging. I wish to describe some of the perils and promises of this experience as it may occur in adulthood by tracing three discrete strands of

development: form of cognition, form of dependence and form of community." Though we are from different times and places and use different analytical tools, our common effort to understand what she terms "the journey toward mature faith" has resulted in remarkably similar conclusions. Park, *The Critical Years,* p. 43.

[21]Those terms offer us contours to understand the historical and social embodiment of ideas, and yet at the same time they can sometimes mislead us if we think too much about the uniqueness of our own moment. While we ought to listen carefully to our own time, working hard to understand centuries and generations and the ways that they are unique, it is possible to make too much of the differences. For example, we will never become a "postmodern" world, having moved beyond the "modern" world as long as Dulles International Airport requires the services of air traffic controllers who rely on mutually agreed upon mathematical models to chart the course of airplanes flying miles overhead. In some situations, the "whatever" of postmodernism is simply silly—and so, even at its best, its understanding of narratives, perspectives and voices offers very little insight into why and how we live, still rooted as we are and must be in the "modern" world.

[22]Ellul, *Reason for Being,* pp. 282-83.

Chapter 2: The Problem and Its Parameters

[1]Robert Bellah et al., *Habits of the Heart: Individualism and Commitment in American Life* (San Francisco: Harper & Row, 1986), p. 276.

[2]Joe Matthews, "Beavis, Butthead & Budding Nihilists: Will Western Civilization Survive?" *Washington Post,* October 3, 1993, p. C1.

[3]Alasdair MacIntyre, *After Virtue: A Study in Moral Theory* (Notre Dame, Ind.: University of Notre Dame Press, 1984); Richard Bernstein, *Beyond Objectivism and Relativism: Science, Hermeneutics and Praxis* (Philadelphia: University of Philadelphia Press, 1983).

[4]Walker Percy, *The Second Coming* (New York: Farrar, Straus & Giroux, 1980), pp. 32, 93.

[5]Robert Altman, director, *The Player,* with Tim Robbins, Greta Scacchi and Whoopi Goldberg (Guild Avenue, 1992).

[6]Graham Swift, director, *Waterland,* with Jeremy Irons, Sinead Cusack and Ethan Hawke (Mayfair/Palace/Pandora/Channel 4 Films/British Screen, 1992).

[7]Aristotle, *Nicomachean Ethics,* trans. Martin Ostwald (Indianapolis: The Library of Liberal Arts/Bobbs-Merrill Educational Publishing, 1962), pp. 3-4.

[8]W. F. R. Hardie, *Aristotle's Ethical Theory* (Oxford: Clarendon Press, 1980), p. 12.

[9]Aristotle, *Nicomachean Ethics,* pp. 17-18.

[10]Jacques Ellul, *The Technological Society* (New York: Vintage Books, 1964), p. 134.

[11]Aleksandr Solzhenitsyn, "The Relentless Cult of Novelty and How It Wrecked the

Century," *New York Times Book Review,* February 7, 1993, pp. 3, 17.
[12]Ibid., pp. 11-12.
[13]Bernstein, *Beyond Objectivism and Relativism,* p. 18.
[14]MacIntyre, *After Virtue,* p. 82.
[15]Bernstein, *Beyond Objectivism and Relativism,* p. 46.
[16]Henry Grunwald, "The Year 2000," *Time,* March 30, 1992, p. 75.
[17]George Steiner, *In Bluebeard's Castle: Some Notes Towards the Redefinition of Culture* (New Haven, Conn.: Yale University Press, 1971), p. 30.
[18]Ibid., p. 86.
[19]Ibid., p. 93.
[20]Ibid., p. 91.
[21]Ibid., p. 88.
[22]Robert Bellah, "The True and Final End: Bellah Responds to Bachelard," *Ethics and Policy* (Berkeley, Calif.: Center for Ethics and Social Policy, Fall 1994), p. 11.
[23]Lesslie Newbigin, *The Gospel in a Pluralist Society* (Grand Rapids: Eerdmans, 1989), p. 5.
[24]Thomas Kuhn, *The Structure of Scientific Revolutions* (Chicago: University of Chicago Press, 1986); Michael Polanyi, *Personal Knowledge: Towards a Post-Critical Philosophy* (Chicago: University of Chicago Press, 1958).
[25]Newbigin, *Gospel in a Pluralist Society,* pp. 37-38.
[26]Milan Kundera, *The Book of Laughter and Forgetting,* trans. Michael Henry Heim (New York: Penguin Books, 1981), p. 232.
[27]Robert Fryling, "Campus Portrait." Address presented at the National Staff Conference of InterVarsity Christian Fellowship, December 1992.
[28]Darren Walhof, letter to author, February 5, 1992.
[29]Mark Schwehn, *Exiles from Eden: Religion and the Academic Vocation in America* (New York: Oxford University Press, 1993), p. 94.
[30]Newbigin, *Gospel in a Pluralist Society,* p. 89.
[31]Ibid., p. 91.

Chapter 3: Education for What Purpose? Comepetence to What End?

[1]Robert Wuthnow, *The Consciousness Reformation* (Berkeley: University of California Press, 1976), p. 71.
[2]FOCUS (Fellowship of Christians in Universities and Schools) is a ministry to students in private, independent schools all along the Eastern seaboard, from Massachusetts to Florida. Its headquarters and its study center, the camp setting for its summer programs, are on Martha's Vineyard, Massachusetts.
[3]Fyodor Dostoyevsky, *Crime and Punishment* (New York: Penguin Books, 1951), p. 275.

[4]Ibid., p. 277.

[5]Ibid., p. 537.

[6]Leo Tolstoy, *Resurrection* (New York: Penguin Books, 1966), p. 74.

[7]Ibid., pp. 73-74.

[8]Ibid., p. 57.

[9]Aleksandr Solzhenitsyn, *The First Circle* (New York: Harper & Row, 1968), p. 493.

[10]Gordon Clark, *Thales to Dewey* (Boston: Houghton Mifflin, 1957), p. 150.

[11]Solzhenitsyn, *First Circle*, p. 553.

[12]Thomas Hardy, *Jude the Obscure* (New York: Penguin Books, 1985).

[13]Oliver Stone, director, *Platoon*, with Tom Berenger, Willem DaFoe and Charlie Sheen (Hemdale, 1986).

[14]Oliver Stone, director, *Wall Street*, with Charlie Sheen, Michael Douglas and Daryl Hannah (Edward R. Pressman/American, 1987).

[15]Fareed Zakaria, "Ethics for Greedheads: B.S. at Business School," *The New Republic*, October 19, 1987, pp. 18-20. For an analysis of this article and the larger questions it raises for American education, see Steve Garber, "The Question of Character," *Eternity*, September 1988, pp. 70-71.

[16]Zakaria, "Ethics for Greedheads," p. 20.

[17]In April 1991 I was invited by Deputy Assistant Secretary of the Navy Daniel Heimbach to join a small team of educators from throughout the Washington area to study the ethics curriculum at the Naval Academy. A more formal report done by the Office of the Assistant Secretary of Defense was submitted to the Senate Committee on Armed Services, "Ethics Instruction at the Service Academies" (March 1991). Our assessment was that the ethics instruction was steeped in moral skepticism and yet was still trying to develop in midshipmen the virtues "of duty, honor and loyalty." A year later I spoke at the Naval Academy to a group of seventy-five midshipmen; after my lecture several told me that "that is precisely the tension we feel ourselves in here."

[18]Ernest Boyer, *College: The Undergraduate Experience in America* (New York: Harper & Row, 1987), p. 283. For an interview with Boyer about his book, see Steve Garber, "Bringing Transcendent Values Back on Our Nation's College Campuses," *Eternity*, September 1987, p. 27. In addition, for an essay on the meaning of Boyer's book for people who care about higher education, see Steve Garber, "Interested in the University?" *Eternity*, September 1987, p. 28.

[19]Denys Arcand, director, *Jesus of Montreal*, with Lothaire Bluteau, Catherine Wilkening and Johanne-Marie Tremblay (Max Films/Gerard Mital Productions/NFB Canada, 1989).

[20]Ben Stiller, director, *Reality Bites*, with Winona Ryder, Ethan Hawke and Janeane Garofalo (Universal/Jersey Films, 1994).

[21]Milan Kundera, *The Book of Laughter and Forgetting*, trans. Michael Henry Heim

(New York: Penguin Books, 1981), p. 232.

[22]George Steiner, *Real Presences* (Chicago: University of Chicago Press, 1989), p. 4.

[23]Ibid., p. 6.

[24]Neil Postman and Charles Weingartner, *Teaching as a Subversive Activity* (New York: Delacorte Press, 1969); Neil Postman, *Amusing Ourselves to Death: Public Discourse in the Age of Show Business* (New York: Penguin Books, 1985); *The End of Education: Redefining the Value of School* (New York: Knopf, 1995).

[25]Neil Postman, *Technopoly: The Surrender of Culture to Technology* (New York: Knopf, 1992), p. xii.

[26]Ibid., pp. 185-86.

[27]Also see Henry Grunwald, who in his essay "The Year 2000" (*Time,* March 30, 1992) argues that "the ultimate irony, or perhaps tragedy, is that secularism has not led to humanism." For a longer look at his essay, see chapter 2.

[28]Robert Bellah et al., *Habits of the Heart: Individualism and Commitment in American Life* (San Francisco: Harper & Row, 1986); *The Good Society* (New York: Knopf, 1991).

[29]Bellah et al., *The Good Society,* p. 170.

[30]William Willimon and Thomas Naylor, *The Abandoned Generation: Rethinking Higher Education* (Grand Rapids: Eerdmans, 1995), p. 65.

[31]Ibid., pp. 38-39.

[32]Ibid., p. 61.

[33]Ibid.

[34]Ibid., p. 42.

[35]A fascinating analysis of Duke's motto and the educational debate over its meaning is taken up by two Duke graduates in the journal *Communio.* They note the irony in the inaugural address of its new president, Nannerl Keohane, "who took the occasion . . . to speak about this motto, which, she admitted, left her immediately 'uneasy' when she learned about it after taking the job. She noted that 'the motto has an archaic sound if one provides a literal translation—erudition and religion.' But it was not the archaic vocabulary that made Keohane uneasy. 'The emphasis on religion,' she confessed, 'seemed hard to square with the restless yearning for discovery, the staunch and fearless commitment to seek for truth wherever truth may be found that is the hallmark of a great university.' Religion, in other words, is hard to square with good scholarship." They go on to say, "The driving assumption behind scholarship in the modern academy has been that true, authentic scholarship can flourish only in an environment of 'academic freedom,' commonly understood as freedom of intellectual inquiry from all prior assumptions about nature, the world, human society, human destiny and especially God." Most of their essay is a thoughtful *apologia* for Catholic scholarship, arguing for "a spirituality of academic life" rooted in Bonaventure's insights. Michael Baxter and Frederick Bauerschmidt,

"*Erudito* Without *Religio?*: The Dilemma of Catholics in the Academy," *Communio: International Catholic Review,* Summer 1995.

[36]Marvin R. Wilson, *Our Father Abraham: Jewish Roots of the Christian Faith* (Grand Rapids: Eerdmans, 1989), pp. 298-300.

[37]H. I. Marrou, *A History of Education in Antiquity* (Madison: University of Wisconsin Press, 1994), pp. 186-91.

[38]Ibid., pp. 299-301.

[39]Ibid., pp. 334-35.

[40]Bertrand Russell, *Education and the Good Life* (New York: Boni & Liveright, 1926); Alfred North Whitehead, *The Aims of Education* (New York: New American Library, 1929); John Dewey, *Experience and Education* (New York: Collier, 1963); C. S. Lewis, *The Abolition of Man* (New York: Macmillan, 1947), and *That Hideous Strength: A Modern Fairy Tale for Grown-Ups* (New York: Macmillan, 1946); Jacques Barzun, *The American University* (New York: Harper & Row, 1968); Mortimer Adler, *Reforming Education: The Opening of the American Mind* (New York: Collier, 1990). In addition, these are excellent analyses: Allan Bloom, *The Closing of the American Mind: How Higher Education Has Failed Democracy and Impoverished the Souls of Today's Students* (New York: Simon & Schuster, 1987); Charles Habib Malik, *A Christian Critique of the University* (Downers Grove, Ill.: InterVarsity Press, 1982); George Marsden, *The Soul of the University: From Protestant Establishment to Established Nonbelief* (New York: Oxford University Press, 1994); Page Smith, *Killing the Spirit: Higher Education in America* (New York: Penguin Books, 1990).

[41]T. S. Eliot, "The Aims of Education," in *To Criticize a Critic* (New York: Farrar, Straus & Giroux, 1965), pp. 75-76.

[42]A number of satisfying critiques of this dominant myth have been written in the last generation. Included are Herman Dooyeweerd, *Roots of Western Culture: Pagan, Secular and Christian Options,* trans. John Kraay (Toronto: Wedge Publishing Foundation, 1979); Michael Polanyi, *Personal Knowledge: Towards a Post-Critical Philosophy* (Chicago: University of Chicago Press, 1958); Richard John Neuhaus, *The Naked Public Square: Religion and Democracy in America* (Grand Rapids: Eerdmans, 1984); and Roy Clouser, *The Myth of Religious Neutrality: An Essay on the Hidden Role of Religious Belief in Theories* (Notre Dame, Ind.: University of Notre Dame Press, 1991).

[43]Sharon Parks, *The Critical Years: Young Adults and the Search for Meaning, Faith and Commitment* (San Francisco: Harper & Row, 1986).

[44]In my own musings over this question, I have concluded that something like "discovering meaning" more accurately gets at the reality of life in God's world than does the image of "meaning-making." See Parks, *The Critical Years,* p. 14.

[45]Ibid., p. 133.

[46]Kundera, *Book of Laughter and Forgetting.*

[47]Peter Berger et al., *The Homeless Mind: Modernization and Consciousness* (New York: Random House, 1974), p. 94.

Chapter 4: Making Sense of It All

[1]Peter Berger et al., *The Homeless Mind: Modernization and Consciousness* (New York: Random House, 1974), p. 185.

[2]Basil Mitchell, *How to Play Theological Ping-Pong: Essays on Faith and Reason* (Grand Rapids: Eerdmans, 1990), pp. 32-33.

[3]Ibid., p. 33.

[4]Steve Turner, *Up to Date* (London: Hodder & Stoughton, 1985), pp. 138-39.

[5]Thomas Oden, "Then and Now: The Recovery of Patristic Wisdom," *The Christian Century,* December 12, 1990, p. 1168.

[6]Thomas Oden, *Two Worlds: Notes on the Death of Modernity in America and Russia* (Downers Grove, Ill.: InterVarsity Press, 1992), pp. 12-13.

[7]Ibid., pp. 32-33.

[8]Ibid., p. 36.

[9]Ibid., pp. 36-37.

[10]Robert Bellah et al., *The Good Society* (New York: Knopf, 1991), pp. 43-44.

[11]Robert Fryling, "Campus Portrait," from an address given by the Director of Campus Ministries of InterVarsity Christian Fellowship at their National Staff Conference, December 1992.

[12]Stanley Hauerwas, *Vision and Virtue: Essays in Christian Ethical Reflection* (Notre Dame, Ind.: University of Notre Dame Press, 1981).

[13]Ibid., p. 42.

[14]Ibid., p. 53.

[15]Stanley Hauerwas, with David Burrell, "Self-Deception and Autobiography: Reflections on Speer's *Inside the Third Reich*," in *Truthfulness and Tragedy* (Notre Dame, Ind.: University of Notre Dame Press, 1977).

[16]Ibid., p. 91.

[17]Ibid., pp. 93-94.

[18]Bill Moyers, taken from transcript of TV production, "The Truth About Lies," p. 15.

[19]Ibid., p. 95.

[20]Stanley Hauerwas and Thomas Shaffer, "Hope Faces Power: Thomas More and the King of England," *Christian Existence Today: Essays on Church, World and Living in Between* (Durham, N.C.: Labyrinth Press, 1988).

[21]Ibid., p. 199.

[22]Ibid.

[23]Ibid., p. 217.

[24]Ibid., pp. 200-201.

[25]Ibid.

[26]From a student's journal, done as an assignment for the American Studies Program. The words *telos* and *teleios* were used in a lecture that day. The first speaks to "the end or purpose of history" while the second speaks to "the end or purpose of an individual life." The question for the day had been, What is the relationship between my aspirations and ambitions, on the one hand, and my understanding of the meaning of history? To quote from the lecture: Do you have a *telos* sufficient to meaningfully orient your *praxis*, personally and publicly, over the course of life?

[27]Berger et al., *The Homeless Mind*, p. 40.

[28]Peter Berger and Thomas Luckman, *The Social Construction of Reality: A Treatise in the Sociology of Knowledge* (New York: Doubleday, 1966).

[29]Berger et al., *The Homeless Mind*, p. 12.

[30]Ibid., p. 158.

[31]Ibid., pp. 152-53.

[32]See Berger's analysis of "modernity and its discontents" where he argues, "Because of the religious crisis in modern society, social 'homelessness' has become metaphysical—that is, it has become 'homelessness' in the cosmos. This is very difficult to bear" (Berger et al., *The Homeless Mind*, p. 185). For Percy, who died in 1990, the first major biography tells his story with great skill, showing him to be a man situated in his century—in a sense "feeling" it in his very soul—as he wrote so knowingly about it. "Percy's imagination is most impressive in its power to show how we are quite literally constructed by our social and cultural ideolects" (Jay Tolson, *Pilgrim in the Ruins: A Life of Walker Percy* [Chapel Hill: University of North Carolina Press, 1992], p. 279).

[33]Gregory Wolfe, "A Stranger and a Pilgrim," *The Catholic World Report,* November 1991, p. 64.

[34]Tolson, *Pilgrim in the Ruins,* p. 245.

[35]Paul Gray, "Implications of Apocalypse: A Review of *The Thanatos Syndrome* by Walker Percy," *Time,* March 30, 1987, p. 71.

[36]Berger et al., "Pluralization of Social Life-Worlds," in *The Homeless Mind,* pp. 63-82.

[37]Robert Wuthnow et al., *Cultural Analysis: The Work of Peter Berger, Mary Douglas, Michel Foucalt and Jurgen Habermas* (Boston: Routledge Kegan Paul, 1984), p. 68.

[38]Laura Blumenfield, "X Marks His Spot: Author Doug Coupland and the Twenty-somethings," *Washington Post,* July 7, 1991, p. B1.

[39]Mike Royko, "Time Is on the Side of Generation X," *Chicago Tribune,* July 30, 1993, p. A3.

Chapter 5: A Worldview, a Way of Life

[1]Francis Schaeffer, *The God Who Is There* (Downers Grove, Ill.: InterVarsity Press, 1968), p. 169.

[2]James Ivory, director, *Howards End,* with Anthony Hopkins, Vanessa Redgrave, Helena Bonham Carter and Emma Thompson (Merchant Ivory/Film Four, 1992).

[3]E. M. Forster, *Howards End* (New York: Bantam Classic, 1985), p. 331.

[4]Jacques Ellul, *Reason for Being: A Meditation on Ecclesiastes* (Grand Rapids: Eerdmans,1990), pp. 282-83.

[5]Iris Murdoch, *The Sovereignty of Good* (New York: Schocken Books, 1971), p. 37.

[6]Basil Mitchell, *How to Play Theological Ping-Pong: Essays on Faith and Reason* (Grand Rapids: Eerdmans, 1990), p. 33.

[7]Woody Allen, director, *Annie Hall,* with Woody Allen and Diane Keaton (UA/Jack Rollins-Charles Joffe, 1977).

[8]Woody Allen, director, *The Purple Rose of Cairo,* with Mia Farrow, Jeff Daniels and Dianne Wiest (Orion/Jack Rollins-Charles Joffe, 1984).

[9]Woody Allen, director, *Hannah and Her Sisters,* with Woody Allen, Mia Farrow, Dianne Wiest and Michael Caine (Orion/Charles Joffe, Jack Rollins, 1979).

[10]Ellen Goodman, "Moral Lobotomy," *Washington Post,* April 3,1993, p. A23.

[11]Philip Rieff, *The Triumph of the Therapeutic* (New York: Harper & Row, 1966).

[12]Goodman, "Moral Lobotomy," p. A23.

[13]Milan Kundera, *The Unbearable Lightness of Being* (New York: Harper & Row, 1991), p. 4.

[14]Jerry London, director, *The Scarlet and the Black,* with Gregory Peck, Christopher Plummer and John Gielgud (1983).

[15]C. S. Lewis, *That Hideous Strength. A Modern Fairy Tale for Grown-Ups* (New York: Macmillan, 1946), p. 348.

[16]See his account of this at the end of chapter 2.

[17]See introduction to chapter 3.

[18]Lesslie Newbigin, "Certain Faith: What Kind of Certainty?" *Tyndale Bulletin* 44, no. 2 (1993): 339-50.

[19]Lesslie Newbigin, *Foolishness to the Greeks* (Grand Rapids: Eerdmans, 1986), and *The Gospel in a Pluralist Society* (Grand Rapids: Eerdmans, 1989).

[20]Steven Garber, "But We Don't Blink," *World,* May 18, 1991, p. 21.

Chapter 6: Masters, Mentors and Moral Meaning

[1]Oliver O'Donovan, *Resurrection and Moral Order* (Grand Rapids: Eerdmans, 1986), p. 92.

[2]Mark Schwehn, *Exiles from Eden: Religion and the Academic Vocation in America* (New York: Oxford University Press, 1993), pp. 5-9; Robert Bellah et al., *Habits of the Heart: Individualism and Commitment in American Life* (San Francisco: Harper & Row, 1986), p. 299.

[3]Richard Morrill, *Teaching Values in College: Facilitating Development of Ethical, Moral*

and Value Awareness in Students (San Francisco: Jossey-Bass, 1980), p. 113.

[4]Ibid., p. 115.

[5]For how various "student specialists" understand this difference, see Steven Garber, "Going First Class on the Titanic," *Christianity Today,* November 20, 1987, pp. 25-27.

[6]Alasdair MacIntyre, *After Virtue: A Study in Moral Theory* (Notre Dame, Ind.: University of Notre Dame Press, 1984), p. 38.

[7]Werner Jaeger, *Paideia: The Ideals of Greek Culture,* trans. Gilbert Highet (New York: Oxford University Press, 1986).

[8]I am grateful to Al Zambone, a graduate student at Catholic University, for his "heart and mind" friendship, which includes regular contributions to my reading, these letters being among them. John Leinenweber, *The Letters of Augustine* (Liguori, Mo.: Triumph Books, 1992), pp. 92-107.

[9]Ibid., p. 93.

[10]Ibid., p. 99.

[11]Richard John Neuhaus, ed., *Virtue Public & Private* (Grand Rapids: Eerdmans, 1984), p. 58.

[12]Stanley Hauerwas and Thomas Shaffer, "Hope Faces Power: Thomas More and the King of England," *Christian Existence Today: Essays on Church, World and Living in Between* (Durham, N.C.: Labyrinth Press, 1988), p. 217.

[13]Schwehn, *Exiles from Eden,* p. 13.

[14]Ibid., pp. 58-59.

[15]Ibid., pp. 60-61.

[16]Ibid., p. 61.

[17]For an examination of this thesis, see Steven Garber, "The Teacher as Revealer and Role Model: Education as a Reflection of the Incarnation," in *Faith Goes to Work: Reflections from the Marketplace,* ed. Robert Banks (Washington, D.C.: Alban Institute, 1993), pp. 93-106.

[18]Akira Kurosawa, director, *Red Beard,* with Toshiro Mifune, Yuzo Kayama and Yoshio Tsuchiya (Toho Company, 1965).

[19]James Goodwin, *Akira Kurosawa and Intertextual Cinema* (Baltimore, Md.: Johns Hopkins University Press, 1994), p. 139.

Chapter 7: The Context of a Common Life

[1]Langdon Gilkey, *Shantung Compound: The Story of Men and Women Under Pressure* (New York: Harper & Row, 1966), p. 233.

[2]Ben Stiller, director, *Reality Bites,* with Winona Ryder, Ethan Hawke and Janeane Garofalo (Universal/Jersey Films, 1994).

[3]Robert Jenson, "How the World Lost Its Story," *First Things,* October 1993, p. 20.

[4]Lesslie Newbigin, *The Gospel in a Pluralist Society* (Grand Rapids: Eerdmans, 1989), p. 91.

[5]Jenson, "How the World Lost Its Story," p. 21.

[6]Alasdair MacIntyre, *After Virtue: A Study in Moral Theory* (Notre Dame, Ind.: University of Notre Dame Press, 1984), pp. 33-34.

[7]James Davison Hunter, *The Culture Wars: The Struggle to Define America* (New York: HarperCollins/Basic,1991); and *Before the Shooting Begins* (New York: Free Press, 1994).

[8]Robert Bellah et al., *Habits of the Heart: Individualism and Commitment in American Life* (San Francisco: Harper & Row, 1986), p. vii.

[9]Ibid., p. 84.

[10]Peter Berger and Thomas Luckman, *The Social Construction of Reality: A Treatise in the Sociology of Knowledge* (New York: Doubleday, 1966), p. 163.

[11]Stanley Hauerwas, *The Community of Character: Toward a Constructive Christian Social Ethic* (Notre Dame, Ind.: University of Notre Dame Press, 1991), pp. 148-49.

[12]Berger and Luckman, *Social Construction of Reality*, p. 158.

Chapter 8: Conviction, Character, Community Incarnate

[1]Iris Murdoch, *The Sovereignty of Good* (New York: Schocken Books, 1971), p. 37.

[2]Michael Verhoeven, director, *The White Rose*, with Lena Stolze, Martin Benrath and Wulf Kessler (Teleculture Films/MGM/UA, 1983).

[3]Mark Schwehn, *Exiles from Eden: Religion and the Academic Vocation in America* (New York: Oxford University Press, 1993), p. 94.

[4]Inge Jens, ed., *At the Heart of the White Rose: Letters and Diaries of Hans and Sophie Scholl* (New York: Harper & Row, 1987), p. xi.

[5]Ibid., p. 112.

[6]Ibid., p. xii.

[7]Ibid.

[8]Ibid.

[9]Ibid.

[10]Ibid., p. xiii.

[11]Inge Scholl, *The White Rose: Munich 1942-43* (Middletown, Conn.: Wesleyan University Press, 1983), p. 31.

[12]Jens, *At the Heart of the White Rose,* p. 251.

[13]Ibid., p. 161.

[14]Ibid., pp. 301-2.

[15]Annette Dumbach and Jud Newborn, *Shattering the German Night: The Story of the White Rose* (Boston: Little, Brown, 1986), p. 99.

[16]Ibid., p. 117

[17]Samuel and Pearl Oliner, *The Altruistic Personality: Rescuers of Jews in Nazi Europe* (New York: Free Press, 1988), p. 187.

[18]Scholl, *The White Rose,* p. 42.

[19]Ibid., p. 87.

[20]Dumbach and Newborn, *Shattering the German Night,* p. 9.

[21]Jens, *At the Heart of the White Rose,* pp. 301-2.

[22]Scholl, *The White Rose,* p. 65.

[23]Richard Hanser, *A Noble Treason: The Revolt of the Munich Students Against Hitler* (New York: Putnam, 1979), p. 274.

[24]Albert Camus, *Resistance, Rebellion and Death,* trans. Justin O'Brien (New York: Alfred A. Knopf, 1961), p. 71.

[25]C. S. Lewis, *The Magician's Nephew* (New York: Collier/Macmillan,1970), p. 125.

[26]Craig Dykstra, *Vision and Character: A Christian Educator's Alternative to Kohlberg* (New York: Paulist Press, 1981), p. 77.

[27]Murdoch, *Sovereignty of Good,* p. 37.

[28]Sam Phillips, "Gimmie Some Truth," *Martinis and Bikinis* (Virgin Records, 1994).

Bibliography

Allen, Woody, director. *Annie Hall*. With Woody Allen and Diane Keaton. UA/Jack Rollins-Charles Joffe, 1977.

————. *Hannah and Her Sisters*. With Woody Allen, Mia Farrow, Dianne Wiest and Michael Caine. Orion/Charles Joffe, Jack Rollins, 1979.

————. *The Purple Rose of Cairo*. With Mia Farrow, Jeff Daniels and Dianne Wiest. Orion/Jack Rollins-Charles Joffe, 1984.

Altman, Robert, director. *The Player*. With Tim Robbins, Greta Scacchi and Whoopi Goldberg. Guild Avenue, 1992.

Arcand, Denys, director. *Jesus of Montreal*. With Lothaire Bluteau, Catherine Wilkening and Johanne-Marie Tremblay. Max Films/Gerard Mital Productions/NFB Canada, 1989.

Aristotle. *Nicomachean Ethics*. Trans. Martin Ostwald. Indianapolis: Library of Liberal Arts/Bobbs-Merrill, 1962.

Augustine. *Confessions*. Trans. F. J. Sheed. York: Sheed & Ward, 1943.

————. *Letters of St. Augustine*, translated by John Leinenweber. Liguori, Mo.: Triumph, 1992.

Barbash, Uri, director. *Beyond the Walls*. With Arnoh Zadok, Muhamad Bakri and Assi Dayan. Israel, 1984.

Barzun, Jacques. *The American University*. New York: Harper & Row/Colophon, 1968.

Baxter, Michael, and Frederick Bauerschmidt. "*Eruditio* Without *Religio?* The Dilemma of Catholics in the Academy." *Communio: International Catholic Review* (summer 1995).

Bellah, Robert. "The True and Final End: Bellah Responds to Bachelard." In *Ethics and Policy*. Berkeley, Calif.: Center for Ethics and Social Policy, Fall 1994.

Bellah, Robert, et al. *The Good Society.* New York: Alfred A. Knopf, 1991.

————. *Habits of the Heart: Individualism and Commitment in American Life.* San Francisco: Harper & Row/Perennial, 1985.

Berger, Peter. *The Noise of Solemn Assemblies: Christian Commitment and the Religious Establishment in America.* Garden City, N.Y: Doubleday, 1961.

————. *The Sacred Canopy: Elements of Sociological Theory of Religion.* Garden City, N.Y: Doubleday, 1967.

Berger, Peter, and Thomas Luckman. *The Social Construction of Reality: A Treatise in the Sociology of Knowledge.* New York: Doubleday/Anchor, 1966.

Berger, Peter, Brigitte Berger and Hansfried Kellner. *The Homeless Mind: Modernization and Consciousness.* New York: Random House/Vintage, 1974.

Bernstein, Richard. *Beyond Objectivism and Relativism: Science, Hermeneutics and Praxis.* Philadelphia: University of Philadelphia Press, 1983.

Blamires, Harry. *The Christian Mind.* London: SPCK, 1963.

Bloom, Allen. *The Closing of the American Mind: How Higher Education Has Failed Democracy and Impoverished the Souls of Today's Students.* New York: Simon & Schuster, 1987.

Blumenfield, Laura. "X Marks His Spot: Author Doug Coupland and the Twentysomethings." *Washington Post,* July 7,1991, p. B1.

Boyer, Ernest. "Bringing Transcendent Values Back on Our Nation's College Campuses." Interview by Steven Garber. *Eternity,* September 1987, p. 27.

————. *College: The Undergraduate Experience in America.* New York: Harper & Row, 1987.

Clark, Gordon. *Thales to Dewey.* Boston: Houghton Mifflin, 1957.

Clouser, Roy. *The Myth of Religious Neutrality: An Essay on the Hidden Belief in Theories.* Notre Dame, Ind.: University of Notre Dame Press, 1991.

Dooyeweerd, Herman. *Roots of Western Culture: Pagan, Secular and Christian Options,* translated by John Kraay. Toronto: Wedge, 1979.

Dostoyevsky, Fyodor. *Crime and Punishment.* New York: Penguin, 1951.

Drew, Donald. *Images of Man: A Critique of the Contemporary Cinema.* Downers Grove, Ill.: InterVarsity Press, 1974.

Dumbach, Anisette, and Jud Newborn. *Shattering the German Night: The Story of the White Rose.* Boston: Little, Brown, 1986.

Dykstra, Craig. *Vision and Character: A Christian Educator's Alternative to Kohlberg.* New York: Paulist, 1981.

Dykstra, Craig, and Sharon Parks, eds. *Faith Development and Fowler.* Birmingham: Religious Education Press, 1986.

Eliot, T. S. "The Aims of Education." In *To Criticize the Critic.* New York: Farrar, Straus & Giroux, 1965.

Ellul, Jacques. *Reason for Being: A Meditation on Ecclesiastes.* Grand Rapids: Eerdmans, 1990.

————. *In Season, Out of Season.* San Francisco: Harper & Row, 1982.

————. *The Technological Society.* New York: Random House/Vintage, 1964.

Erikson, Erik. *Insight and Responsibility: Lectures on the Ethical Implications of Psychoanalytic Insight.* New York: W. W. Norton, 1964.

Forster, E. M. *Howards End.* New York: Bantam Classic, 1985.

Fowler, James. *Becoming Adult, Becoming Christian: Adult Development and Christian Faith.* San Francisco: Harper & Row, 1984.

————. *Stages of Faith: The Psychology of Human Development and the Quest for Meaning.* San Francisco: Harper & Row, 1981.

————. *Weaving the New Creation: Stages of Faith and the Public Church.* New York: HarperCollins, 1991.

Fowler, James, and Sam Keen. *Life-Maps: Conversations on the Journey of Faith.* Waco, Tex.: Word, 1978.

Fricke, David. "Smashing Pumpkins: The *Rolling Stone* Interview with Billy Corgan." *Rolling Stone,* November 16, 1995, p. 52.

Friere, Paulo. *Pedagogy of the Oppressed.* New York: Herder & Herder, 1972.

Fryling, Robert. "Campus Portrait." Address presented at the National Staff Conference of InterVarsity Christian Fellowship, December 1992.

Garber, Steven. "Bringing Transcendent Values Back on Our Nation's College Campuses." *Eternity,* September 1987, p. 27.

————. "Going First Class on the *Titanic.*" *Christianity Today,* November 20, 1987, pp. 25-27.

————. "Interested in the University?" *Eternity,* September 1987, p. 28.

————. "The Question of Character." *Eternity,* September 1988, pp. 70-71.

————. "The Teacher as Revealer and Role Model: Education as a Reflection of the Incarnation." In *Faith Goes to Work: Reflections from the Marketplace,* edited by Robert Banks, pp. 93-106. Washington, D.C.: Alban Institute, 1993.

―――. "But We Don't Blink." *World,* May 18, 1991, p. 21.

Gilkey, Langdon. *Shantung Compound: The Story of Men and Women Under Pressure.* New York: Harper & Row, 1966.

Goodman, Ellen. "Moral Lobotomy." *The Washington Post,* April 3, 1993, p. A23.

Goodwin, James. *Akira Kurosawa and Intertextual Cinema.* Baltimore: Johns Hopkins University Press, 1994.

Gray, Paul. "Implications of Apocalypse: A Review of *The Thanatos Syndrome* by Walker Percy." *Time,* March 30, 1987, p. 71.

Grunwald, Henry. "The Year 2000." *Time,* March 30,1992, p. 75.

Guinness, Os. *The Dust of Death.* Downers Grove, Ill.: InterVarsity Press, 1973.

Hardie, W. F. R. *Aristotle's Ethical Theory.* Oxford: Clarendon, 1980.

Hardy, Thomas. *Jude the Obscure.* New York: Penguin, 1985.

Hauerwas, Stanley. *The Community of Character: Toward a Constructive Christian Social Ethic.* Notre Dame, Ind.: University of Notre Dame Press, 1981.

―――. *Vision and Virtue: Essays in Christian Ethical Reflection.* Notre Dame, Ind.: Fides, 1974.

Hauerwas, Stanley, and Thomas Shaffer. "Hope Faces Power: Thomas More and the King of England." In *Christian Existence Today: Essays on Church, World and Living in Between,* edited by Stanley Hauerwas. Durham, N.C.: Labyrinth Press, 1988.

Hauerwas, Stanley, with David Burrell. "Self-Deception and Autobiography: Reflections on Speer's *Inside the Third Reich.*" In *Truthfulness and Tragedy,* edited by Stanley Hauerwas et al. Notre Dame, Ind.: University of Notre Dame Press, 1977.

Hunter, James Davison. *Before the Shooting Begins.* New York: Free Press, 1994.

―――. *The Culture Wars: The Struggle to Define America.* New York: BasicBooks, 1991.

Ivory, James, director. *Howards End.* With Anthony Hopkins, Vanessa Redgrave, Helena Bonham Carter and Emma Thompson. Merchant Ivory/ Film Four, 1992.

Jaeger, Werner. *Paideia: The Ideals of Greek Culture,* translated by Gilbert Highet. New York: Oxford University Press, 1986.

Jardine, Andre. *Tocqueville: A Biography.* Trans. Lydia Davis and Robert Hemenway. New York: Farrar, Straus & Giroux, 1988.

Jens, Inge, ed. *At the Heart of the White Rose: Letters and Diaries of Hans and Sophie Scholl.* New York: Harper & Row, 1987.

Jenson, Robert. "How the World Lost Its Story." *First Things,* October 1993, pp. 19-24.

Kaufman, Philip, director. *The Unbearable Lightness of Being.* With Daniel Day-Lewis, Juliette Binoche and Lena Olin. Saul Zaentz, 1987.

Kuhn, Thomas. *The Structure of Scientific Revolutions.* Chicago: University of Chicago Press, 1970.

Kundera, Milan. *The Book of Laughter and Forgetting,* translated by Michael Henry Heim. New York: Penguin Books, 1981.

———. *The Unbearable Lightness of Being.* New York: Harper & Row/Perennial, 1991.

Kurosawa, Akira, director. *Red Beard.* With Toshiro Mifune, Yuzo Kayama and Yoshio Tsuchiya. Toho, 1965.

Levinson, Daniel. *The Seasons of a Man's Life.* New York: Alfred A. Knopf, 1978.

Lewis, C. S. *The Abolition of Man.* New York: Macmillan, 1947.

———. *That Hideous Strength: A Modern Fairy Tale for Grown-Ups.* New York: Macmillan, 1946

London, Jerry, director. *The Scarlet and the Black.* With Gregory Peck, Christopher Plummer and John Gielgud. [From J. P Gallagher, *The Scarlet Pimpernel of the Vatican.*] ITC-RAI Radiotelevisione Italiana, 1983.

Macaulay, Ranald, and Jerram Barrs. *Being Human: The Nature of Spiritual Experience.* Downers Grove, Ill.: InterVarsity Press, 1978.

MacIntyre, Alasdair. *After Virtue: A Study in Moral Theory.* Notre Dame, Ind.: University of Notre Dame Press, 1984.

Malik, Charles Habib. *A Christian Critque of the University.* Downers Grove, Ill.: InterVarsity Press, 1982.

Marrou, H. I. *A History of Education in Antiquity.* Madison: University of Wisconsin Press, 1956.

Marsden, George. *The Soul of the American University: From Protestant Establishment to Established Nonbelief.* New York: Oxford University Press, 1994.

Matthews, Joe. "Beavis, Butthead and Budding Nihilists: Will Western Civilization Survive?" *Washington Post,* October 3, 1993, p. C1.

Mitchell, Basil. *How to Play Theological Ping-Pong: Essays on Faith and Reason.* Grand Rapids: Eerdmans, 1990.

Morrill, Richard. *Teaching Values in College: Facilitating Development of Ethical, Moral and Value Awareness in Students.* San Francisco: Jossey-Bass, 1980.

Moyers, Bill, producer. "The Truth About Lies." New York: Public Affairs Television, 1989.

Murdoch, Iris. *The Sovereignty of Good.* New York: Schocken Books, 1971.

Neuhaus, Richard John. *The Naked Public Square: Religion and Democracy in America.* Grand Rapids: Eerdmans, 1984.

Neuhaus, Richard John, ed. *Virtue Public and Private.* Grand Rapids: Eerdmans, 1986.

Newbigin, Lesslie. "Certain Faith: What Kind of Certainty?" *Tyndale Bulletin* 44, no. 2 (1993): 339-50.

————. *Foolishness to the Greeks.* Grand Rapids: Eerdmans, 1986.

————. *The Gospel in a Pluralist Society.* Grand Rapids: Eerdmans, 1989.

O'Donovan, Oliver. *Resurrection and Moral Order.* Grand Rapids: Eerdmans, 1986.

Oden, Thomas. *After Modernity, What? Agenda for Theology.* Grand Rapids: Zondervan, 1990.

————. "Then and Now: The Recovery of Patristic Wisdom." *The Christian Century,* December 12, 1990, p. 1168.

————. *Two Worlds: Notes on the Death of Modernity in America and Russia.* Downers Grove, Ill.: InterVarsity Press, 1992.

Oliner, Samuel, and Pearl Oliner. *The Altruistic Personality: Rescuers of Jews in Nazi Europe.* New York: Free Press, 1988.

Parks, Sharon. *The Critical Years: Young Adults and the Search for Meaning, Faith and Commitment.* San Francisco: Harper & Row, 1986.

Percy, Walker. *The Second Coming.* New York: Farrar, Straus & Giroux, 1980.

Perry, William. *Forms of Intellectual and Ethical Development in the College Years: A Scheme.* New York: Holt, Rinehart & Winston, 1968.

Phillips, Sam. "Gimme Some Truth." *Martinis and Bikinis.* Virgin Records, 1994.

Polanyi, Michael. *Personal Knowledge: Towards a Post-critical Philosophy.* Chicago: University of Chicago Press, 1958.

Postman, Neil. *Amusing Ourselves to Death: Public Discourse in the Age of Show Business.* New York: Penguin, 1985.

———. *The End of Education: Redefining the Value of School.* New York: Knopf, 1995.

———. *Technopoly: The Surrender of Culture to Technology.* New York: Alfred A. Knopf, 1992.

Postman, Neil, and Charles Weingartner. *Teaching as a Subversive Activity.* New York: Delacorte, 1969.

Rieff, Phillip. *The Triumph of the Therapeutic.* New York: Harper & Row, 1966.

Rookmaaker, Hans. *Modern Art and the Death of a Culture.* Downers Grove, Ill.: InterVarsity Press, 1970.

Royko, Mike. "Time Is on the Side of Generation X." *Chicago Tribune,* July 30, 1993, p. A3.

Russell, Bertrand. *Education and the Good Life.* New York: Boni & Liveright, 1926.

Schaeffer, Francis. *Escape from Reason.* Downers Grove, Ill.: InterVarsity Press, 1968.

———. *The God Who Is There.* Downers Grove, Ill.: InterVarsity Press, 1968.

———. *He Is There and He Is Not Silent.* Wheaton, Ill.: Tyndale House, 1972.

———. *True Spirituality.* Wheaton, Ill.: Tyndale House, 1971.

Scholl, Inge. *The White Rose: Munich 1942-43.* Middletown, Conn.: Wesleyan University Press, 1983.

Schwehn, Mark. *Exiles from Eden: Religion and the Academic Vocation in America.* New York: Oxford University Press, 1993.

Smashing Pumpkins. "Zero." *Mellon Collie and the Infinite Sadness.* Virgin Records, 1995.

Smith, Page. *Killing the Spirit: Higher Education in America.* New York: Penguin/Viking, 1990.

Solzhenitsyn, Aleksandr. *The First Circle.* New York: Harper & Row, 1968.

———. "The Relentless Cult of Novelty and How It Wrecked the Century."

222   THE FABRIC OF FAITHFULNESS

The New York Times Book Review, February 7, 1993, p. 3.

Steiner, George. *In Bluebeard's Castle: Some Notes Towards the Redefinition of Culture.* New Haven, Conn.: Yale University Press, 1971.

———. *Real Presences.* Chicago: University of Chicago Press, 1989.

Stiller, Ben, director. *Reality Bites.* With Winona Ryder, Ethan Hawke and Janeane Garofalo. Universal/Jersey Films, 1994.

Stone, Oliver, director. *Platoon.* With Tom Berenger, Willem DaFoe and Charlie Sheen. Hemdale, 1986.

———. *Wall Street.* With Charlie Sheen, Michael Douglas and Daryl Hannah. Edward R. Pressman/American, 1987.

Swift, Graham, director. *Waterland.* With Jeremy Irons, Sinead Cusack and Ethan Hawke. Mayfair/Palace/Pandora/Channel 4 Films/British Screen, 1992.

Tolson, Jay. *Pilgrim in the Ruins: A Life of Walker Percy.* Chapel Hill: University of North Carolina Press, 1992.

Tolstoy, Leo. *Resurrection.* New York: Penguin, 1966.

Turner, Steve. *Up to Date.* London: Hodder & Stoughton, 1985.

Verhoeven, Michael, director. *The White Rose.* With Lena Stolze, Martin Benrath and Wulf Kessler. Teleculture Films/MGM/UA, 1983.

Whitehead, Alfred North. *The Aims of Education.* New York: New American Library, 1929.

Willimon, William, and Thomas Naylor. *The Abandoned Generation: Rethinking Higher Education.* Grand Rapids: Eerdmans, 1995.

Wolfe, Gregory. "A Stranger and a Pilgrim." *The Catholic World Report,* November 1991, p. 64.

Wuthnow, Robert. *The Consciousness Reformation.* Berkeley: University of California Press, 1976.

———. *Meaning and Moral Order: Explorations in Cultural Analysis.* Berkeley: University of California Press, 1987.

Wuthnow, Robert, et al. *Cultural Analysis: The Work of Peter Berger, Mary Douglas, Michel Foucalt and Jurgen Habermas.* Boston: Routledge Kegan Paul, 1984.

Zakaria, Fareed. "Ethics for Greedheads: B.S. at Business School." *The New Republic,* October 19, 1987, pp. 18-20.